THE ULTIMA
GUITAR
CHORDS
BOOK

THE ULTIMATE
GUITaR
CHORDS
BOOK

Compiled by Nick Freeth

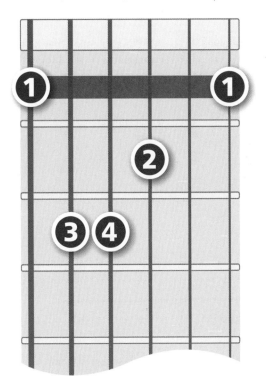

Bath · New York · Singapore · Hong Kong · Cologne · Delhi · Melbourne

First published by Parragon in 2010

Parragon
Queen Street House
4 Queen Street
Bath BA1 1HE, UK

Designed, produced and packaged by
Stonecastle Graphics Limited

Compiled by Nick Freeth
Edited by Philip de Ste. Croix
Chord diagrams by Stonecastle Graphics

ISBN 978-1-4454-1632-8

Printed in China

Contents

How to use this book

In its main section, this book displays fingerings for 360 guitar chords: 30 for each of the 12 musical notes, from A to G#/Ab. It's designed for clarity and ease of use, and provides rapid access to chord diagrams relating to any note.

Here's how it's arranged: bold capital letters in the text below correspond to the labelled lines on the 'example' on page 7.

A is the **keynote heading**, listing the alphabetical names, with, where appropriate, sharp (#) and flat (b) symbols, for all 12 notes. Chords for each specified note are grouped together in the directory, and the heading's **yellow-shaded area (B)** identifies the key to which the chord displayed on a page belongs.

Some notes and keys (A#/Bb, C#/Db, D#/Eb, F#/Gb, G#/Ab) have two names: each name in these pairs refers to a note of identical pitch, which can be described in either 'sharp' or 'flat' form. (See **B** and **C**: there's more about alternative note and chord names on page 11.)

Among the 30 chords per keynote are:

- **Majors** – chords with four semitones (a 'major third') between their 1st (root) and 3rd notes;
- **Minors** – chords with three semitones (a 'minor third') between their root and 3rd notes;
- Other, more 'exotic' harmonies, explained more fully on pages 9–11.

The keynote's name appears as each page's **main heading (C)**. The specific chord being illustrated and described is named on the line below **(D)**. Widely used chords appear in several different versions **(E)**.

The central diagram shows the fingering for a given chord. Its horizontal lines **(F)** represent individual frets – although the area where the finger actually holds a string down lies immediately below the fret itself, and this space is also commonly termed 'the nth fret' (where 'n' is the number of the fret in question). Strings themselves are represented by images like the one labelled **G**. For the purposes of this book, it's assumed that standard (EADGBE) tuning is being used.

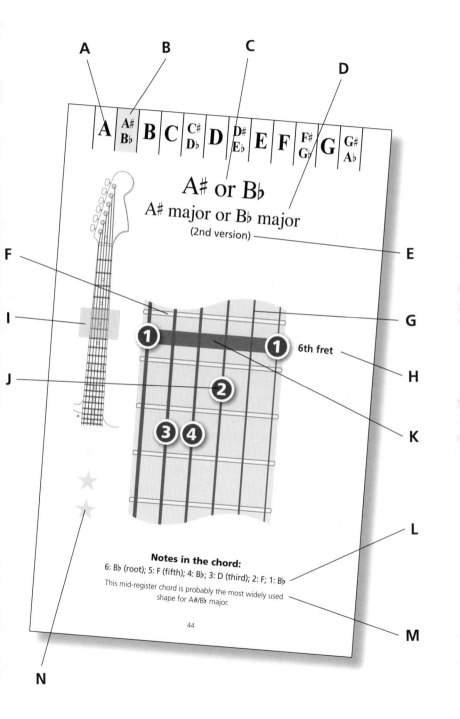

| A | A♯ B♭ | B | C | C♯ D♭ | D | D♯ E♭ | E | F | F♯ G♭ | G | G♯ A♭ |

A♯ or B♭

A♯ major or B♭ major
(2nd version)

6th fret

Notes in the chord:
6: B♭ (root); 5: F (fifth); 4: B♭; 3: D (third); 2: F; 1: B♭

This mid-register chord is probably the most widely used shape for A#/B♭ major.

44

When the main diagram is topped by an image of the guitar's 'nut' (the grooved block over which the strings pass *en route* to the headstock – see diagram below), the illustrated chord is fingered between the nut and the fourth fret. The required fret position for shapes higher up the neck is specified by a line of text beside the fingerboard graphic (**H**). A chord's placement on the neck is also indicated by the shaded diagram to the left of the main diagram (**I**).

Fingering numbers are displayed by white numerals on a circular red background (**J**). '1' refers to the index finger of the left (or fretting) hand; '2' the middle finger; '3' the ring finger; and '4' the little finger. A red bar with a single number (**K**) indicates a 'barré': this involves an individual finger (usually, but not always, the index) fretting two or more strings simultaneously.

Strings that are to be played open (unfretted), carry an 'O' above them and those that aren't to be sounded for the chord have an 'X' above them (see diagram below).

'Notes in the chord' towards the bottom of each page (**L**) names the individual notes that comprise a chord, and shows how they relate to the scale of that chord's keynote. (Some notes can simply be described as, say, the scale's 3rd or 5th 'degree', but others require a little more elaboration: you can read about the musical theory behind this on pages 9–11.) Beneath the 'Notes in the chord' section are a few lines of more general information about the chord appearing on the page (**M**)…and above and to the left, a series of up to three gold stars (**N**) 'grades' each shape for technical difficulty: one star = easy, two stars = medium and three stars = difficult.

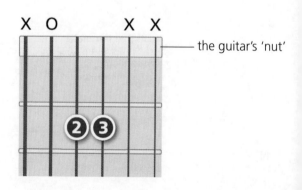
the guitar's 'nut'

All about the chords in this book

The musically simplest chords are formed from the eight **degrees** or notes of a **major scale**. These degrees are a sequence of **semitones** and **tones**, starting and finishing with the **keynote** (first and eighth degree) of the scale: the **semitone** is the smallest 'official' distance between pitches in Western music, and is the interval produced by raising or lowering a guitar fingering by a single fret; a **tone** equals two semitones.

All major scales comprise the same set of intervals: the one shown below is for the key of C major (see pages 103-5).

Note	C	D	E	F	G	A	B	C
Degree	1st	2nd	3rd	4th	5th	6th	7th	8th/1st
Interval		tone	tone	s/t	tone	tone	tone	s/t

Major chords comprise the **first** (also called the '**tonic**' or '**root**'), **third** and **fifth** degrees of the major scale: in C, these are C (first), E (third) and G (fifth). The notes may appear in any order, and there can be as many tonics, thirds and fifths as you want. However, if the lowest note is the keynote itself (C in C major), the chord is said to be in the **root position**; with the third (E in C major) in the bass, the chord is a **first inversion**; and with the fifth (G in C major) in the bass, it's a **second inversion**.

Several other major-type chords featured in this book are just slight modifications of the first-third-fifth 'triad'.

- In a '**sus 4**' or **suspended fourth**, the third is replaced with the fourth, creating an unsettled musical feel that is 'resolved' when the player returns to a standard triad.
- An **added sixth** involves – as you'll have guessed! – the introduction of the sixth degree of the scale (A in C major) into a regular major chord.
- The **6/9** is a little more complex: in the key of C, it features both an added sixth (A) and a D (counted here as the ninth degree) – see page 109.
- In a **major seventh**, the seventh degree of the scale (B in C major: see pages 110–11) is played with the tonic, third and fifth, resulting in a mild but tasty dissonance.

A second group of majors are the **dominant seventh** chords produced by lowering the scale's normal seventh note by a semitone (making it a B♭ in C major) and adding it to the basic triad. Within the book, these flattened seventh notes are themselves described, for simplicity's sake, as 'dominant sevenths', although this isn't strictly correct; the potentially confusing technical term for them is **minor sevenths**.

• The basic **dominant seventh** is a major triad with the lowered seventh note that's just been described. In C, its notes are C, E, G and B♭: see pages 112–14.
• **Ninth**, **eleventh** and **thirteenth** chords are jazzy 'extensions' of the 'dom 7'. In a **ninth** chord, a ninth (D in the key of C) is added to the 'dom 7' notes; strictly speaking, an **eleventh** chord is a ninth chord that also incorporates an eleventh (F in the key of C); while a **thirteenth** is a 'dom seventh' with a ninth, eleventh *and* a thirteenth (A in the key of C). However, it often isn't physically possible to include all these notes in a guitar chord, so some are omitted … though it's essential that the root, the 'dom 7' tone itself, and the note specified by the number in the chord name, are always sounded.
• The **7+9** chord is yet another 'dom 7' variant: the + sign indicates that its extra ninth note should be 'augmented' (raised by a semitone): this produces a juicy, funky chord of (in C major) C-E-B♭-D# (see page 115).

Minor chords are based on the eight notes of the **minor scale** – whose construction is more complex than its major cousin's. We'll focus here on the notes and intervals of the **melodic minor** scale, which vary slightly as it rises and falls. This is a list of the notes comprising a melodic minor scale of C:

Rising Melodic Minor

Note	C	D	E♭	F	G	A	B	C
Degree	1st	2nd	3rd	4th	5th	6th	7th	8th/1st
Interval		tone	s/t	tone	tone	tone	tone	s/t

Descending Melodic Minor

Note	C	B♭	A♭	G	F	E♭	D	C
Degree	8th/1st	7th	6th	5th	4th	3rd	2nd	1st
Interval		tone	tone	s/t	tone	tone	s/t	tone

As well as standard minor triads (comprising the first, third and fifth degrees of the scale), this directory includes:

• Chords in which the sixth note of the rising melodic minor scale is combined with the notes of the minor triad: a Cm6 chord contains C, E♭, G and A (see pages 126–7).
• Minor triads with a dominant seventh (comprising C, E♭, G, and B♭ in C minor – see pages 128–130).

• Minor triads with a dominant seventh, also incorporating a ninth
(D in C minor – see page 131).

In the book, you'll also find three other chord categories:

• **Diminished** chords, made up entirely of notes separated by **minor thirds**
(intervals of three semitones).
• **Augmented** chords, made up entirely of notes separated by **major thirds**
(intervals of four semitones).
• 'Bare', '**open fifth**' or '**power**' chords (see page102 for a so-called **C5** – this
name for an 'open fifth' chord is widely used, but disliked by purists). Open fifths
are neither major nor minor, as they contain no third degree of the scale at all!
Power chords are identified throughout the book by this graphic symbol:

Finally, a word about the confusing topic of notes and chords with alternative
names. When a C is raised in pitch by a semitone, it's said to have been **sharpened**.
However, if you take a D (one tone above the C) and lower it by a semitone
(i.e. **flatten** it), the result is a note that's identical in pitch to a C#, but can also be
called D♭. In some musical contexts, it makes more sense to use 'sharp' terminology;
at other times, it's clearer and more helpful to refer to notes, chords and keys by
their 'flat' names: but you need to remember that (for example) a scale or chord of
C# major is exactly the same as one of D♭ major, even though the names for their
constituent notes are quite different!

Notes for C# major: C# D# E# F# G# A# B# C#
=
Notes for D♭ major: D♭ E♭ F G♭ A♭ B♭ C D♭

A
'Bare' A (A5)

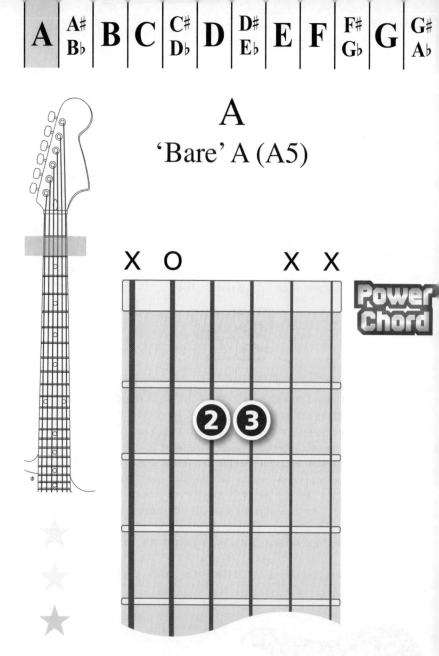

Power Chord

Notes in the chord:
5: A (root); 4: E (fifth); 3: A

This chord contains no third, and is therefore neither major nor minor. The 6th, 2nd and 1st strings aren't played.

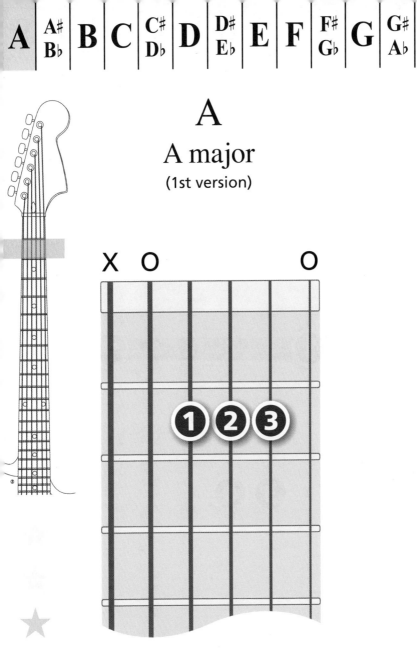

A
A major
(1st version)

Notes in the chord:
5: A (root); 4: E (fifth); 3: A; 2: C# (third);1: E

The 6th string isn't normally sounded here, but may be
included to produce a second inversion of the chord.

13

A
A major
(2nd version)

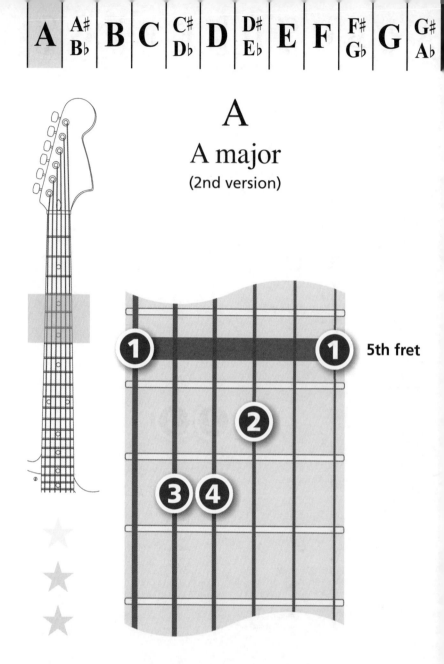

5th fret

Notes in the chord:
6: A (root); 5: E (fifth); 4: A; 3: C# (third); 2: E; 1: A

As all the strings are fretted in this barréd fingering, your left hand can control how long the notes ring.

A

A major

(3rd version)

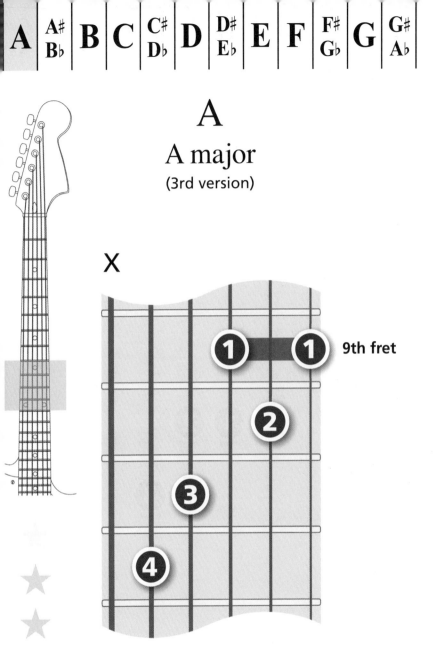

X

9th fret

Notes in the chord:

5: A (root); 4: C# (third); 3: E (fifth); 2: A; 1: C#

This higher pitched form of A provides a lighter sound. Avoid playing the 6th string: its low E won't sound very good here.

A

A sus4

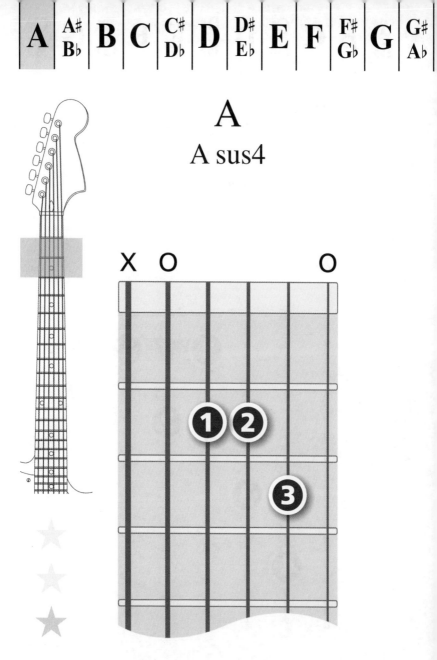

Notes in the chord:

5: A (root); 4: E (fifth); 3 A; 2: D (sus fourth); 1: E

The third (C#) is replaced here with a 'suspension' – the D a semitone above it. This chord usually 'resolves' to a standard A major (or minor).

A

A6

(1st version)

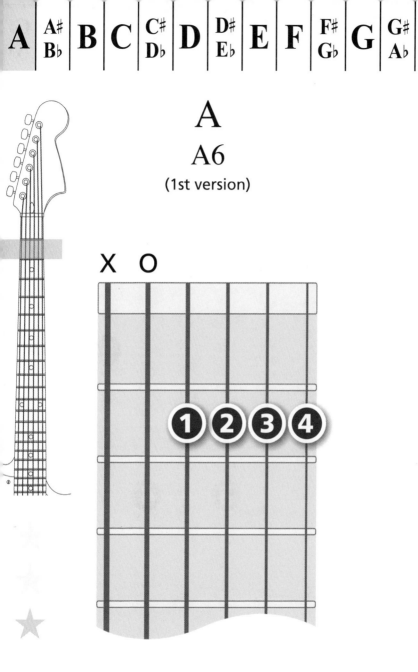

X O

① ② ③ ④

Notes in the chord:

5: A (root); 4: E (fifth); 3: A; 2: C# (third); 1: F# (added sixth)

'Added sixths' can either be used within a song, or as a distinctive final chord. You could play all four fretted notes with a barré.

A
A6
(2nd version)

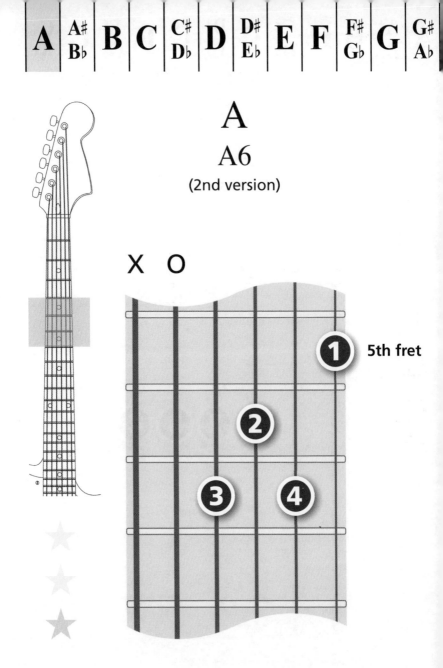

X   O

1 — 5th fret

2

3   **4**

Notes in the chord:

5: A (root); 4: A; 3: C# (third); 2: F# (added sixth); 1: A

A higher voicing of the 'added 6th' chord – the open 5th
string conveniently supplies the root bass note.

A
A6/9

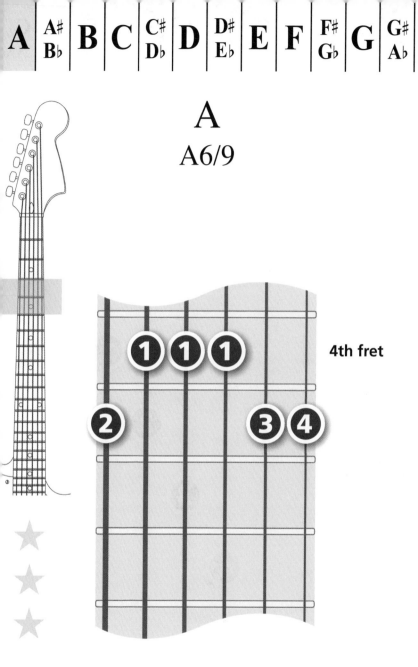

4th fret

Notes in the chord:
6: A (root); 5: C# (third); 4: F# (sixth); 3: B (ninth); 2: E (fifth); 1: A

A jazzy chord that's sometimes used to conclude a number.

A
A maj7
(1st version)

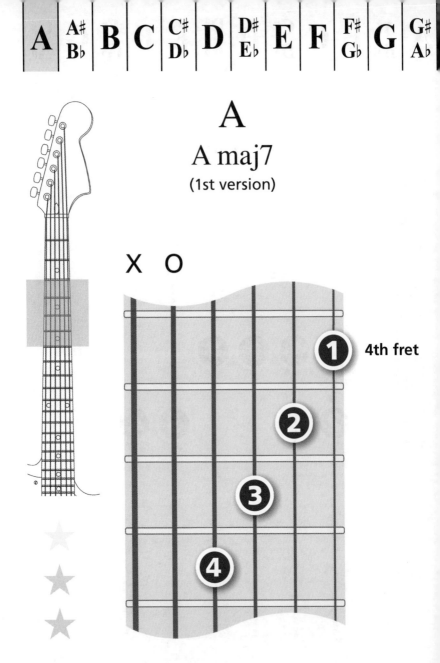

Notes in the chord:

5: A (root); 4: A; 3: C# (third); 2: E (fifth); 1 G# (maj seventh)

This 'maj7' is formed by adding a top string G#
to a regular A chord.

A

A maj7

(2nd version)

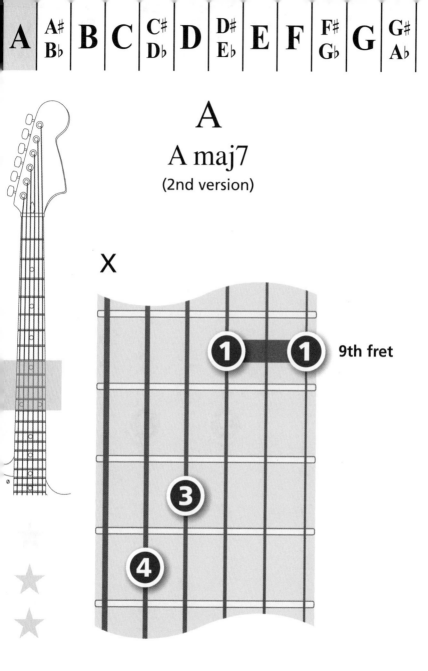

Notes in the chord:

5: A (root); 4: C# (third); 3: E (fifth); 2: G# (maj seventh); 1: C#

You can use this 'A maj7' to precede or follow the A chord
on page 15 by simply releasing your second finger!

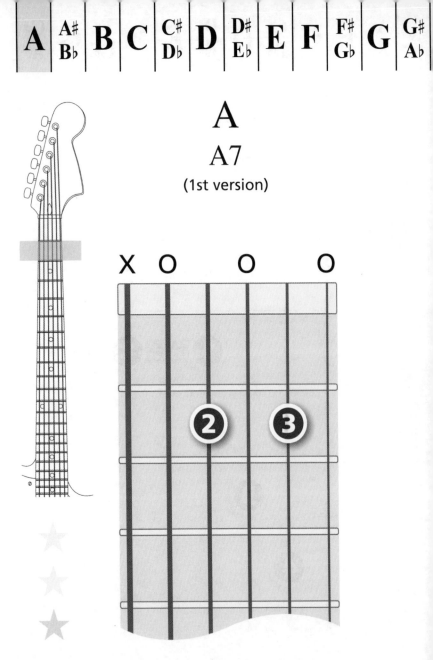

A
A7
(1st version)

Notes in the chord:

5: A (root); 4: E (fifth); 3: G (dom seventh); 2: C# (third); 1: E

A7 gives a bluesy feel when used as a keynote chord, and also provides a 'stepping-stone' to root chords of D major or minor.

A
A7
(2nd version)

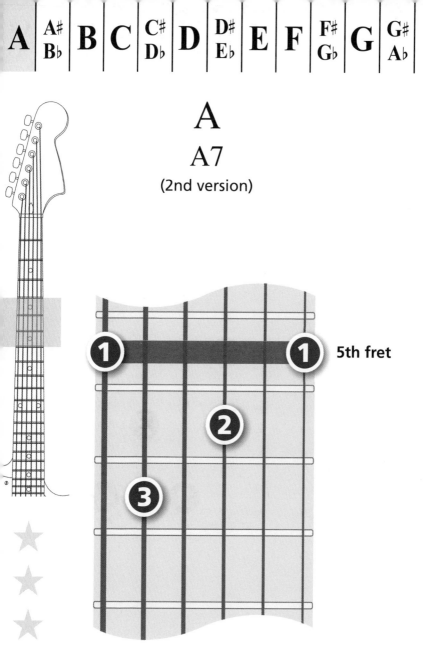

5th fret

Notes in the chord:

6: A (root); 5: E (fifth); 4: G (dom seventh); 3: C# (third); 2: E; 1: A

This shape can be very effective if you use it to 'slide up' to
the chord, especially in hard rock and heavy metal!

A	A# Bb	B	C	C# Db	D	D# Eb	E	F	F# Gb	G	G# Ab

A

A7

(3rd version)

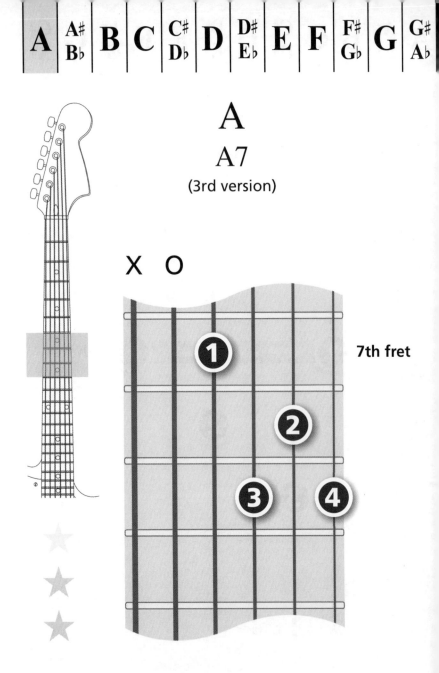

X O

7th fret

Notes in the chord:

5: A (root); 4: A; 3: E (fifth); 2: G (dom seventh); 1: C# (third)

You'll have heard this great-sounding shape on many classic funk records.

A
A7+9

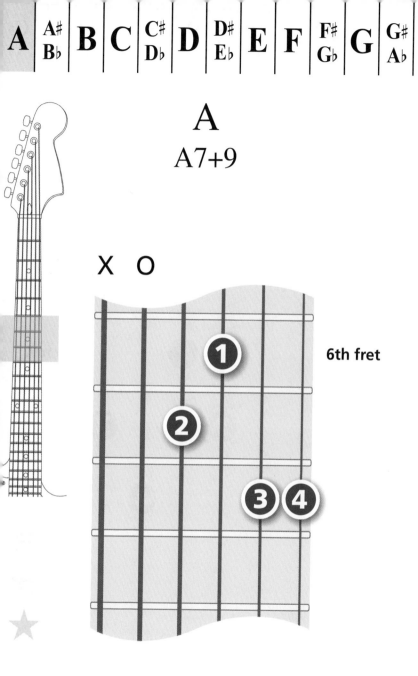

6th fret

Notes in the chord:

5: A (root); 4: A; 3: C# (third); 2: G (dom seventh); 1: B# (aug ninth)

The 'clash' produced here results from combining the
C# on the 3rd string with a B# – or, more simply, C –
on the 1st.

25

A
A9

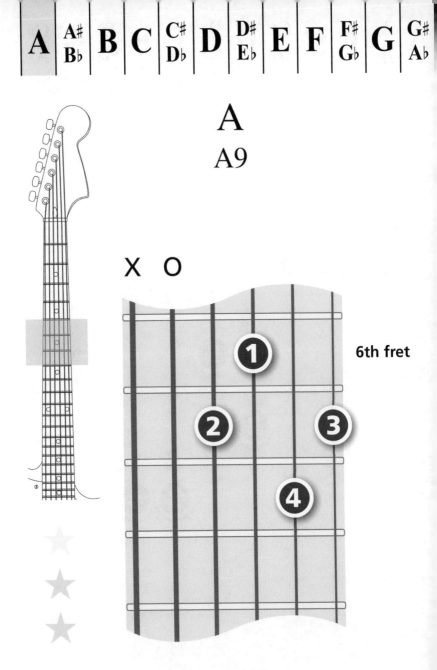

6th fret

Notes in the chord:
5: A (root); 4: A; 3: C# (third); 2: G (dom seventh); 1: B (ninth)

The ninth on the top string creates a juicy 'extension' to a regular dominant seventh chord.

A
A11

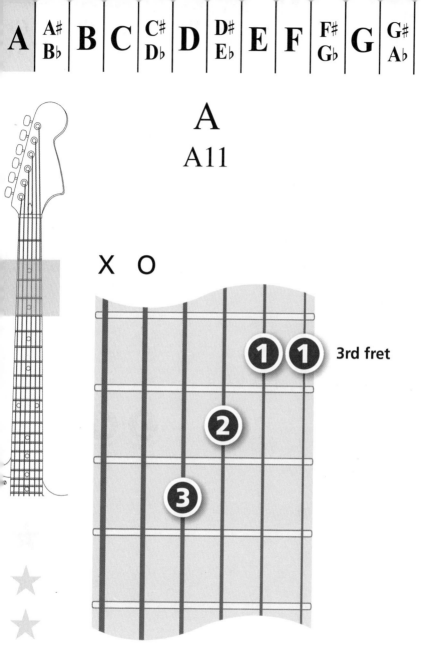

3rd fret

Notes in the chord:

5: A (root); 4: G (dom seventh); 3: B (ninth); 2: D (eleventh); 1: G

A further 'extension' of the basic dominant seventh,
with the D on the 2nd string supplying its characteristic
musical flavour.

27

A
A13

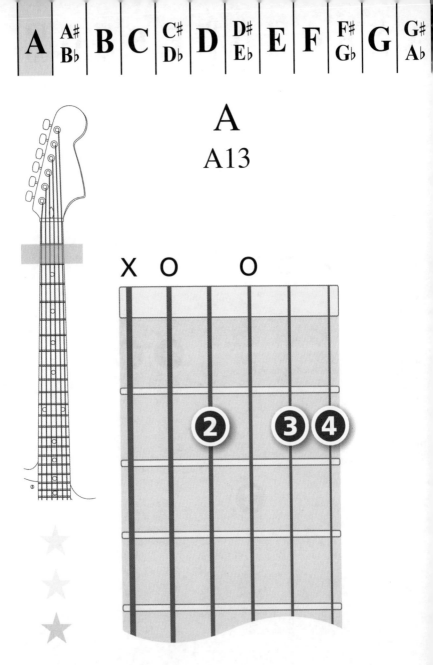

Notes in the chord:

5: A (root); 4: E (fifth); 3: G (dom seventh); 2: C# (third); 1: F# (thirteenth)

The ultimate extension of a standard dominant seventh
chord; a favourite with jazz players!

A

A diminished (A dim, A°)

(1st version)

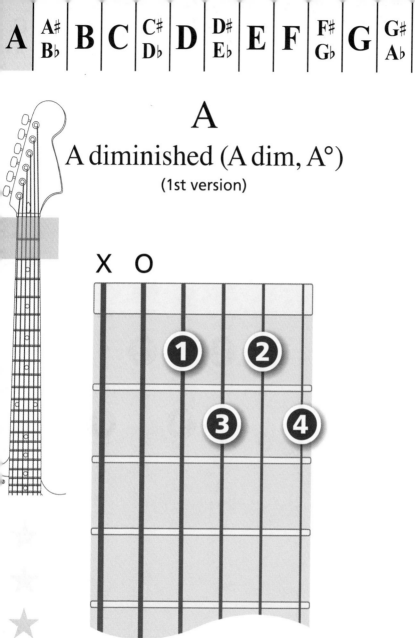

X O

Notes in the chord:

5: A (root); 4: D# (dim fifth); 3: A; 2: C (minor third); 1: F# (dim seventh)

A useful diminished fingering; the open A on the 5th
string makes it especially easy.

A
A diminished (A dim, A°)
(2nd version)

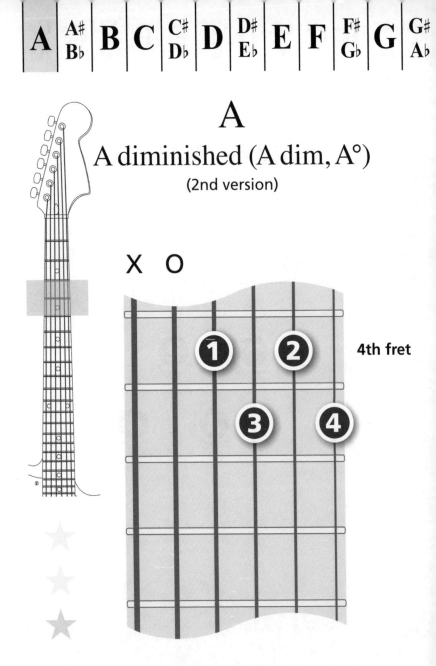

Notes in the chord:

5: A (root); 4: F# (dim seventh); 3: C (minor third); 2: D# (dim fifth); 1: A

A higher-pitched voicing, with the open-string A still in
the bass.

A

A augmented (A aug, A+)

(1st version)

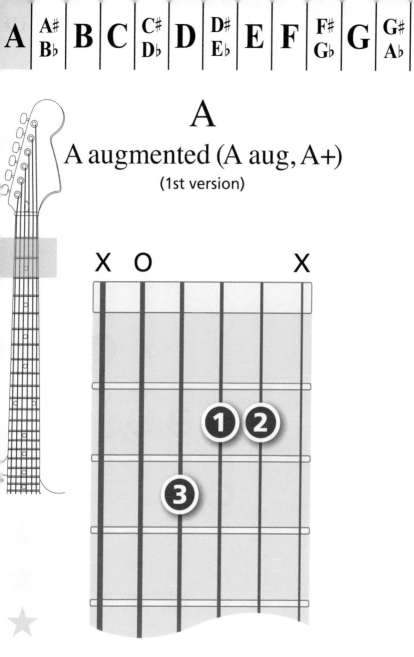

Notes in the chord:

5: A (root); 4: F (aug fifth); 3: A; 2: C# (third)

A very simple fingering for an augmented chord.

A
A augmented (A aug, A+)
(2nd version)

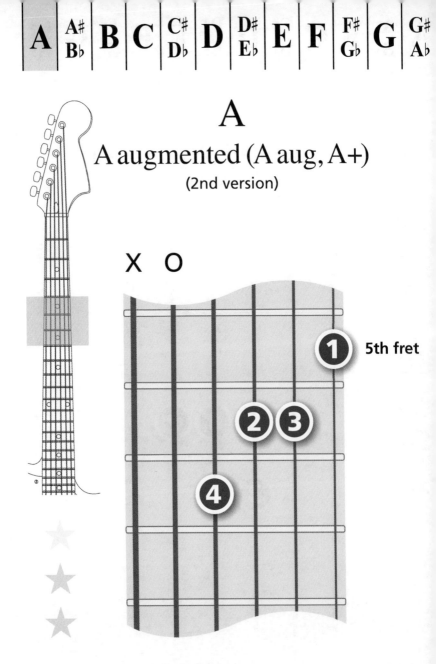

X O

5th fret

Notes in the chord:
5: A (root); 4: A; 3: C# (third); 2: F (aug fifth); 1: A

Another effective augmented chord, using a shape that can be 'shifted' up and down the neck to produce 'augs' in other keys.

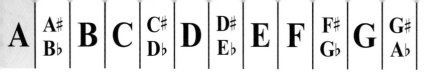

A

A minor (Am)

(1st version)

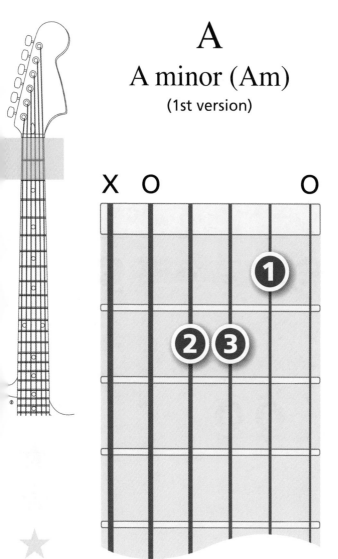

Notes in the chord:

5: A (root); 4: E (fifth); 3: A; 2: C (third); 1: E

A basic, but always useful fingering.

33

A	A# B♭	B	C	C# D♭	D	D# E♭	E	F	F# G♭	G	G# A♭

A
A minor (Am)
(2nd version)

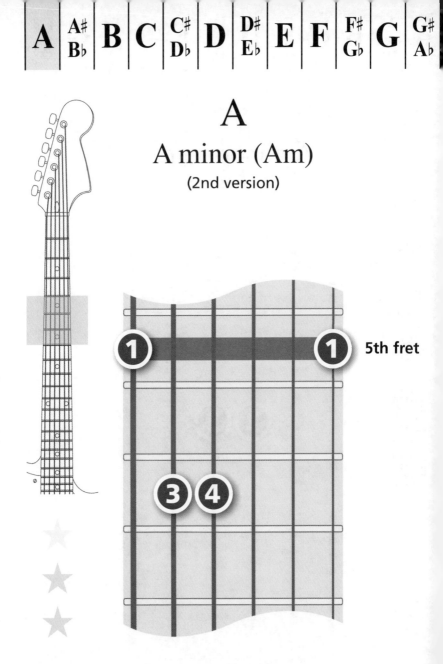

5th fret

Notes in the chord:
6: A (root); 5: E (fifth); 4: A; 3: C (third); 2: E; 1: A

Press your index finger down firmly to ensure the 3rd and
2nd strings don't buzz on this barré shape.

A

A minor (Am)

(3rd version)

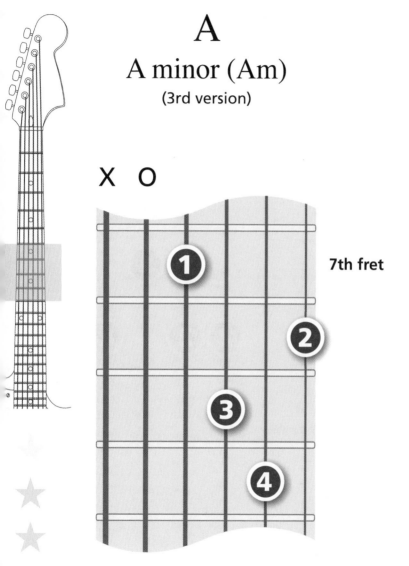

7th fret

Notes in the chord:

5: A (root); 4: A; 3: E (fifth); 2: A; 1: C (third)

Not the easiest of fingerings – but it produces a nice higher-register A minor.

A
Am6
(1st version)

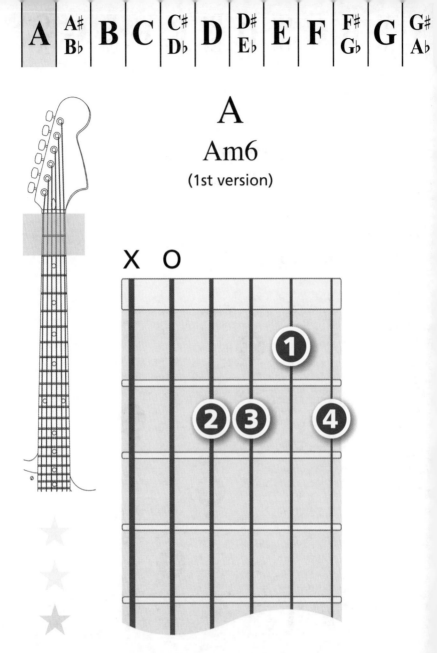

Notes in the chord:

5: A (root); 4: E (fifth); 3: A; 2: C (third); 1: F# (sixth)

By lifting your little finger from the second fret here, you can alternate between Am6 and a standard A minor.

A
Am6
(2nd version)

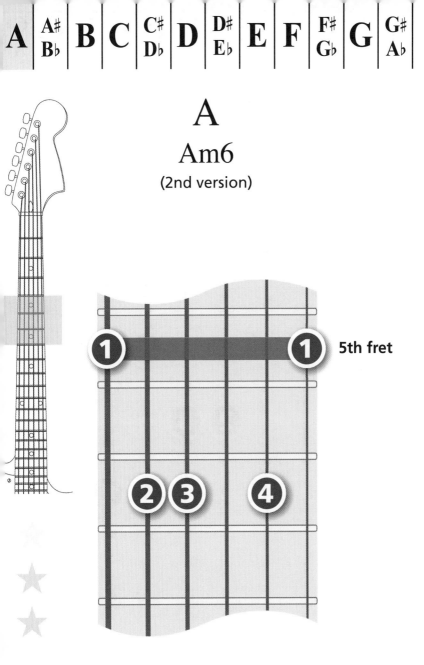

5th fret

Notes in the chord:
6: A (root); 5: E (fifth); 4: A; 3: C (third); 2: F# (sixth); 1: A

Take care with your barré, or the 3rd string won't
sound cleanly.

A
Am7
(1st version)

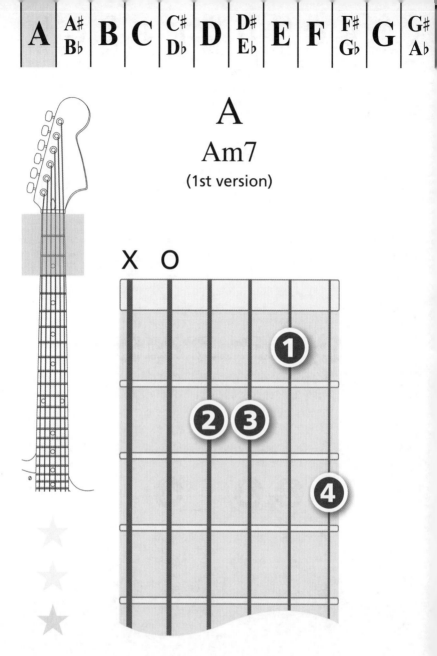

X   O

Notes in the chord:
5: A (root); 4: E (fifth); 3: A; 2: C (third); 1: G (dom seventh)

Though the 6th string is marked as silent here, including
it enables you to alternate between A and E in the bass
when fingerpicking.

A
Am7
(2nd version)

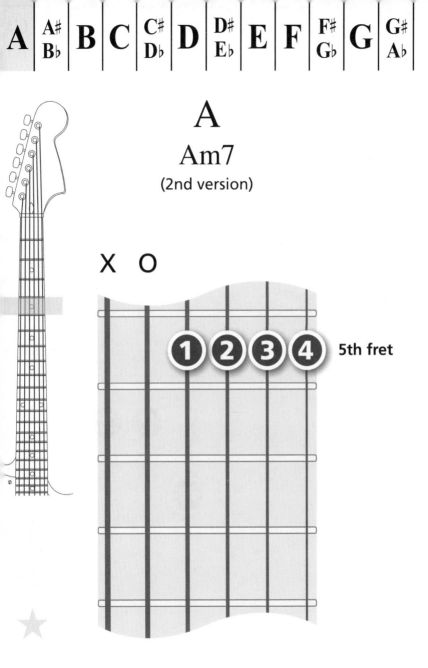

5th fret

Notes in the chord:

5: A (root); 4: G (dom seventh); 3: C (third); 2: E (fifth); 1: A

This shape could also be fingered by a barré across the top four strings at the 5th fret.

A
Am7
(3rd version)

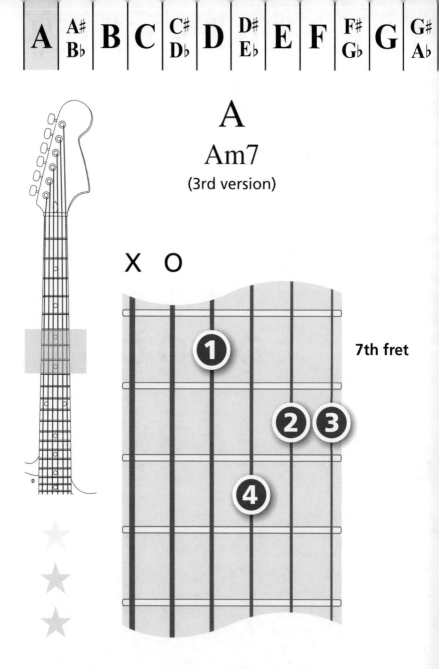

X O

7th fret

Notes in the chord:
5: A (root); 4: A; 3: E (fifth); 2: G (dom seventh); 1: C (third)

This higher-pitched Am7 can be very effective in the right musical context.

A
Am9

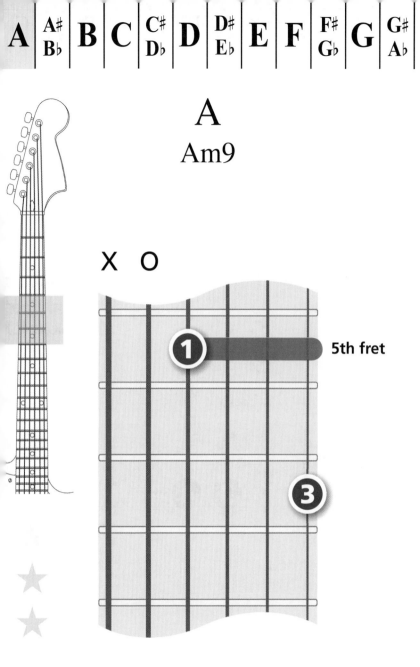

X   O

1   **5th fret**

3

Notes in the chord:

5: A (root); 4: G (dom seventh); 3: C (third); 2: E (fifth); 1: B (ninth)

A perennially useful, tasty extension of the basic Am7
that exudes a jazzy feel.

41

A♯ or B♭
'Bare' A♯ or 'bare' B♭
(A♯5 or B♭5)

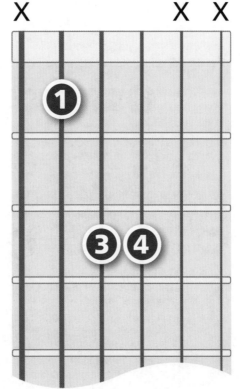

Notes in the chord:
5: B♭ (root); 4: F (fifth); 3: B♭

A powerful three-stringer.

42

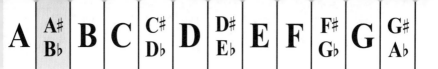

A♯ or B♭
A♯ major or B♭ major
(1st version)

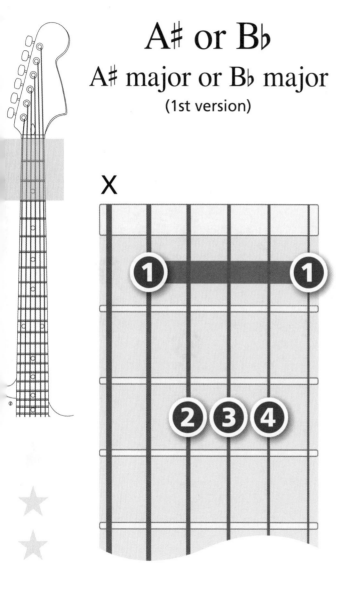

X

Notes in the chord:
5: B♭ (root); 4: F (fifth); 3 B♭; 2: D (third); 1: F

A barré is necessary for most five- and six-string chords
in 'guitar-unfriendly' keys like A♯/B♭.

A# or B♭
A# major or B♭ major
(2nd version)

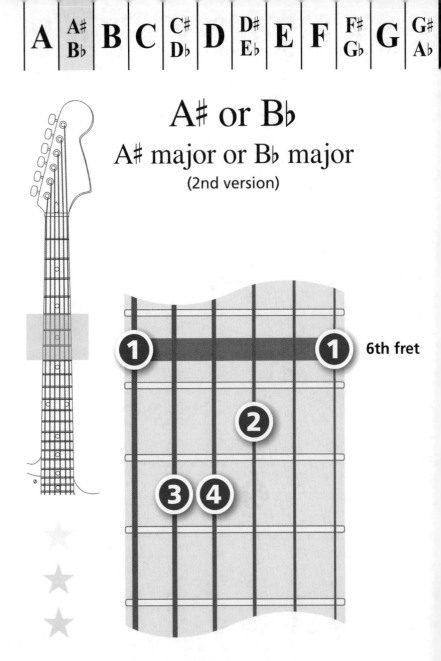

6th fret

Notes in the chord:
6: B♭ (root); 5: F (fifth); 4: B♭; 3: D (third); 2: F; 1: B♭

This mid-register chord is probably the most widely used shape for A#/B♭ major.

A# or B♭
A# major or B♭ major
(3rd version)

X X

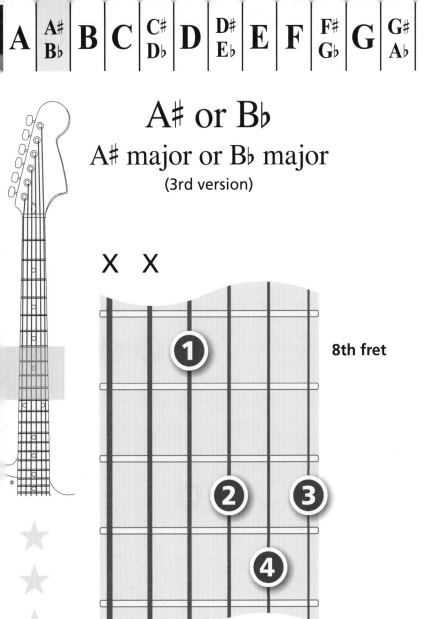

8th fret

Notes in the chord:
4: B♭ (root); 3: F (fifth); 2: B♭; 1: D (third)

An attractive high voicing, though it doesn't fall easily
under the fingers.

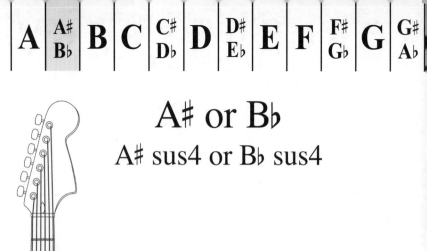

A# or Bb
A# sus4 or Bb sus4

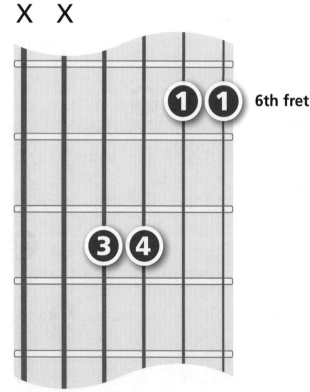

6th fret

Notes in the chord:
4: Bb (root); 3: Eb (sus fourth); 2: F (fifth); 1: Bb

A pleasantly simple shape to play!

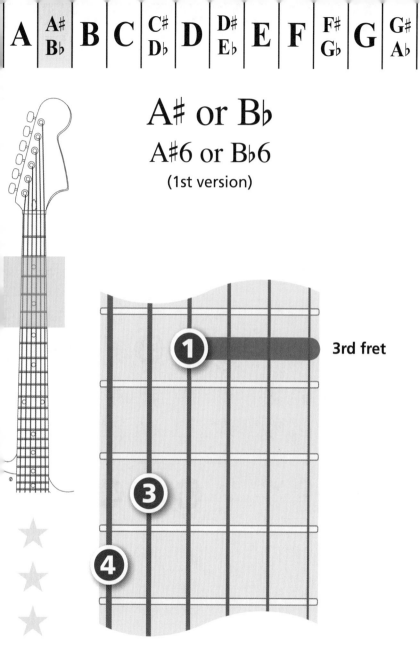

| A | A# Bb | B | C | C# Db | D | D# Eb | E | F | F# Gb | G | G# Ab |

A# or Bb
A#6 or Bb6
(1st version)

3rd fret

Notes in the chord:
6: Bb (root); 5: D (third); 4: F (fifth); 3: Bb; 2: D; 1: G (added sixth)

Effective whether strummed vigorously or played gently as
a broken chord.

47

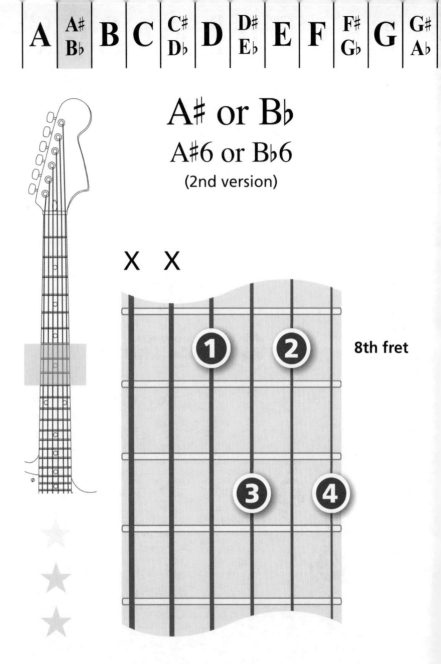

A♯ or B♭
A♯6 or B♭6
(2nd version)

8th fret

Notes in the chord:
4: B♭ (root); 3: F (fifth); 2: G (added sixth); 1: D (third)

A lighter chord – though it retains a cutting edge.

A# or Bb
A# 6/9 or Bb 6/9

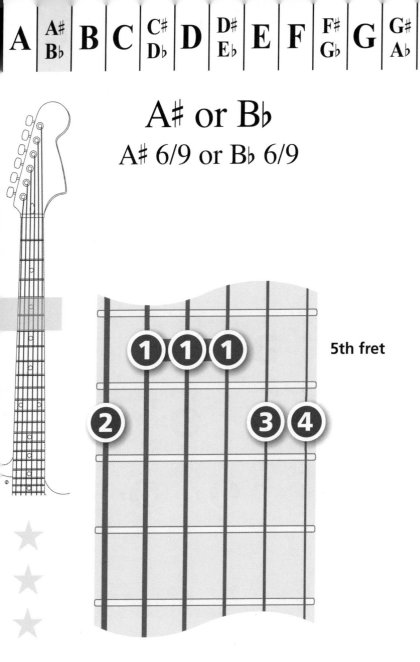

5th fret

Notes in the chord:

6: Bb (root); 5: D (third); 4: G (sixth); 3: C (ninth); 2: F (fifth); 1: Bb

A standard 6/9 fingering, placed here in the 5th position.

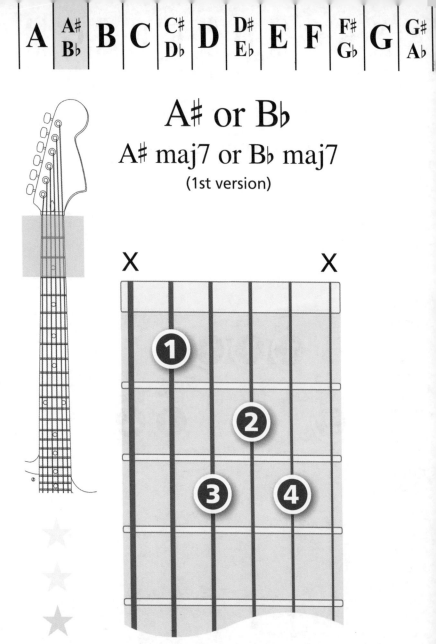

A# or B♭

A# maj7 or B♭ maj7

(1st version)

X   X

① ② ③ ④

Notes in the chord:

5: B♭ (root); 4: F (fifth); 3: A (maj seventh); 2: D (third)

Only the inner strings are required here.

A	A# Bb	B	C	C# Db	D	D# Eb	E	F	F# Gb	G	G# Ab

A# or Bb

A# maj7 or Bb maj7

(2nd version)

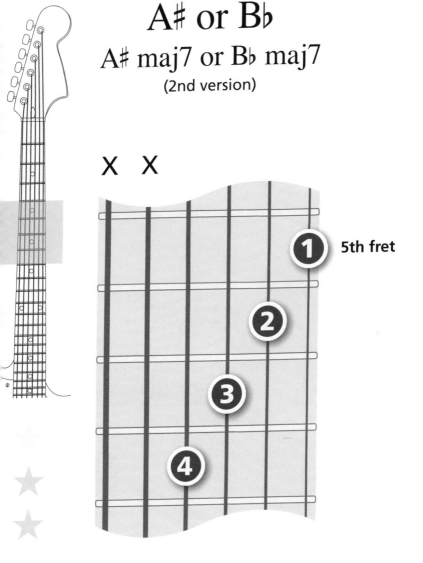

X X

5th fret

Notes in the chord:

4: Bb (root); 3: D (third); 2: F (fifth); 1: A (maj seventh)

No deep bass – but this is a lovely chord in the
right context.

51

A	A#/B♭	B	C	C#/D♭	D	D#/E♭	E	F	F#/G♭	G	G#/A♭

A♯ or B♭
A♯7 or B♭7
(1st version)

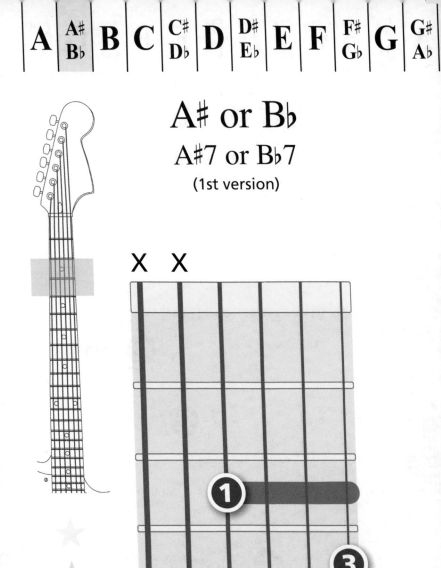

Notes in the chord:
4: F (fifth); 3: B♭; 2: D (third); 1: A♭ (dom seventh)

A comparatively simple second-inversion dominant
seventh, which can be used in other keys when moved
up and down the fingerboard.

A	A# Bb	B	C	C# Db	D	D# Eb	E	F	F# Gb	G	G# Ab

A# or Bb
A#7 or Bb7
(2nd version)

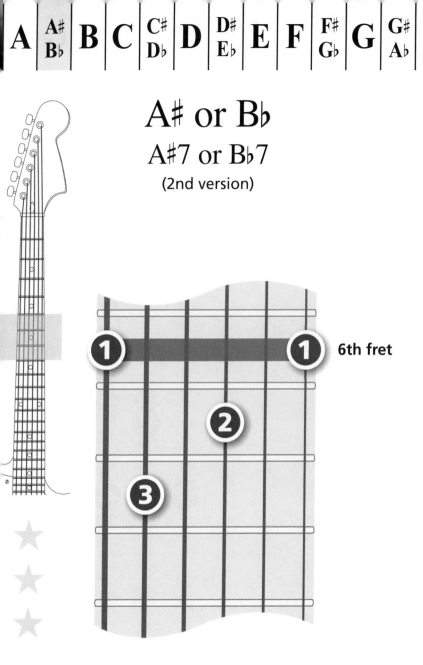

6th fret

Notes in the chord:

6: Bb (root); 5: F (fifth); 4: Ab (dom seventh); 3: D (third); 2: F; 1: Bb

This dominant-seventh shape is another guitarists' staple.

| A | A♯
B♭ | B | C | C♯
D♭ | D | D♯
E♭ | E | F | F♯
G♭ | G | G♯
A♭ |

A♯ or B♭
A♯7 or B♭7
(3rd version)

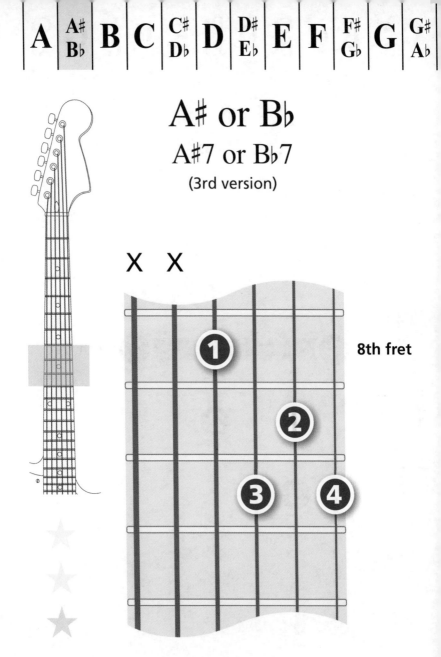

X X

8th fret

Notes in the chord:
4: B♭ (root); 3: F (fifth); 2: A♭ (dom seventh); 1: D (third)

Add a bass F by holding down the 5th string at the 8th fret
with an index finger barré.

A	A# Bb	B	C	C# Db	D	D# Eb	E	F	F# Gb	G	G# Ab

A♯ or B♭
A♯7+9 or B♭7+9

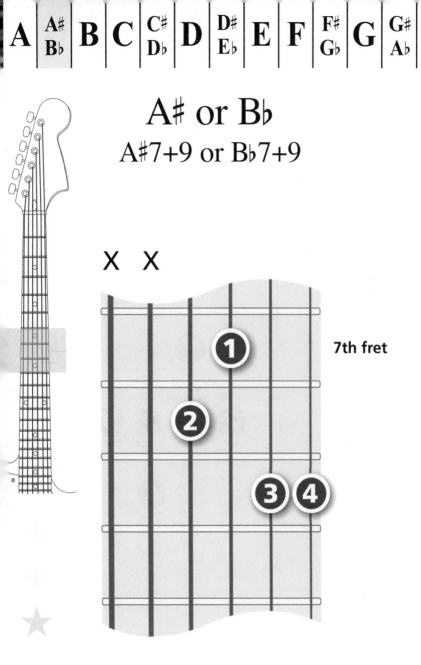

X X

7th fret

Notes in the chord:
4: B♭ (root); 3: D (third); 2: A♭ (dom seventh); 1: C♯ (aug ninth)

The lack of any deep bass doesn't detract from this
tasty chord.

A	A♯ B♭	B	C	C♯ D♭	D	D♯ E♭	E	F	F♯ G♭	G	G♯ A♭

A♯ or B♭
A♯9 or B♭9

X X

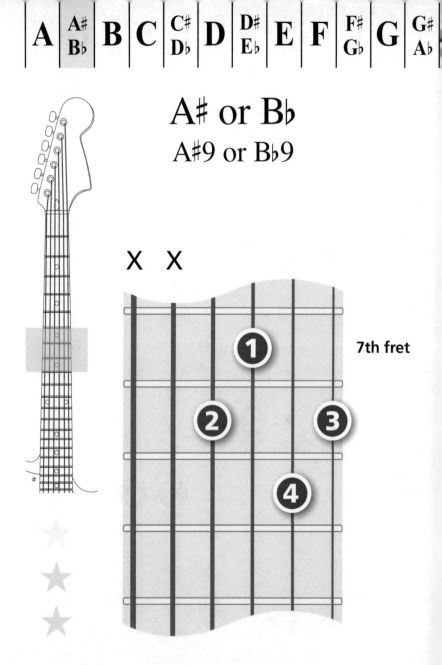

7th fret

Notes in the chord:

4: B♭ (root); 3: D (third); 2: A♭ (dom seventh); 1: C (ninth)

The vital ninth interval forms the top note here.

A♯ or B♭
A♯11 or B♭11

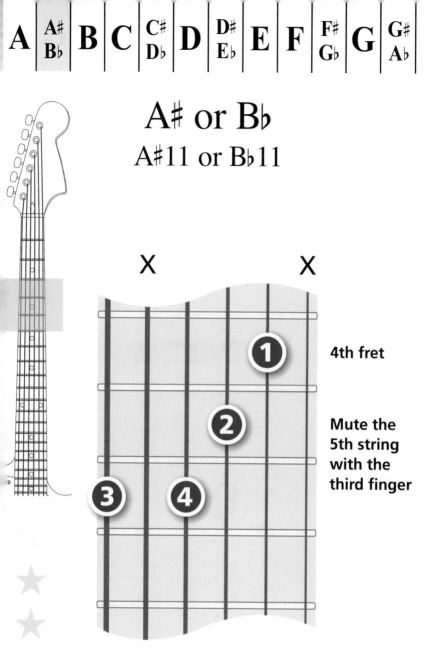

X   X

4th fret

**Mute the
5th string
with the
third finger**

Notes in the chord:
6: B♭ (root); 4: A♭ (dom seventh); 3: C (ninth); 2: E♭(eleventh)

Don't strike the top string, and ensure that the 5th
string is muted.

A# or B♭
A#13 or B♭13

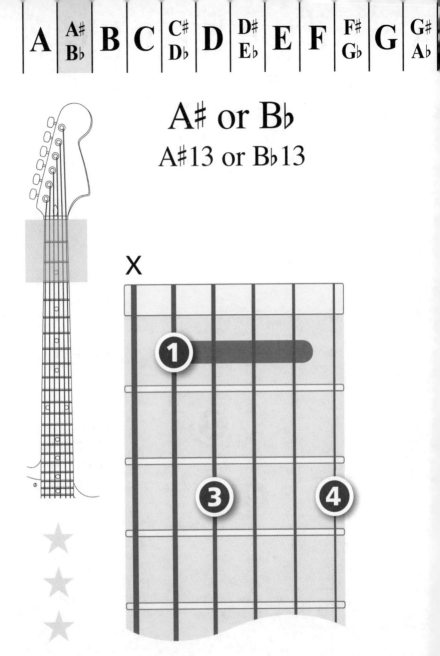

X

Notes in the chord:

5: B♭ (root); 4: F (fifth); 3: A♭ (dom seventh); 2: C (ninth); 1: G (thirteenth)

Not an easy chord to finger – but the resultant sound is worth the effort.

A# or Bb
A# dim or Bb dim
(A#° or Bb°)
(1st version)

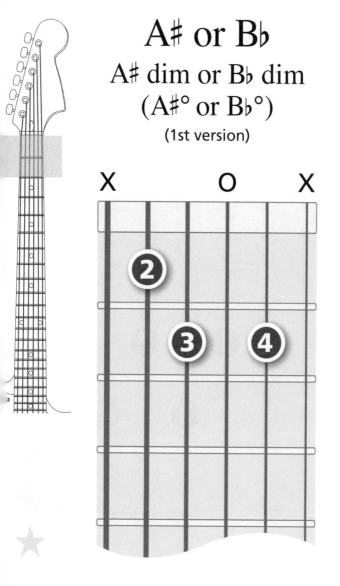

Notes in the chord:

5: Bb (root); 4: E (dim fifth); 3: G (dim seventh); 2: Db (minor third)

A useful root version of this diminished chord.

A# or B♭

A# dim or B♭ dim
(A#° or B♭°)
(2nd version)

X X

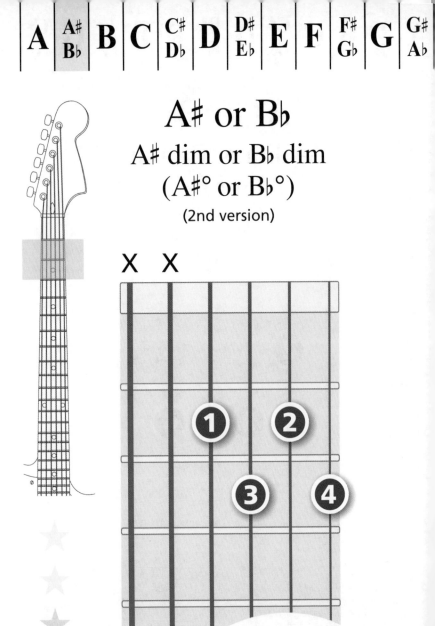

Notes in the chord:
4: E (dim fifth); 3: B♭ (keynote); 2: D♭ (minor third); 1: G (dim seventh)

A slightly higher four-string inversion.

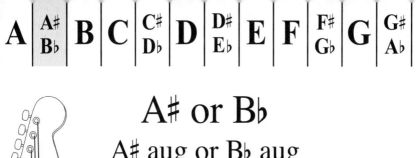

A	A♯ B♭	B	C	C♯ D♭	D	D♯ E♭	E	F	F♯ G♭	G	G♯ A♭

A♯ or B♭

A♯ aug or B♭ aug
(A♯+ or B♭+)
(1st version)

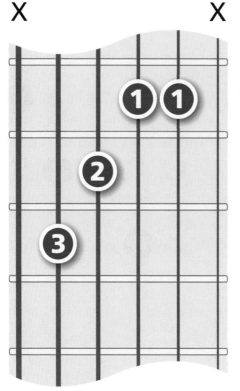

3rd fret

Notes in the chord:

5: D (third); 4: G♭ (aug fifth); 3: B♭ (keynote); 2: D

Augmented chords, like diminished ones, can be named after any of the notes they contain, so this can also serve as D+ or G♭+.

A♯ or B♭
A♯ aug or B♭ aug
(A♯+ or B♭+)
(2nd version)

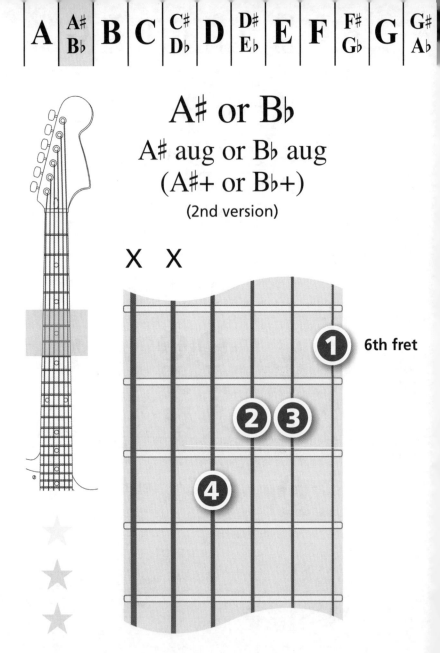

X X

1 6th fret

2 **3**

4

Notes in the chord:
4: B♭ (keynote); 3: D (third); 2: G♭ (aug fifth); 1: B♭

The key note appears at the top and bottom of the voicing shown here.

A♯ or B♭
A♯ minor or B♭ minor
(A♯m or B♭m)
(1st version)

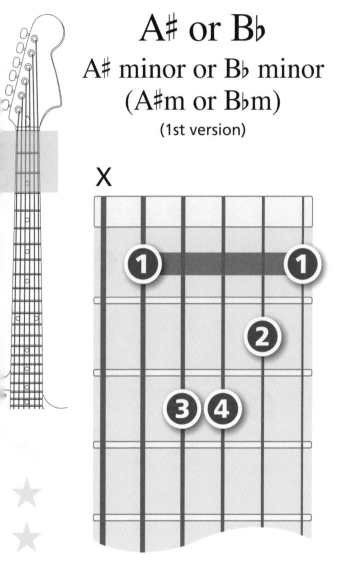

Notes in the chord:
5: B♭ (root); 4: F (fifth); 3: B♭; 2: D♭ (third); 1: F

In some situations, you can simplify this shape by omitting the bass B♭, and making a barré unnecessary.

63

A# or Bb
A# minor or Bb minor
(A#m or Bbm)
(2nd version)

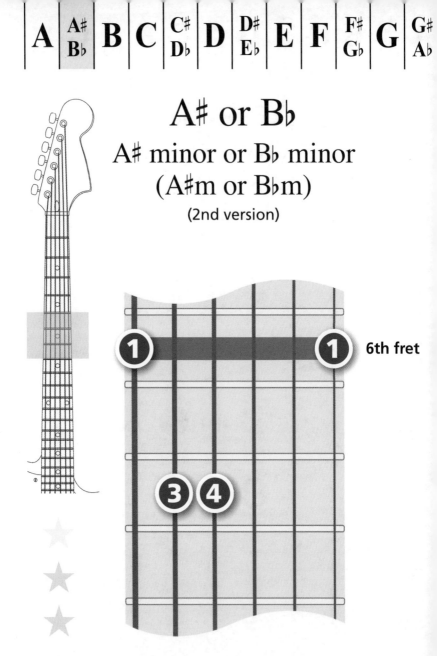

6th fret

Notes in the chord:
6: Bb (root); 5: F (fifth); 4: Bb; 3: Db (third); 2: F; 1: Bb

Like the previous chord, this one can be played as a four-stringer, with the A#/Bb on the 4th string as its bass.

A♯ or B♭
A♯ minor or B♭ minor
(A♯m or B♭m)
(3rd version)

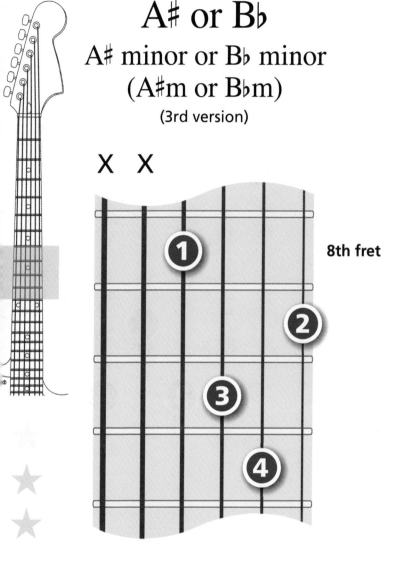

8th fret

Notes in the chord:
4: B♭ (root); 3: F (fifth); 2: B♭; 1: D♭ (third)

A high-position minor; no low A#/B♭ is reachable here.

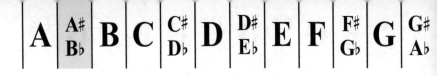

A♯ or B♭
A♯m6 or B♭m6
(1st version)

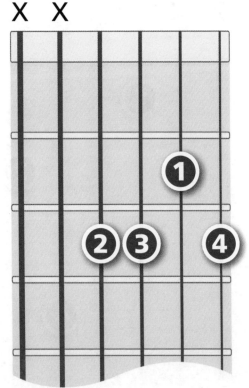

Notes in the chord:
4: F (fifth); 3: B♭; 2: D♭ (third); 1: G (sixth)

This is a second inversion – though the absence of a bass
key note will rarely matter.

A♯ or B♭

A♯m6 or B♭m6

(2nd version)

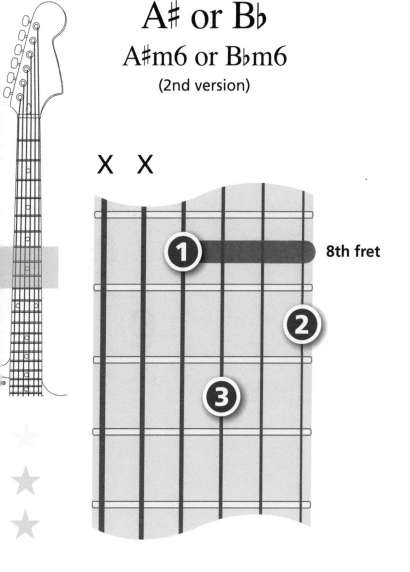

8th fret

Notes in the chord:

4: B♭ (root); 3: F (fifth); 2: G (sixth); 1: D♭ (third)

Even with such a small barré, the 2nd string still has a tendency to buzz!

A# or Bb
A#m7 or Bbm7
(1st version)

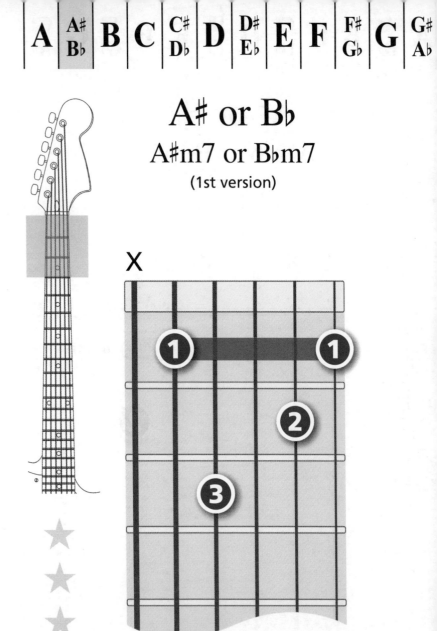

Notes in the chord:

5: Bb (root); 4: F (fifth); 3: Ab (dom seventh); 2: Db (third); 1: F

Another potentially difficult chord to finger, especially if your guitar has a high action.

A	A# Bb	B	C	C# Db	D	D# Eb	E	F	F# Gb	G	G# Ab

A# or Bb

A#m7 or Bbm7

(2nd version)

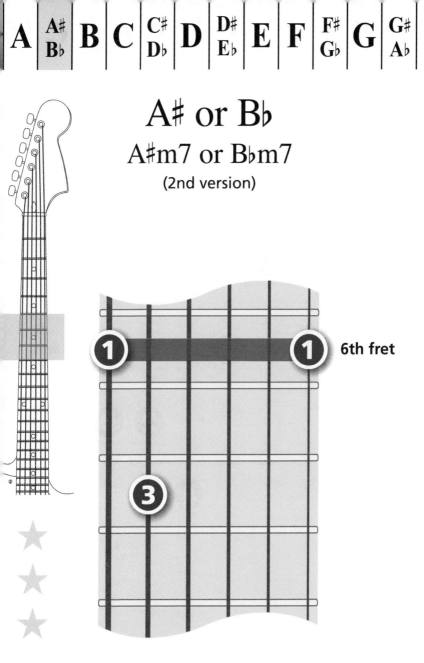

6th fret

Notes in the chord:

6: Bb (root); 5: F (fifth); 4: Ab (dom seventh); 3: Db (third); 2: F; 1: Bb

This rich chord often benefits from being strummed slowly.

A	A♯ B♭	B	C	C♯ D♭	D	D♯ E♭	E	F	F♯ G♭	G	G♯ A♭

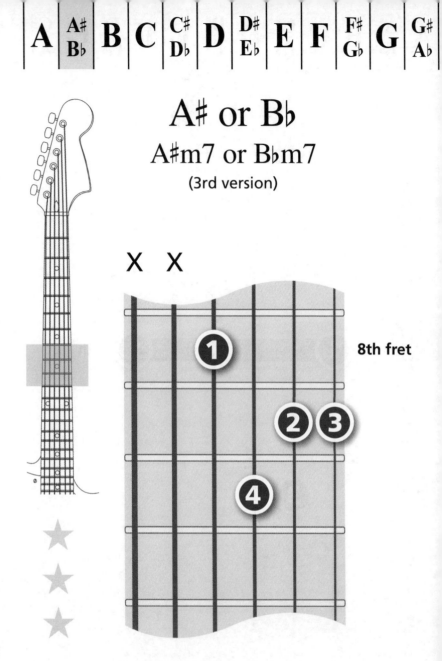

A♯ or B♭
A♯m7 or B♭m7
(3rd version)

8th fret

Notes in the chord:
4: B♭ (root); 3: F (fifth); 2: A♭ (dom seventh); 1: D♭ (third)

An 8th position voicing with all the clarity that the guitar's upper register can bring.

A	A# B♭	B	C	C# D♭	D	D# E♭	E	F	F# G♭	G	G# A♭

A# or B♭
A#m9 or B♭m9

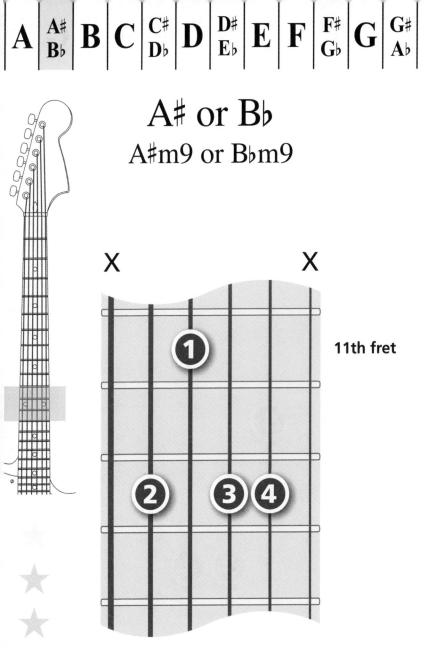

X   X

11th fret

Notes in the chord:
5: B♭ (root); 4: D♭; 3: A♭ (dom seventh); 2: C (ninth)

This takes us all the way up to the 13th fret!

B
'Bare' B (B5)

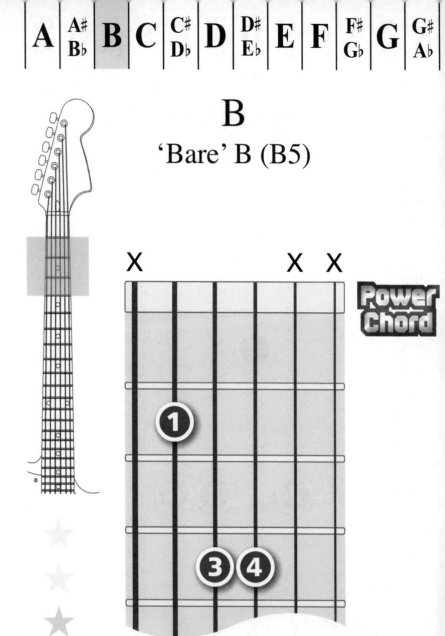

Power Chord

Notes in the chord:
4: B (root); 3: F# (fifth); 3: B

The 6th, 2nd and 1st strings remain silent for this 'power chord'.

A	A#/Bb	B	C	C#/Db	D	D#/Eb	E	F	F#/Gb	G	G#/Ab

B

B major

(1st version)

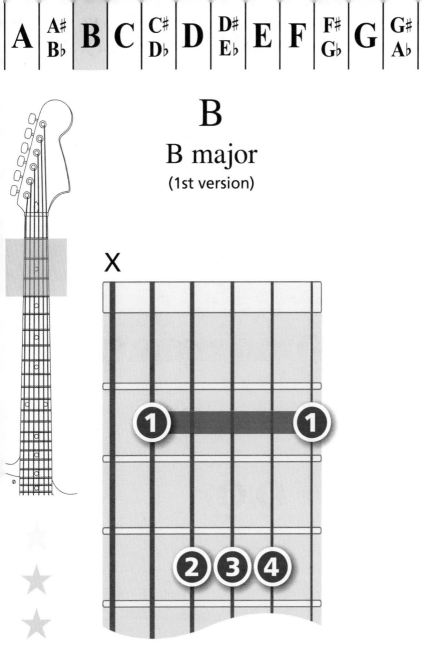

X

Notes in the chord:

5: B (root); 4: F# (fifth); 3: B; 2: D# (third); 1: F#

The key of B major isn't ideal for guitarists, and even this musically simple chord, placed low down on the fingerboard, requires some effort.

A	A# B♭	B	C	C# D♭	D	D# E♭	E	F	F# G♭	G	G# A♭

B
B major
(2nd version)

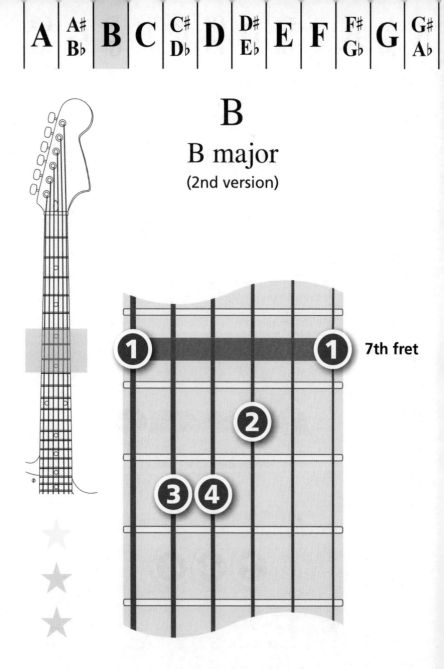

7th fret

Notes in the chord:

6: B (root); 5: F# (fifth); 4: B; 3: D# (third); 2: F# (fifth); 1: B

In a key such as B, higher position chords like this are often no more difficult to manage than those nearer the nut.

B

B major
(3rd version)

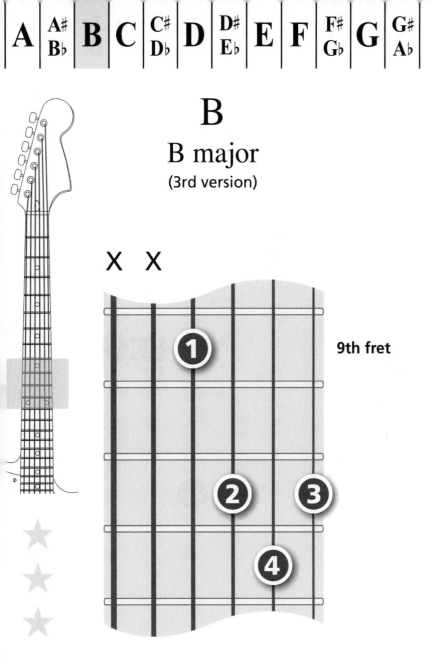

9th fret

Notes in the chord:
4: B (root); 3: F# (fifth); 2: B; 1: D# (third)

This high voicing of B has an attractively light sound.

| **A** | **A#**
B♭ | **B** | **C** | **C#**
D♭ | **D** | **D#**
E♭ | **E** | **F** | **F#**
G♭ | **G** | **G#**
A♭ |

B
B sus4

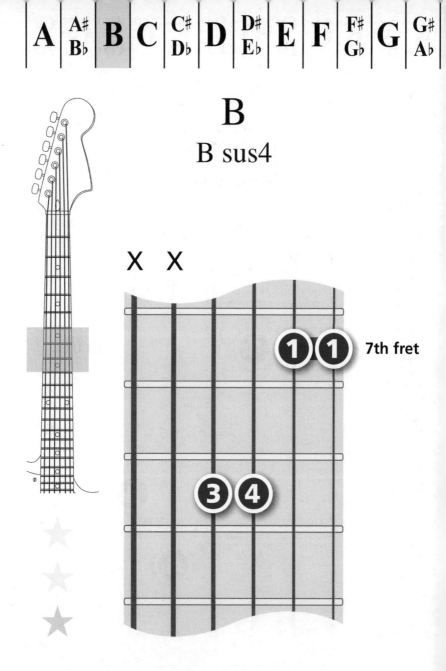

X X

1 1   **7th fret**

3 4

Notes in the chord:
4: B (root); 3: E (sus fourth); 2: F# (fifth); 1: B

The suspended fourth can be resolved by raising your 'pinky', and replacing it at the 8th fret on the 3rd string with your second finger.

B

B6

(1st version)

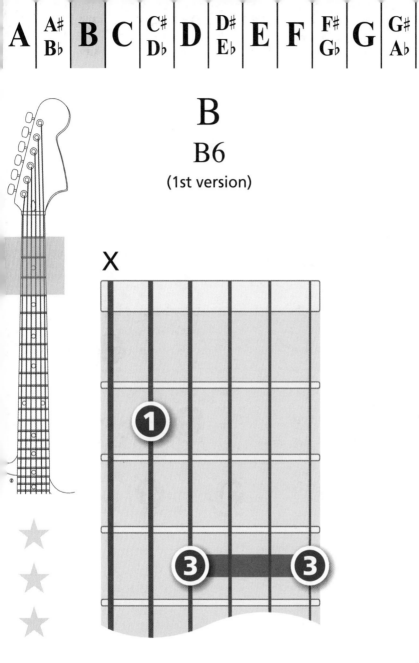

X

Notes in the chord:

5: B (root); 4: F# (fifth); 3: B; 2: D# (third); 1: G# (added sixth)

Some players worry about barréing with a finger other
than the index – but you may find this shape easier than
it looks.

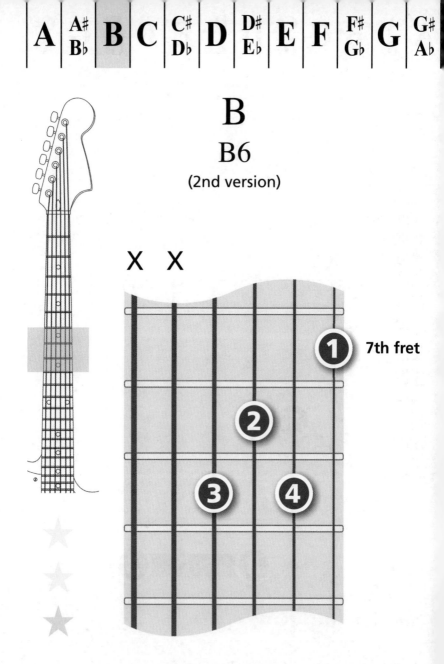

| A | A#
Bb | B | C | C#
Db | D | D#
Eb | E | F | F#
Gb | G | G#
Ab |

B

B6
(2nd version)

X X

1 — 7th fret

2

3 **4**

Notes in the chord:
4: B (root); 3: D# (third); 2: G# (added sixth); 1: B

A much simpler B6, though it omits the fifth note of
the chord (F#).

B
B6/9

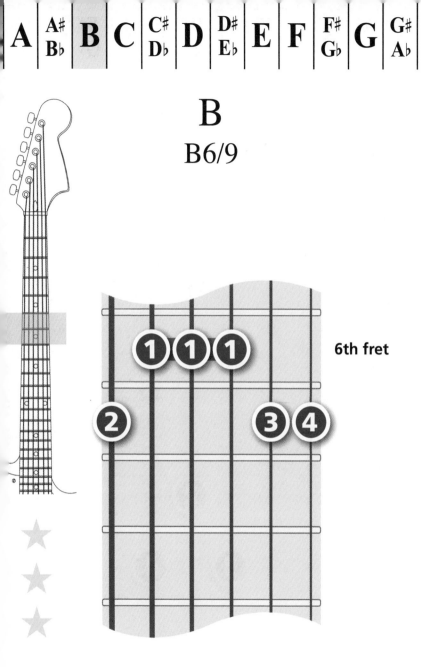

6th fret

Notes in the chord:
6: B (root); 5: D# (third); 4: G# (sixth); 3: C# (ninth); 2: F# (fifth); 1: B

One of the standard 6/9 shapes, played here at the
6th position.

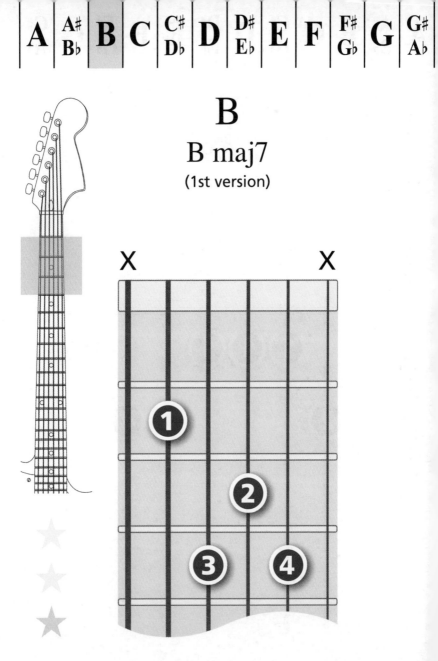

| A | A#
Bb | B | C | C#
Db | D | D#
Eb | E | F | F#
Gb | G | G#
Ab |

B

B maj7

(1st version)

X   X

Notes in the chord:

5: B (root); 4: F# (fifth); 3: A# (maj seventh); 2: D# (third)

Neither of the outer strings is needed here, and the left-hand fingers can control how long the chord vibrates.

B

B maj7
(2nd version)

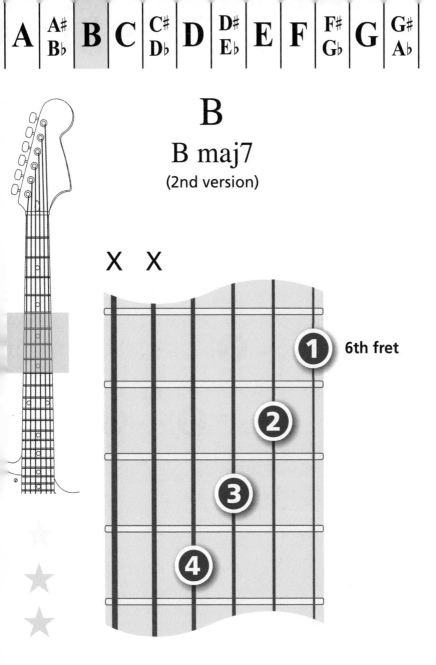

Notes in the chord:

4: B (root); 3: D# (third); 2: F# (fifth); 1: A# (maj seventh)

A higher-pitched chord, with the major seventh as its top note.

B

B7

(1st version)

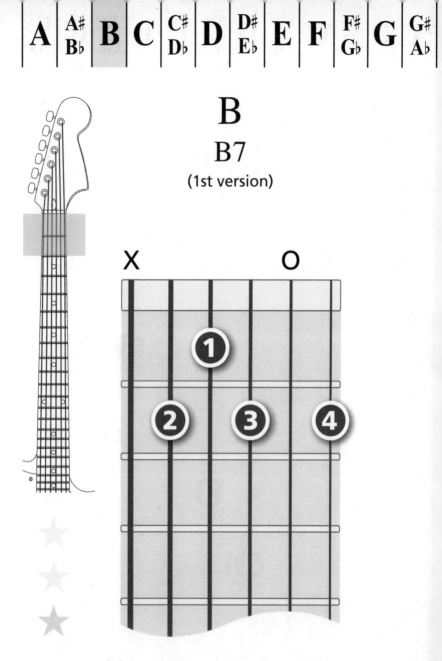

Notes in the chord:

5: B (root); 4: D# (third); 3: A (dom seventh); 2: B; 1: F# (fifth)

Full chords featuring an open string are a rarity in the key of B.

B
B7
(2nd version)

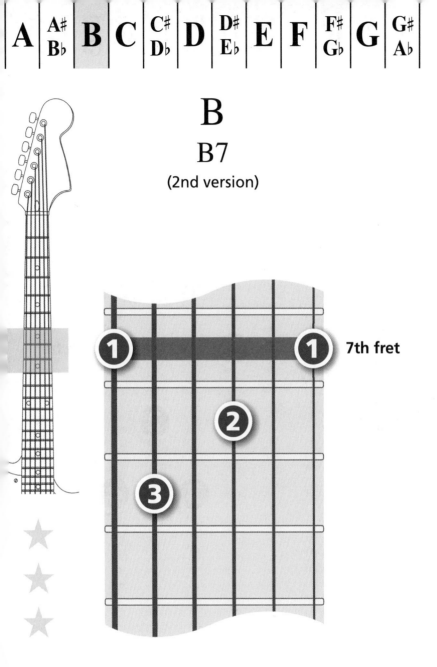

7th fret

Notes in the chord:

6: B (root); 5: F# (fifth); 4: A (dom seventh); 3: D# (third); 2: F# (fifth); 1: B

This shape works well when you slide up to it in blues or
rock playing.

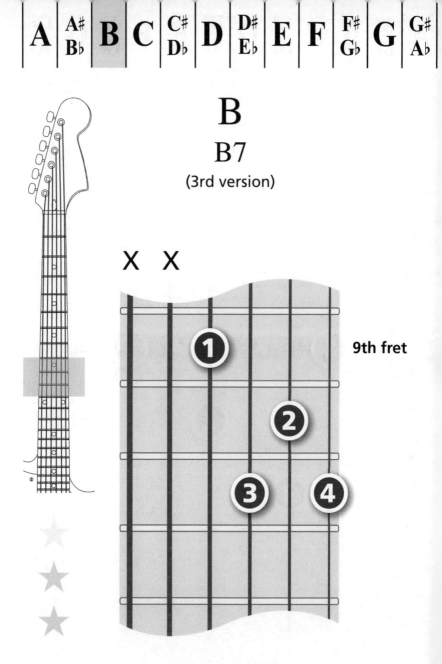

B

B7

(3rd version)

X X

9th fret

Notes in the chord:

4: B (root); 3: F# (fifth); 2: A (dom seventh); 1: D# (third)

Chords like this can be delicate or pack a punch,
depending on how they're struck.

B
B7+9

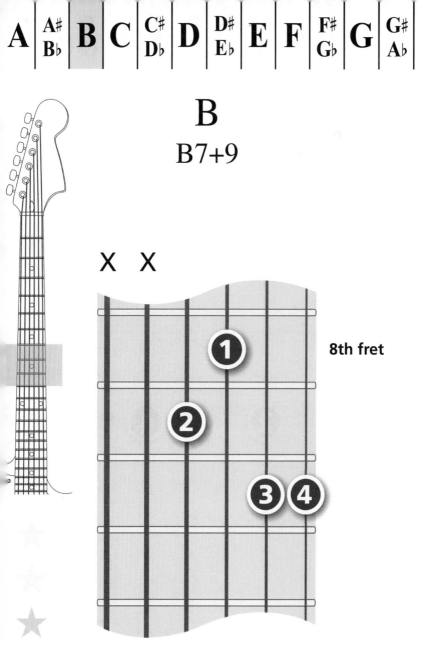

8th fret

Notes in the chord:

: B (root); 3: D# (third); 2: A (dom seventh); 1: C double sharp (D) (aug ninth)

A familiar fingering that sounds great at this high
neck position.

B
B9

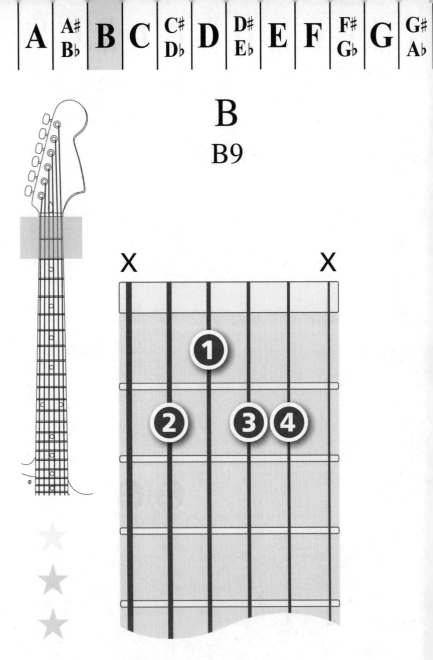

Notes in the chord:
5: B (root); 4: D# (third); 3: A (dom seventh); 2: C# (ninth)

This chord can be followed by a standard B7 – which is played by simply lifting your fourth finger and sounding the 2nd string open.

B

B11

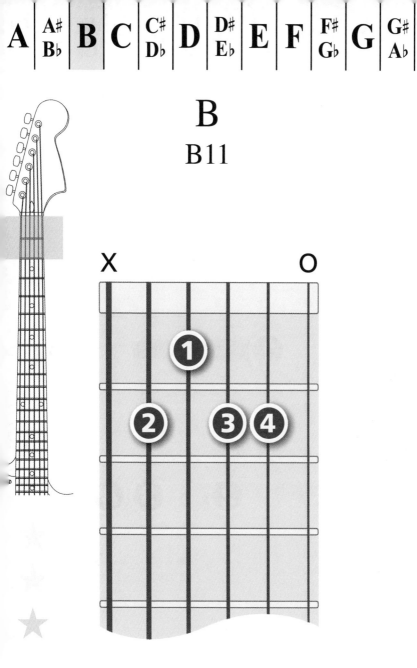

Notes in the chord:

5: B (root); 4: D# (third); 3: A (dom seventh); 2: C# (ninth); 1: E (eleventh)

Adding an open 1st string is all that's needed to convert
the B9 on the previous page to B11.

B
B13

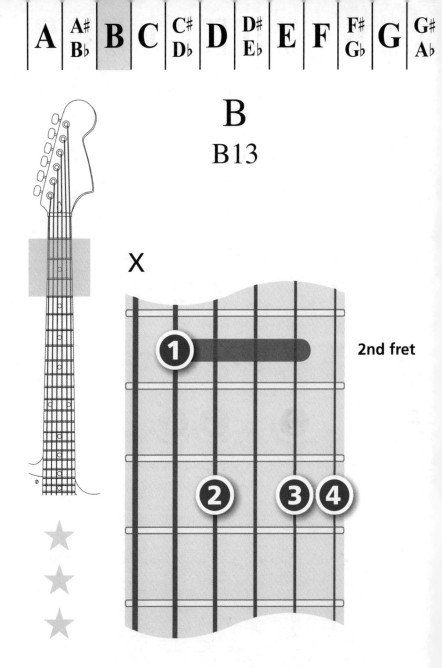

X

2nd fret

Notes in the chord:
5: B (root); 4: F# (fifth); 3: A (dom seventh); 2: D# (third); 1: G# (thirteenth

A chord that sounds especially rich at this low
fingerboard position.

B

B diminished (B dim, B°)

(1st version)

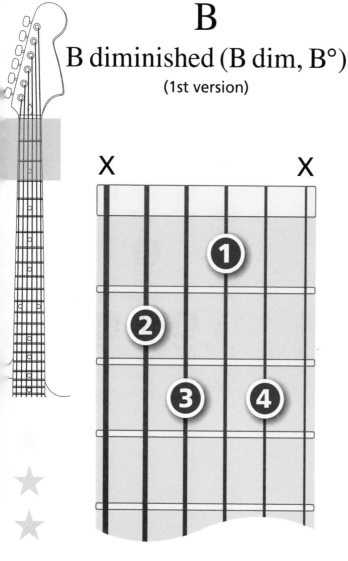

X   X

Notes in the chord:

5: B (root); 4: F (dim fifth); 3: G# (dim seventh); 2: D (minor third)

The inner strings supply the notes for this
diminished chord.

B

B diminished (B dim, B°)

(2nd version)

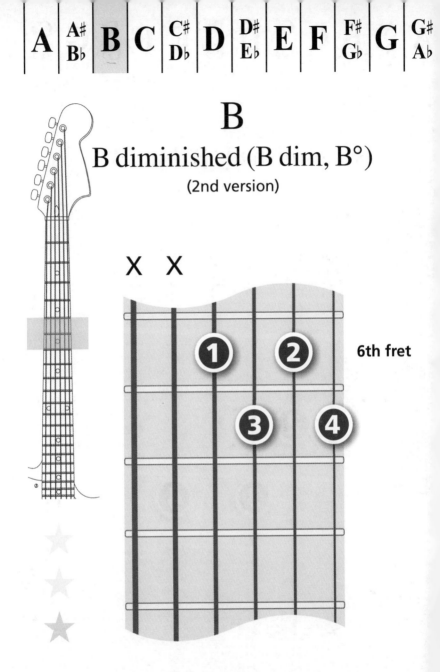

X X

6th fret

Notes in the chord:

4: G# (dim seventh); 3: D (minor third); 2: F (dim fifth); 1: B (keynote)

A handy B° – though it doesn't have the keynote as
its root.

B

B augmented (B aug, B+)

(1st version)

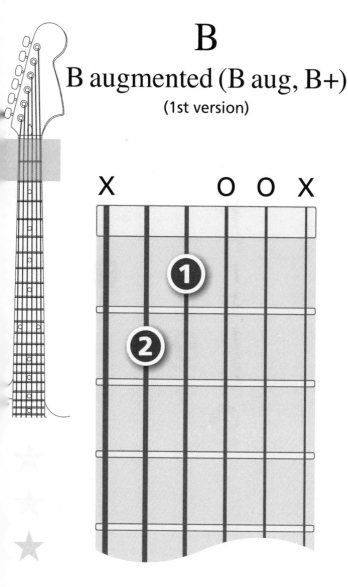

X   O   O   X

Notes in the chord:

5: B (root); 4: D# (third); 3: G (aug fifth); 2: B

Unusually for this key, the augmented chord shown here features two open strings.

B

B augmented (B aug, B+)

(2nd version)

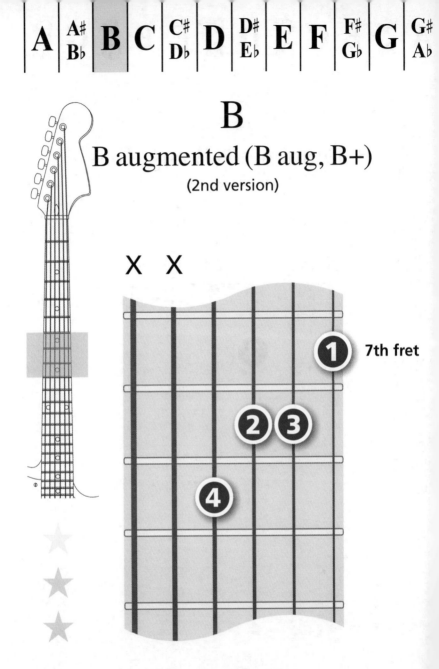

X X

① 7th fret

② ③

④

Notes in the chord:

4: B (root); 3: D# (third); 2: G (aug fifth); 1: B

A standard four-string augmented shape, deployed here at the 7th position.

92

B
B minor (Bm)
(1st version)

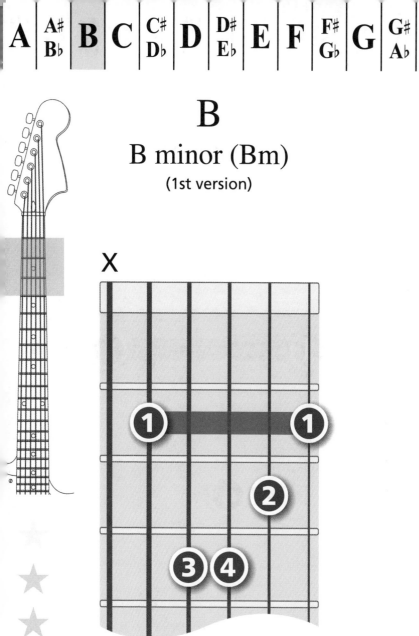

X

Notes in the chord:

5: B (root); 4: F# (fifth); 3: B; 2: D (third); 1: F#

The simplest full B minor on the guitar; for an easier, second inversion chord, omit the barré and strike only the top four strings.

B

B minor (Bm)

(2nd version)

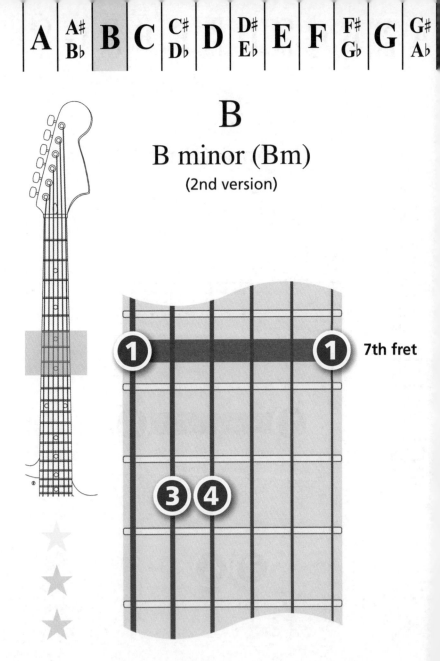

7th fret

Notes in the chord:

6: B (root); 5: F# (fifth); 4: B; 3: D (third); 2: F#; 1: B

To play this shape in a four-string version, barré only the first three strings, and make the B on the 4th string the root.

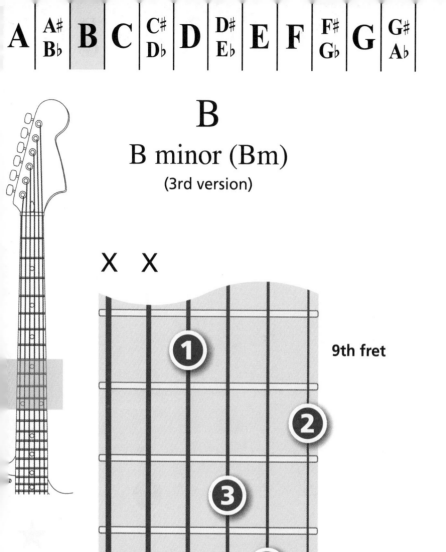

B
B minor (Bm)
(3rd version)

9th fret

Notes in the chord:

4: B (root); 3: F# (fifth); 2: B; 1: D (third)

A higher, four-string voicing of B minor.

95

B
Bm6
(1st version)

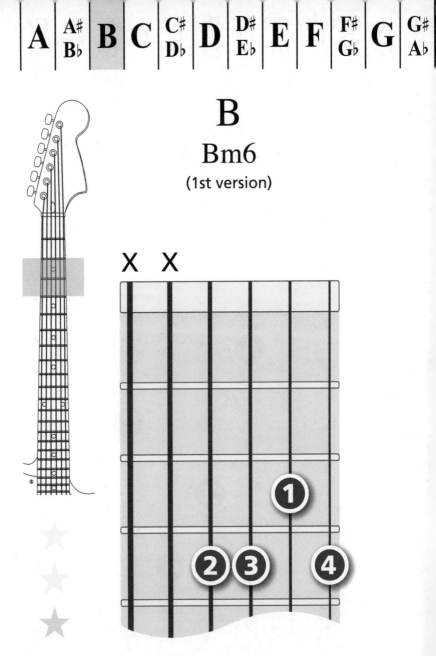

Notes in the chord:

4: F# (fifth); 3: B; 2: D (third); 1: G# (sixth)

A second inversion, with the fifth note of the B minor scale (F#) as its bass.

B

Bm6

(2nd version)

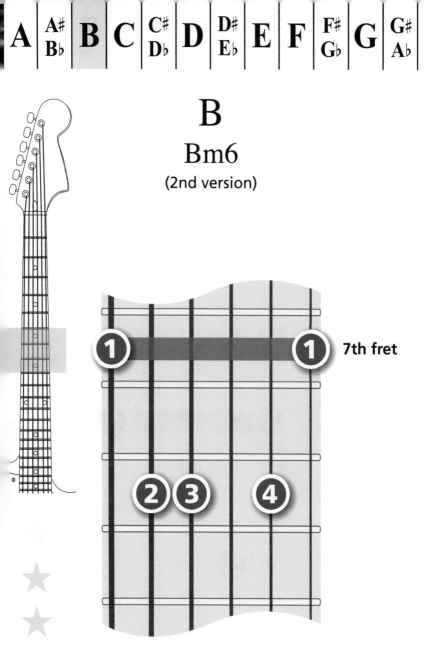

7th fret

Notes in the chord:

6: B (root); 5: F# (fifth); 4: B; 3: D (third); 2: G# (sixth); 1: B

Plenty of power is available from this six-note Bm6.

B

Bm7

(1st version)

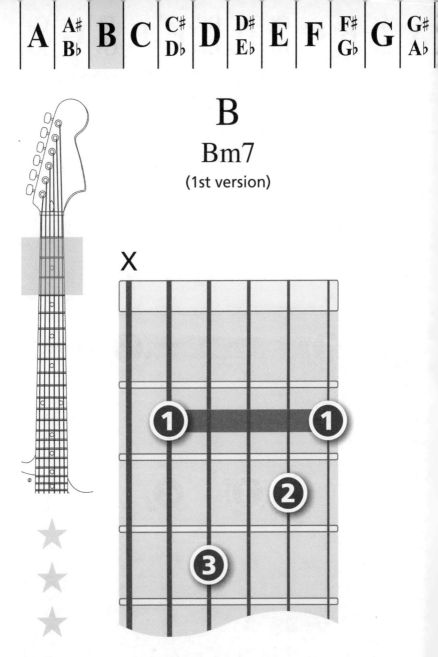

Notes in the chord:

5: B (root); 4: F# (fifth); 3: A (dom seventh); 2: D (third); 1: F#

You can add a low F# here by extending your barré to the
6th string: doing so produces a second inversion.

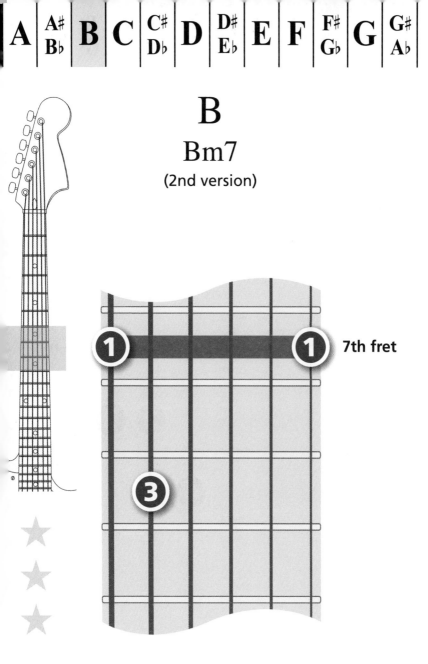

B
Bm7
(2nd version)

7th fret

Notes in the chord:
6: B (root); 5: F# (fifth); 4: A (dom seventh); 3: D (third); 2: F#; 1: B

Ensuring that all the barréd notes ring out cleanly can
sometimes be a problem here.

B
Bm7
(3rd version)

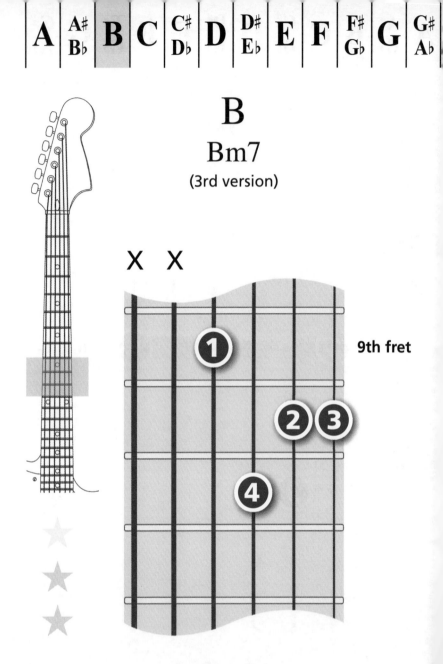

X X

9th fret

Notes in the chord:

4: B (root); 3: F# (fifth); 2: A (dom seventh); 1: D (third)

A versatile higher-pitched Bm7.

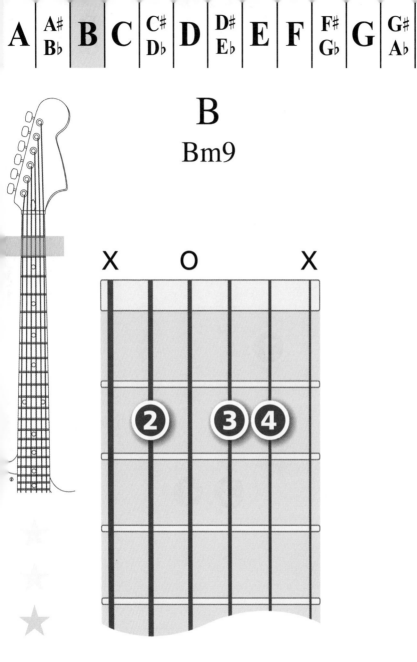

Notes in the chord:

5: B (root); 4: D (third); 3: A (dom seventh); 2: C# (ninth)

This chord gives your index finger a well-earned rest!

C
'Bare' C (C5)

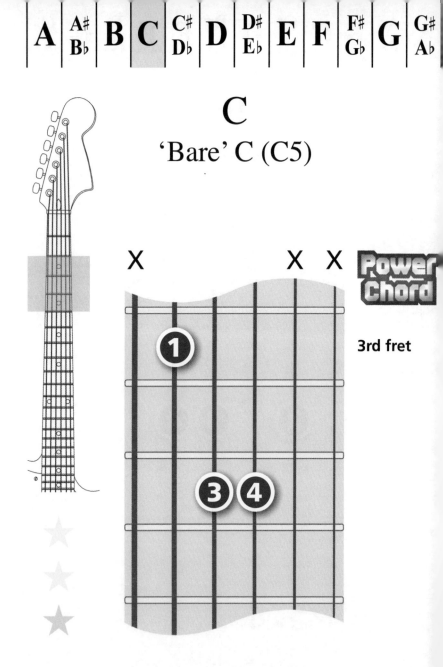

3rd fret

Notes in the chord:
5: C (root); 4: G (fifth); 3: C

This chord contains no third, and is therefore neither major nor minor. The 6th, 2nd and 1st strings aren't played.

A	A# Bb	B	C	C# Db	D	D# Eb	E	F	F# Gb	G	G# Ab

C
C major
(1st version)

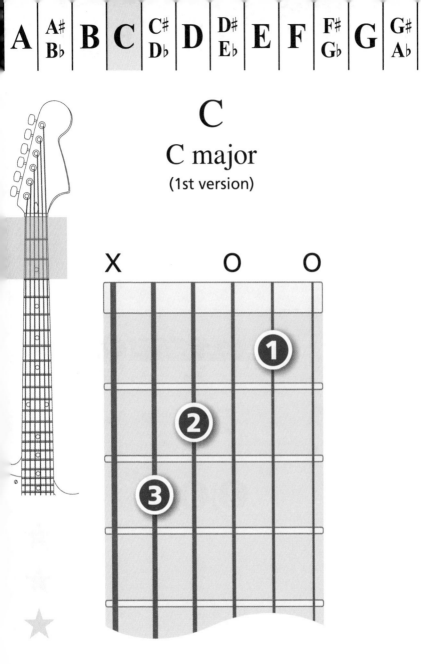

Notes in the chord:
5: C (root); 4: E (third); 3: G (fifth); 2: C; 1: E

Fingering the normally silent 6th string at the 3rd fret gives a G, and produces a second inversion of the C chord.

C

C major
(2nd version)

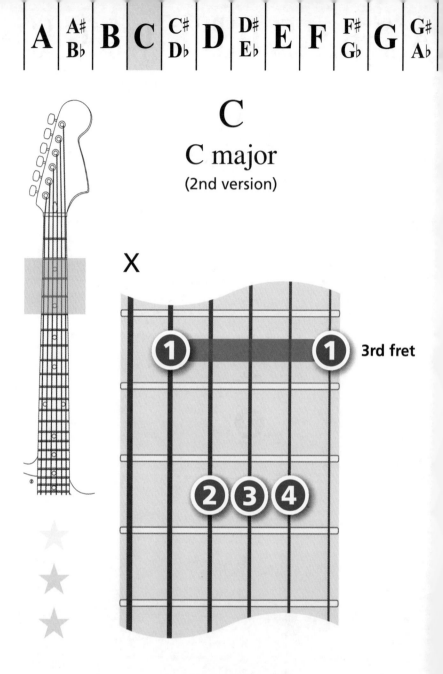

X

3rd fret

Notes in the chord:

5: C (root); 4: G (fifth); 3: C; 2: E (third); 1: G

Playing the 6th string (already fretted by the barré) creates a bass G, and with it a second inversion of the C chord.

C

C major
(3rd version)

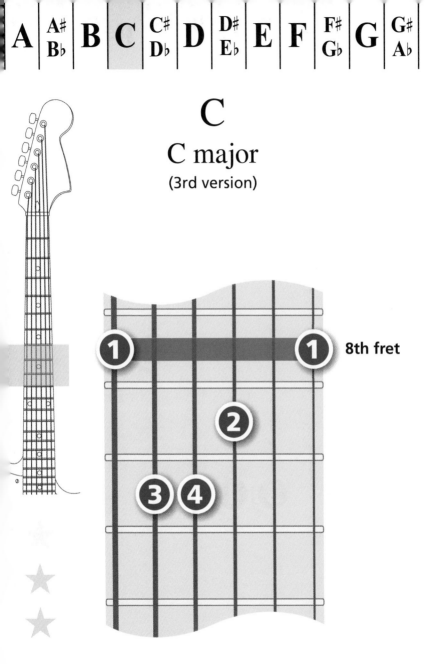

8th fret

Notes in the chord:
6: C (root); 5: G (fifth); 4: C; 3: E (third); 2: G; 1: C

A handy higher-pitched C major chord.

C

C sus4

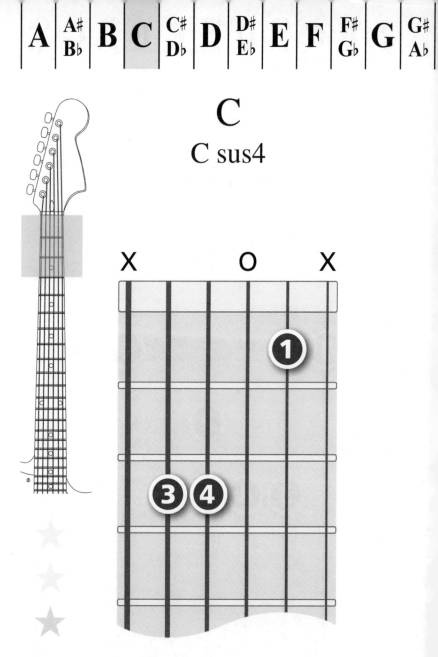

Notes in the chord:

5: C (root); 4: F (sus4); 3: G (fifth); 2: C

Resolve this 'suspended fourth' chord onto 'standard' C (p.103) by lifting your fourth finger, and placing your second finger on the 4th string, 2nd fret.

A	A#/Bb	B	C	C#/Db	D	D#/Eb	E	F	F#/Gb	G	G#/Ab

C

C6

(1st version)

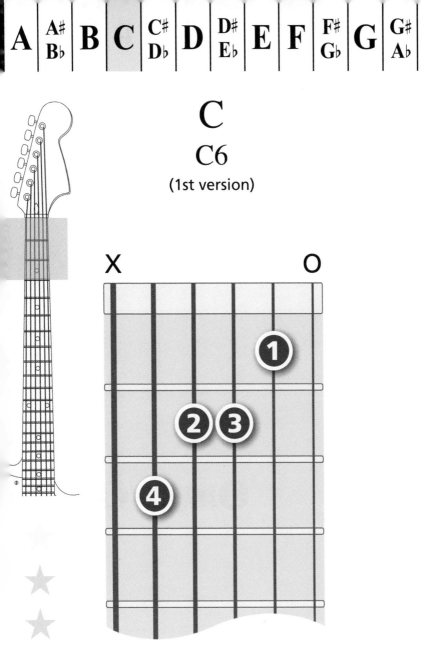

Notes in the chord:

5: C (root); 4: E (third); 3: A (sixth); 2: C; 1: E

A moderately easy 'added sixth' shape.

A	A# Bb	B	C	C# Db	D	D# Eb	E	F	F# Gb	G	G# Ab

C
C6
(2nd version)

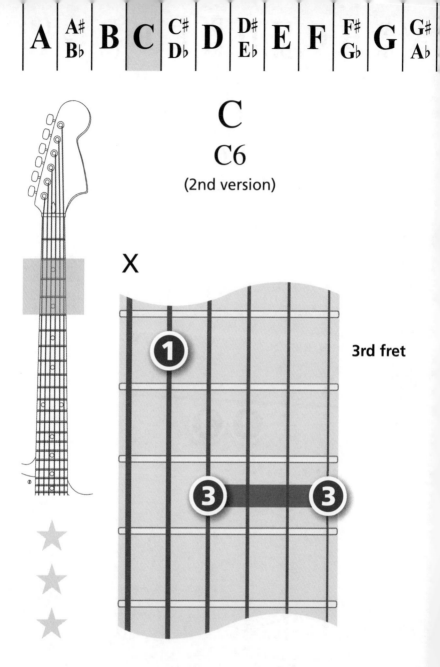

3rd fret

Notes in the chord:
5: C (root); 4: G (fifth); 3: C; 2: E (third); 1: A (sixth)

This voicing places the added sixth at the top of the chord, making it especially prominent.

C
C6/9

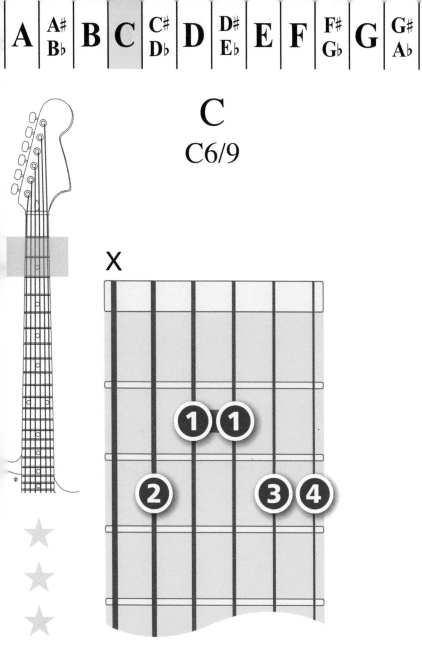

X

Notes in the chord:

5: C (root); 4: E (third); 3: A (sixth); 2: D (ninth); 1: G (fifth)

This fingering can be used for 6/9s all over the fingerboard.

C

C maj7
(1st version)

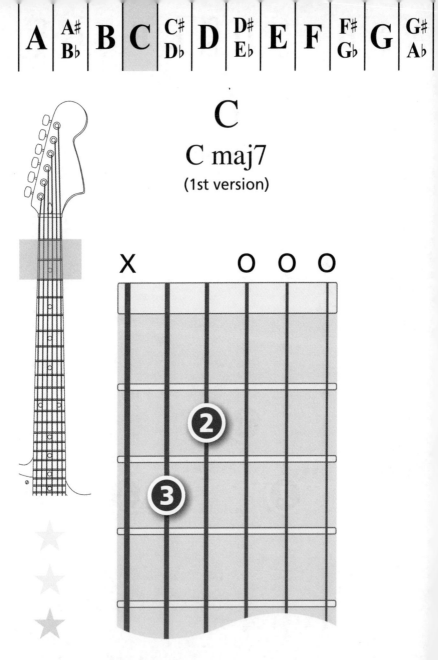

X   O   O   O

Notes in the chord:

5: C (root); 4: E (third); 3: G (fifth); 2: B (maj7); 1: E

All that's needed to resolve this chord onto a standard C is the addition of your index finger at the 2nd string, 1st fret.

C

C maj7
(2nd version)

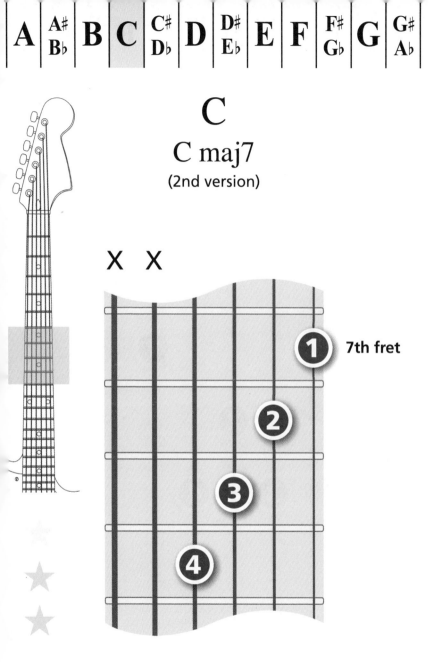

X X

① 7th fret

②

③

④

Notes in the chord:

4: C (root); 3: E (third); 2: G (fifth); 1: B (maj7)

A good C maj7 for when you don't require a deep bass note!

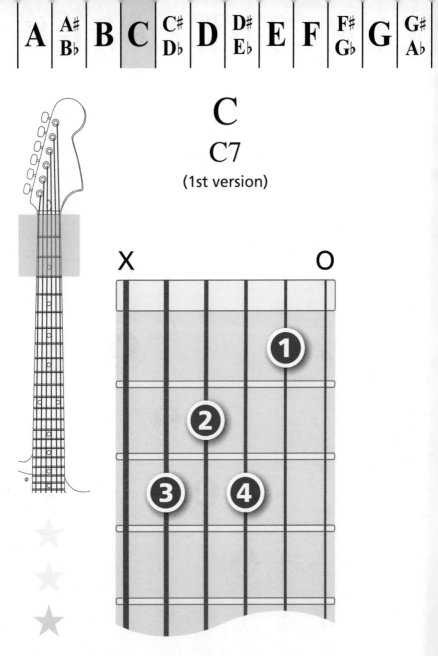

A | A#/Bb | B | C | C#/Db | D | D#/Eb | E | F | F#/Gb | G | G#/Ab

C
C7
(1st version)

X   O

Notes in the chord:
5: C (root); 4: E (3rd); 3: Bb (dom7); 2: C; 1: E

A simple and effective dominant seventh.

C

C7

(2nd version)

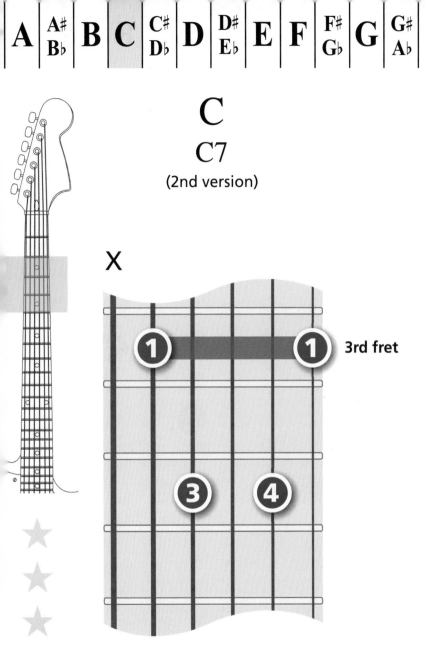

X

3rd fret

Notes in the chord:

5: C (root); 4: G (fifth); 3: B♭ (dom7); 2: E (third); 1: G

Your barré needs to be firm here, or the B♭ at the 3rd string won't sound properly.

C

C7

(3rd version)

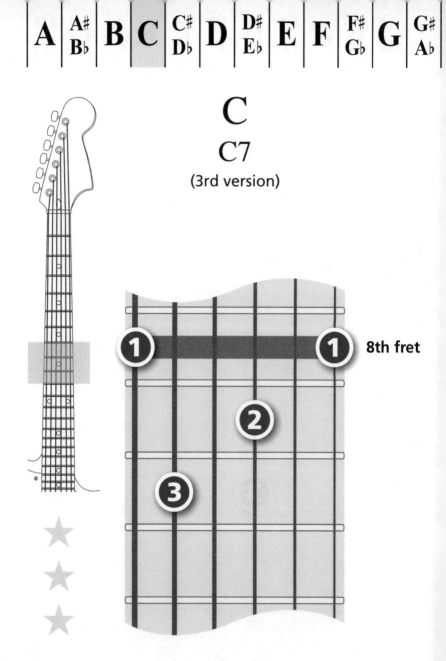

8th fret

Notes in the chord:

6: C (root); 5: G (fifth); 4: Bb (dom7); 3: E (third); 2: G; 1: C

A good shape to 'slide up' to.

C
C7+9

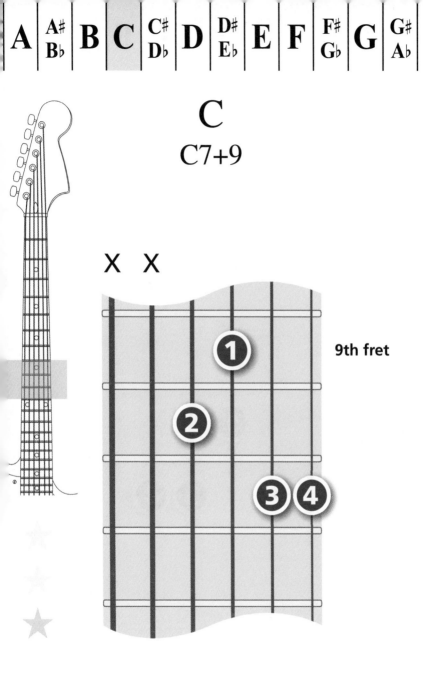

9th fret

Notes in the chord:

4: C (root); 3: E (third); 2: Bb (dom7); 1: D# (aug9)

Chords of this kind were a particular favourite of Jimi Hendrix, and are perennially useful in blues and jazz.

C

C9

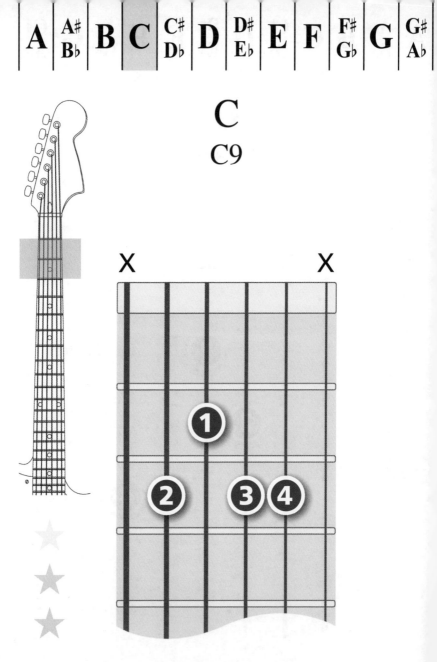

Notes in the chord:

5: C (root); 4: E (third); 3: Bb (dom7); 2: D (ninth)

This C9 is played on the inner strings only; the 1st and 6th are silent.

A	A# Bb	B	C	C# Db	D	D# Eb	E	F	F# Gb	G	G# Ab

C
C11

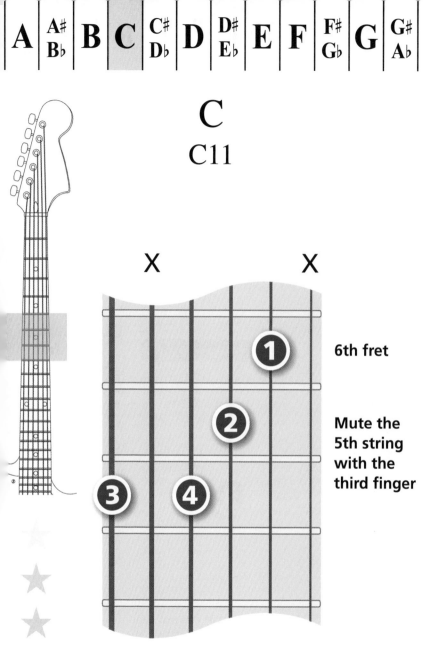

X   X

6th fret

**Mute the
5th string
with the
third finger**

Notes in the chord:

6: C (root); 4: Bb (dom seventh); 3: D (ninth); 2: F (eleventh)

We previously encountered this fingering for A#/Bb11 on
page 57. In this chord it is raised to the 6th position.

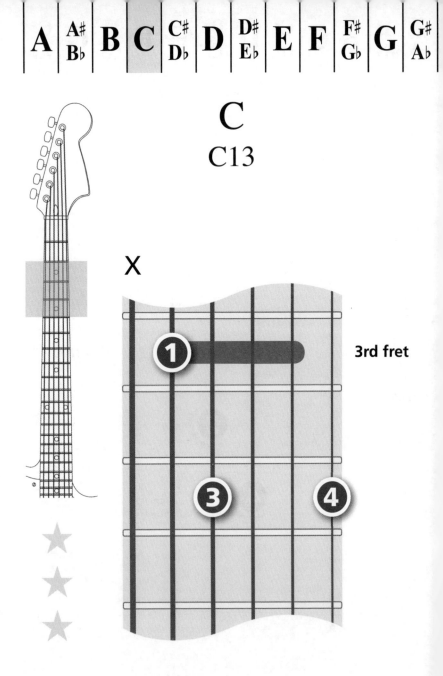

A	A# B♭	B	C	C# D♭	D	D# E♭	E	F	F# G♭	G	G# A♭

C
C13

X

3rd fret

Notes in the chord:
5: C (root); 4: G (fifth); 3: B♭ (dom seventh); 2: D (ninth); 1: A (thirteenth)

The presence of the ninth (absent from some 13th voicings) makes this difficult shape worth practising.

C

C diminished (C dim, C°)

(1st version)

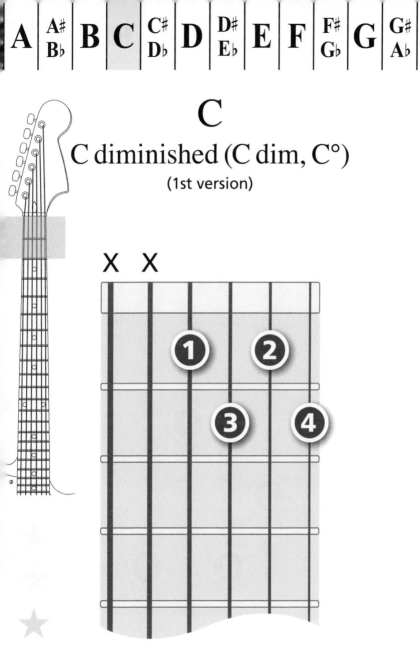

Notes in the chord:

4: E♭ (minor third); 3: A (dim seventh); 2: C (keynote); 1: F# (dim fifth)

This diminished chord doesn't have C as its bass, but is
still suitable in many musical contexts.

C

C diminished (C dim, C°)

(2nd version)

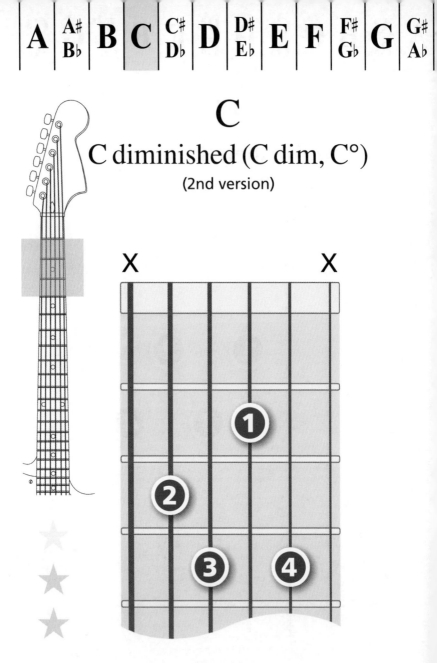

Notes in the chord:

5: C (root); 4: F# (dim fifth); 3: A (dim seventh); 2: E♭ (minor third)

A nice diminished shape, with C firmly established as the root note.

C

C augmented (C aug, C+)

(1st version)

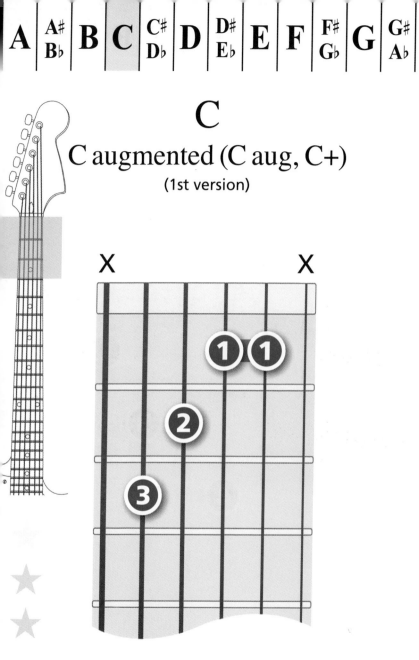

Notes in the chord:

5: C (root); 4: E (third); 3: G# (aug fifth); 2: C

Playing this augmented chord anticipates a move onto F major.

C
C augmented (C aug, C+)
(2nd version)

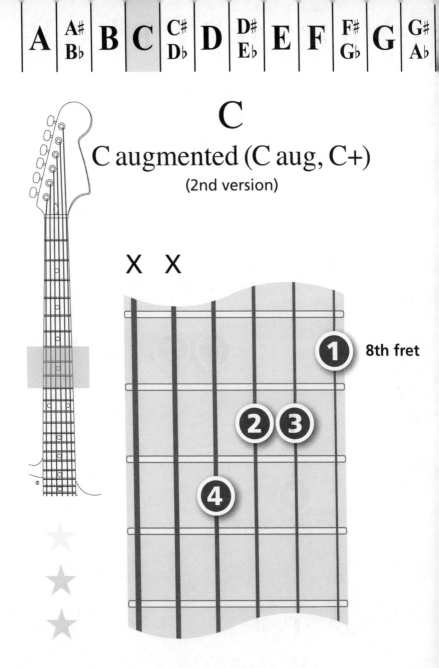

X X

8th fret

Notes in the chord:
4: C (root); 3: E (third); 2: G# (aug fifth); 1: C

The notes here are an octave above their counterparts in
the chord on page 121.

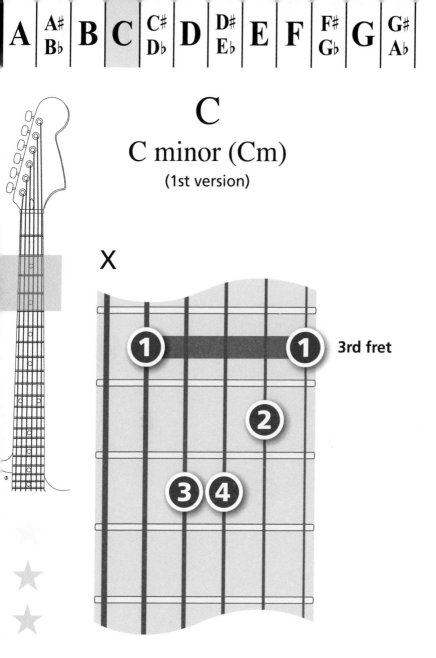

A	A# Bb	B	C	C# Db	D	D# Eb	E	F	F# Gb	G	G# Ab

C
C minor (Cm)
(1st version)

X

1   1   **3rd fret**

2

3 4

Notes in the chord:
5: C (root); 4: G (fifth); 3: C; 2: Eb (third); 1: G

The most convenient five-string C minor chord on the
lower part of the fingerboard.

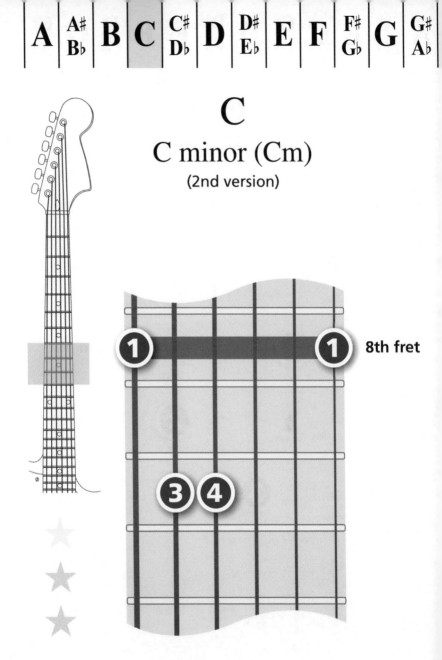

C
C minor (Cm)
(2nd version)

8th fret

Notes in the chord:
6: C (root); 5: G (fifth); 4: C; 3: E♭ (third); 2: G; 1: C

A higher-pitched version of C minor.

A	A# B♭	B	C	C# D♭	D	D# E♭	E	F	F# G♭	G	G# A♭

C
C minor (Cm)
(3rd version)

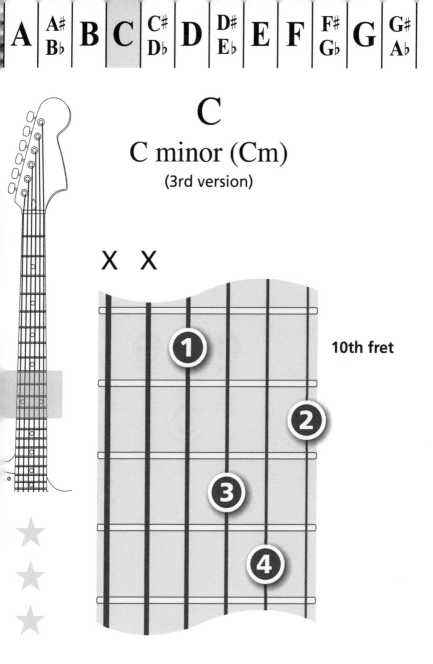

X X

10th fret

Notes in the chord:

4: C (root); 3: G (fifth); 2: C; 1: E♭ (third)

This shape may be hard to play on guitars with only 12
frets clearly accessible – but it sounds great!

C

Cm6

(1st version)

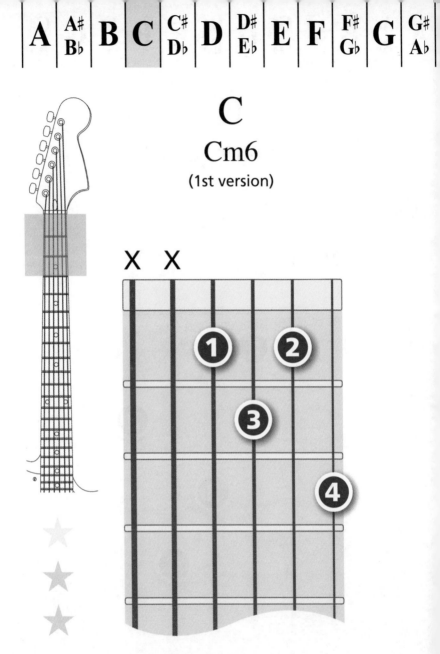

Notes in the chord:

4: E♭ (third); 3: A (sixth); 2: C; 1: G (fifth)

A first inversion of Cm6, with an E♭ as its lowest note.

C

Cm6
(2nd version)

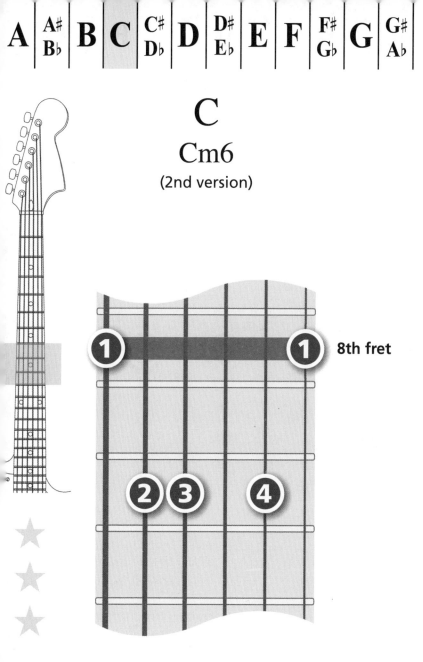

8th fret

Notes in the chord:
6: C (root); 5: G (fifth); 4: C; 3: Eb (third); 2: A (sixth); 1: C

Take care with your barré, or the 3rd string won't sound cleanly.

C

Cm7

(1st version)

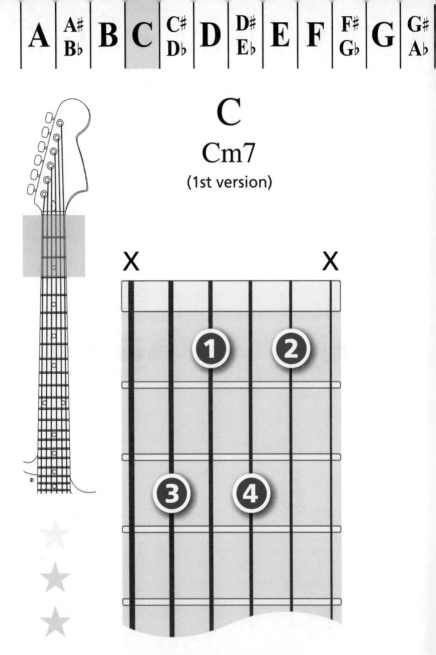

Notes in the chord:

5: C (root); 4: E♭ (third); 3: B♭ (dom7); 2: C

A frequently heard voicing of this chord – although it lacks the G that would supply its fifth.

C
Cm7
(2nd version)

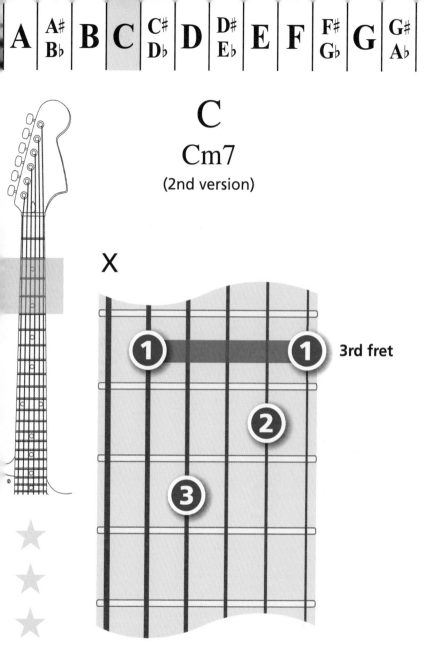

X

3rd fret

Notes in the chord:
5: C (root); 4: G (fifth); 3: Bb (dom7); 2: Eb (third); 1: G

All the constituent notes for a full Cm7 are present here.

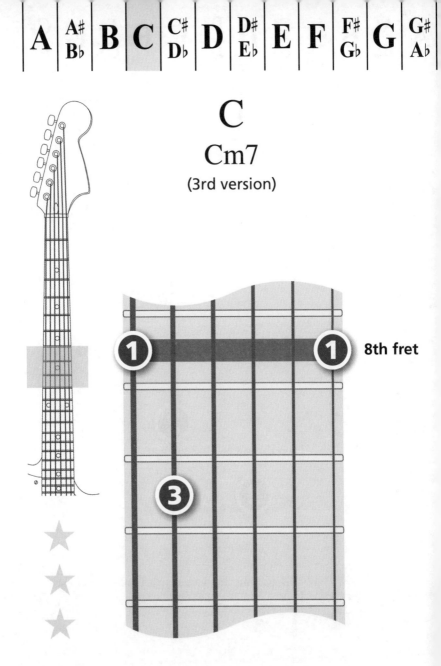

C

Cm7

(3rd version)

8th fret

Notes in the chord:

6: C (root); 5: G (fifth); 4: B♭ (dom7); 3: E♭ (third); 2: G; 1: C

A well-executed first-finger barré is required here –
and for many other higher-position shapes.

A	A# / Bb	B	C	C# / Db	D	D# / Eb	E	F	F# / Gb	G	G# / Ab

C
Cm9

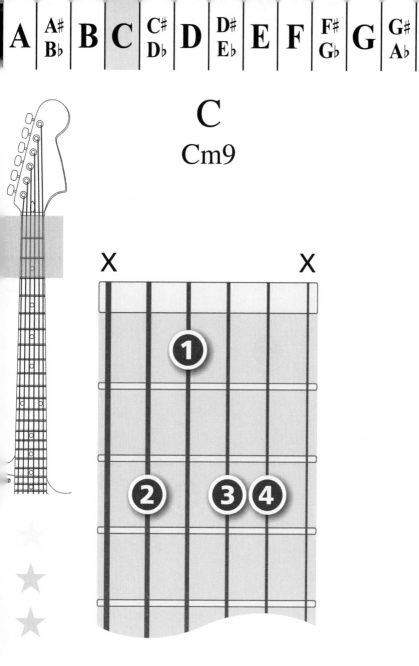

Notes in the chord:
5: C (root); 4: Eb (third); 3: Bb (dom7); 2: D (ninth)

Like the Cm7 on page 128, this fingering omits G (the fifth of the chord), but clearly conveys the required harmony.

C# or D♭

'Bare' C# or 'bare' D♭
(C#5 or D♭5)

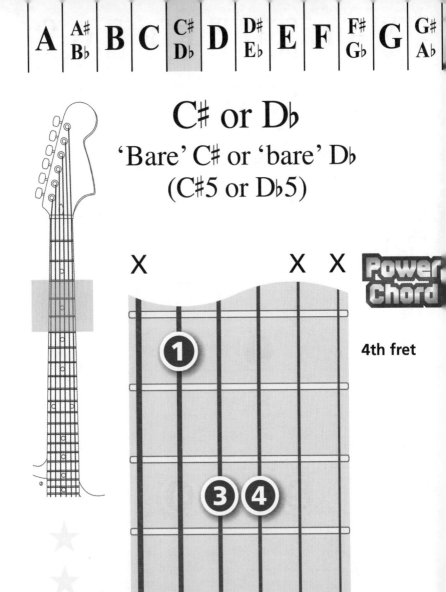

X   X   X

Power Chord

4th fret

Notes in the chord:
5: C# (root); 4: G# (fifth); 3: C#

The 6th, 2nd and 1st strings aren't played here.

C# or Db
C# major or Db major
(1st version)

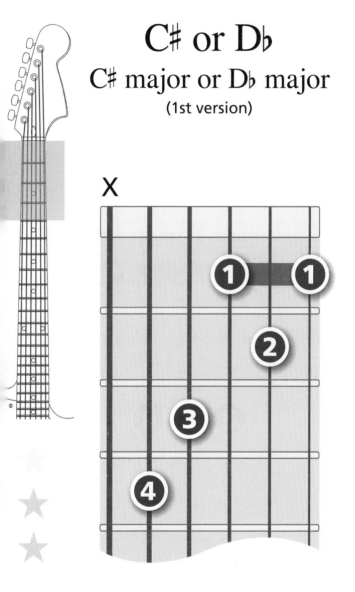

X

Notes in the chord:
5: C# (root); 4: E# (third); 3: G# (fifth); 2: C#; 1: E#

This shape can be moved up the fingerboard to make major chords; it appears here in its lowest possible position.

C# or Db

C# major or Db major

(2nd version)

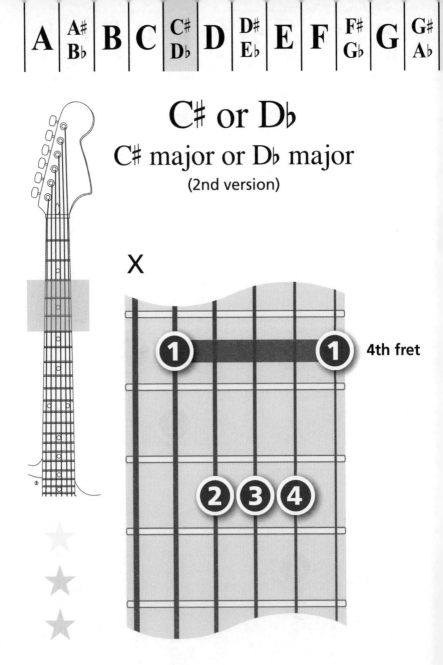

X

4th fret

Notes in the chord:

5: C# (root); 4: G# (fifth); 3: C#; 2: E# (third); 1: G#

Extend your barré to the 6th string to play a low G#, if you wish to convert this root chord to a second inversion.

C♯ or D♭
C♯ major or D♭ major
(3rd version)

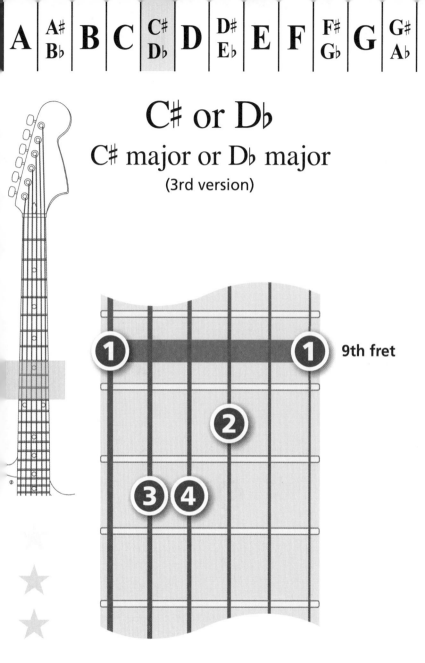

9th fret

Notes in the chord:
6: C# (root); 5: G# (fifth); 4: C#; 3: E# (third); 2: G#; 1: C#

A high voicing of C#/Db.

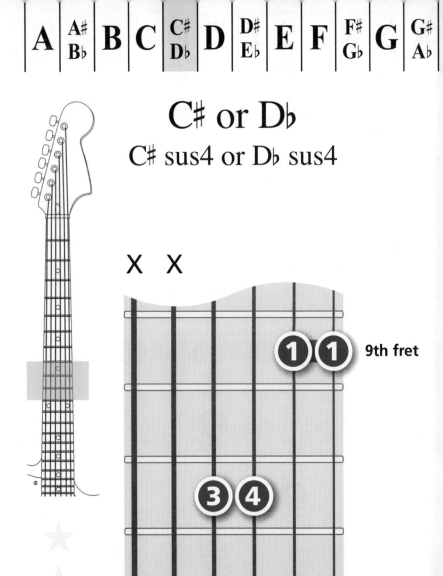

C♯ or D♭

C♯ sus4 or D♭ sus4

X   X

9th fret

Notes in the chord:

4: C# (root); 3: F# (sus fourth); 2: G# (fifth); 1: C#

Resolve this 'sus 4' to a standard major by releasing your
little finger and placing your second at the 10th fret,
3rd string.

C♯ or D♭

C♯6 or D♭6

(1st version)

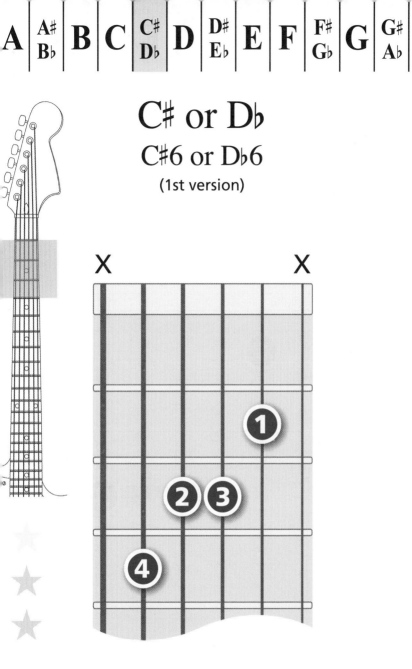

Notes in the chord:

5: C# (root); 4: E# (third); 3: A# (added sixth); 2: C#

A simple added sixth, using a shiftable fingering on the inner strings.

C♯ or D♭

C♯6 or D♭6

(2nd version)

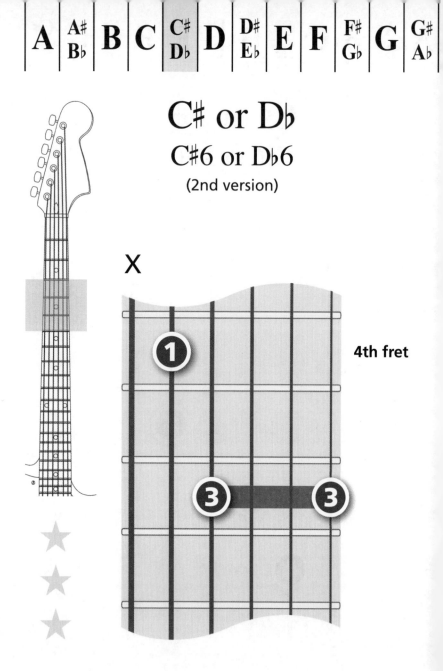

X

4th fret

Notes in the chord:

5: C# (root); 4: G# (fifth); 3: C#; 2: E# (third); 1: A# (added sixth)

This shape is a challenge, but the results are worthwhile!

C# or Db
C#6/9 or Db6/9

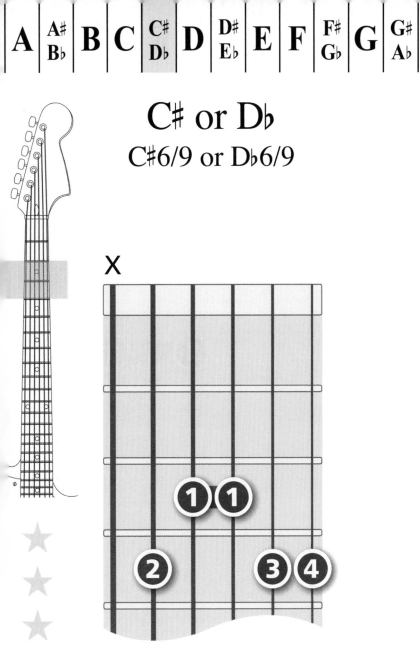

Notes in the chord:
5: C# (root); 4: E# (third); 3: A# (sixth); 2: D# (ninth); 1: G# (fifth)

Like so many fingerings, the one for a five-string 6/9 can
be replicated up and down the neck.

C# or D♭

C# maj7 or D♭ maj7

(1st version)

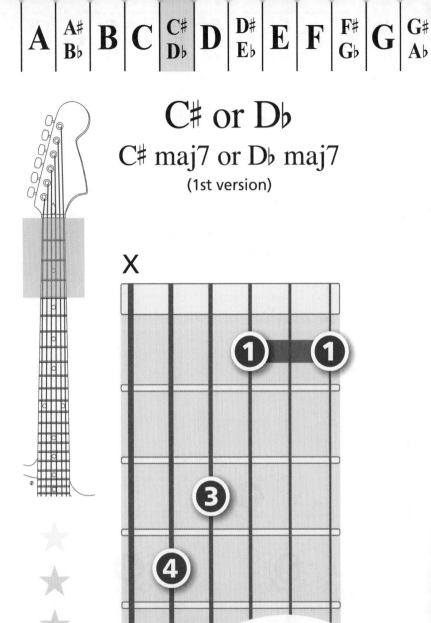

Notes in the chord:

5: C# (root); 4: E# (third); 3: G# (fifth); 2: B# (maj seventh); 1: E#

A 'maj 7' that can be restored to a regular major by
adding your second finger at the 2nd string's 2nd fret
(see page 133).

A	A#/Bb	B	C	C#/Db	D	D#/Eb	E	F	F#/Gb	G	G#/Ab

C# or Db
C# maj7 or Db maj7
(2nd version)

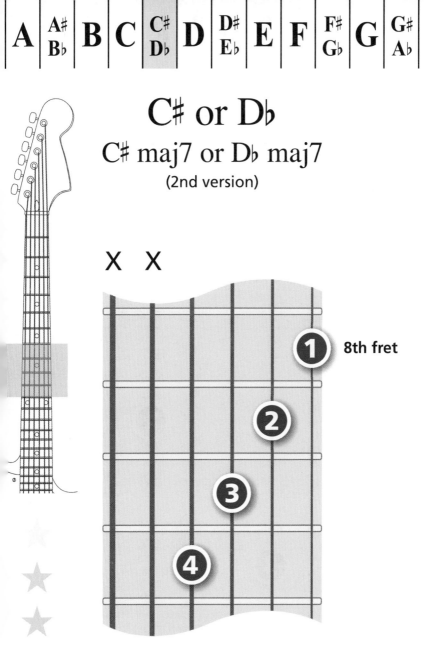

X X

8th fret

Notes in the chord:
4: C# (root); 3: E# (third); 3: G# (fifth); 1: B# (maj seventh)

This chord may be rather a stretch, but the fingers fall into the correct shape easily enough.

141

C# or D♭

C#7 or D♭7

(1st version)

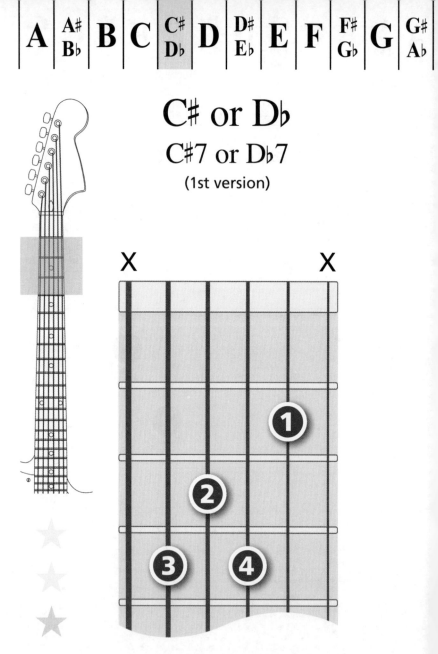

X   **X**

Notes in the chord:

5: C# (root); 4: E# (third); 3: B (dom seventh); 2: C#

A convenient inner-string 'dom 7', although it lacks the fifth note of the chord (G#).

A	A# Bb	B	C	C# Db	D	D# Eb	E	F	F# Gb	G	G# Ab

C# or Db

C#7 or Db7

(2nd version)

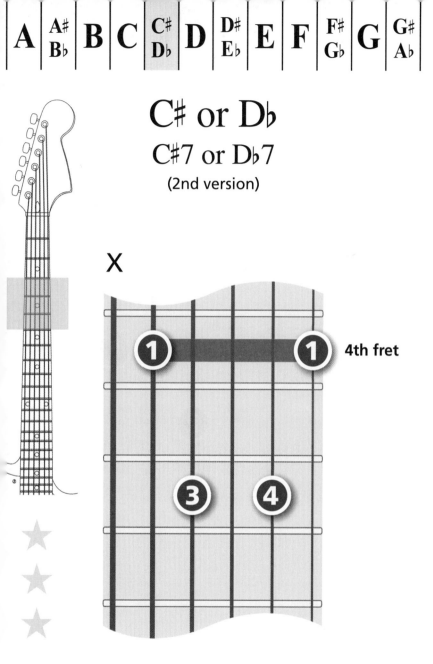

X

1 — 1   **4th fret**

3   4

Notes in the chord:

5: C# (root); 4: G# (fifth); 3: B (dom seventh); 2: E# (third); 1: G#

No shortage of fifths here – and you could add another in
the bass by extending your barré to the 6th string.

143

A	A# Bb	B	C	C# Db	D	D# Eb	E	F	F# Gb	G	G# Ab

C# or Db
C#7 or Db7
(3rd version)

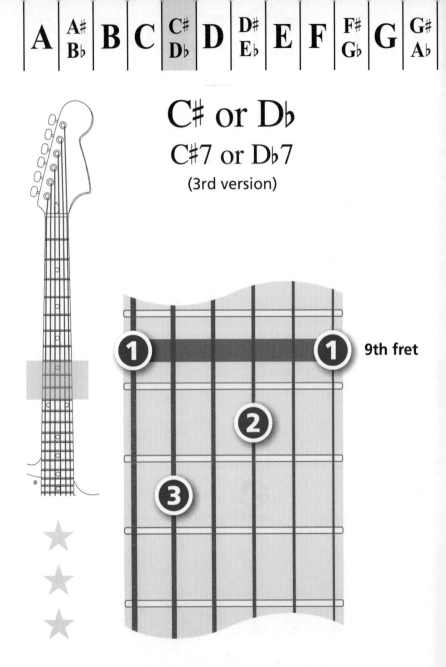

9th fret

Notes in the chord:
6: C# (root); 5: G# (fifth); 4: B (dom seventh); 3: E# (third); 2: G#; 1: C#

A handy 9th position dominant seventh.

| A | A# Bb | B | C | C# Db | D | D# Eb | E | F | F# Gb | G | G# Ab |

C♯ or D♭
C♯7+9 or D♭7+9

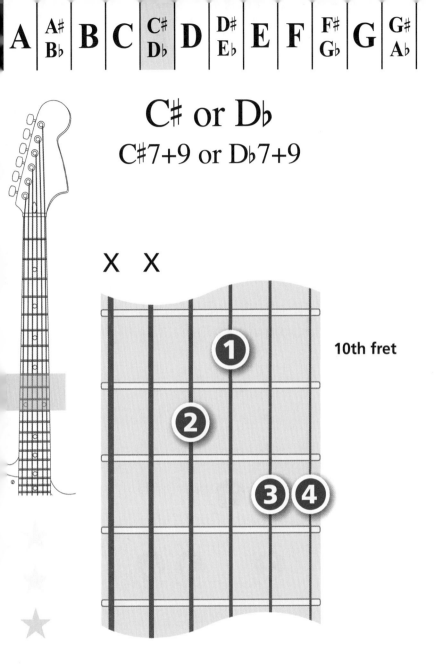

X X

10th fret

Notes in the chord:
4: C# (root); 3: E# (third); 2: B (dom seventh); 1: D double sharp (E) (aug ninth)

Cutting and spicy-sounding, especially at this high pitch!

C♯ or D♭

C♯9 or D♭9

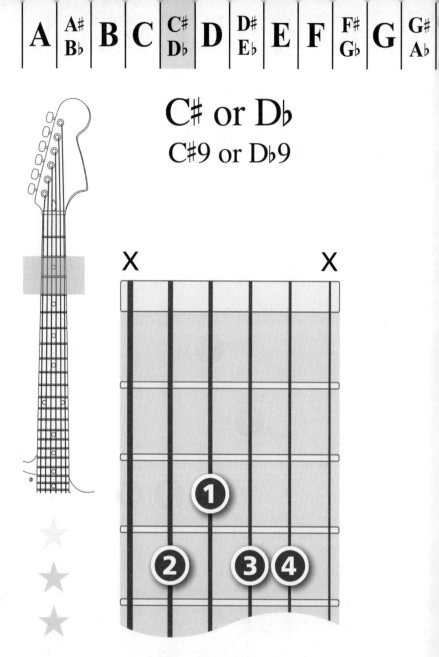

Notes in the chord:

5: C# (root); 4: E# (third); 3: B (dom seventh); 2: D# (ninth)

Playing this four-stringer vigorously on an electric will often produce some tasty distortion!

C# or Db
C#11 or Db11

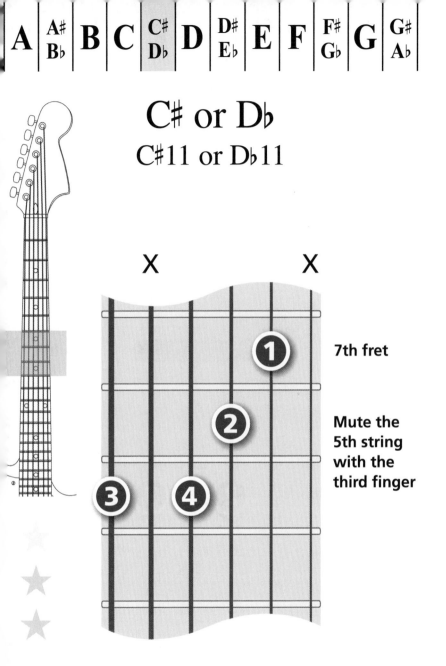

X   X

7th fret

Mute the 5th string with the third finger

Notes in the chord:
6: C# (root); 4: B (dom seventh); 3: D# (ninth); 2: F# (eleventh)

If you're unsure whether the 5th string has been effectively muted, avoid it by picking the bass C# (6th), then strumming the remaining notes.

147

C# or Db
C#13 or Db13

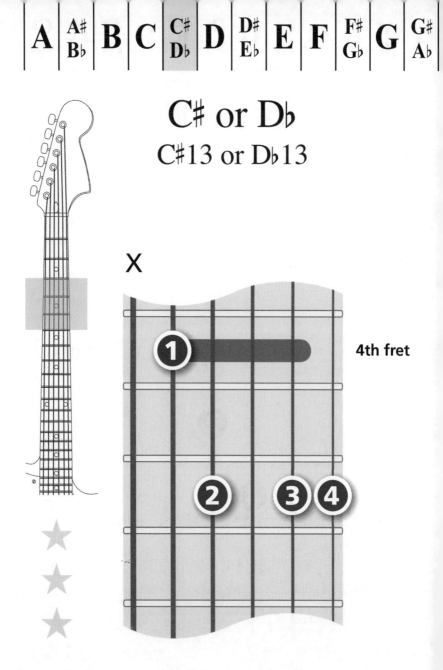

X

4th fret

Notes in the chord:
5: C# (root); 4: G# (fifth); 3: B (dom seventh); 2: E# (third); 1: A# (thirteenth)

This chord requires careful left-hand positioning or
it may not sound clearly.

A	A# Bb	B	C	C# Db	D	D# Eb	E	F	F# Gb	G	G# Ab

C# or Db
C# dim or Db dim
(C#° or Db°)
(1st version)

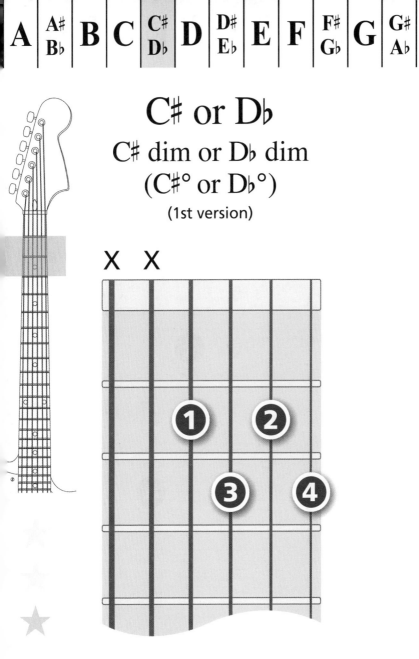

X   X

Notes in the chord:
4: E (minor third); 3: A# (dim seventh); 2: C# (keynote); 1: G (dim fifth)

The only slight drawback with this diminished chord is the
absence of the key note in its bass.

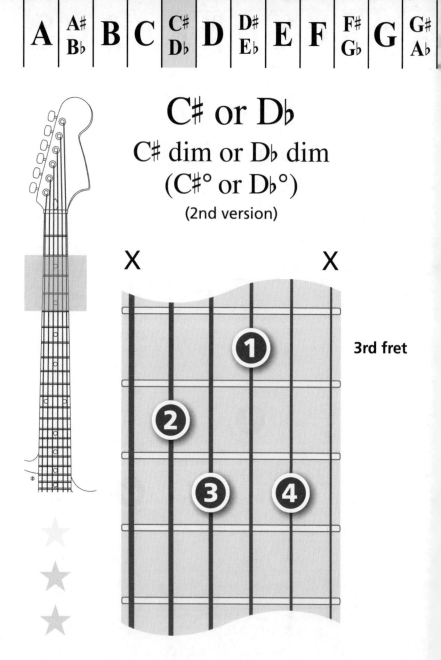

A	A# Bb	B	C	C# Db	D	D# Eb	E	F	F# Gb	G	G# Ab

C# or Db
C# dim or Db dim
(C#° or Db°)
(2nd version)

X   X

1

2

3   **4**

3rd fret

Notes in the chord:
5: C# (root); 4: G (dim fifth); 3: A# (dim seventh); 2: E (minor third)

A C# or Db diminished with its root note in place on the
5th string.

150

A	A# B♭	B	C	C# D♭	D	D# E♭	E	F	F# G♭	G	G# A♭

C# or D♭

C# aug or D♭ aug
(C#+ or D♭+)
(1st version)

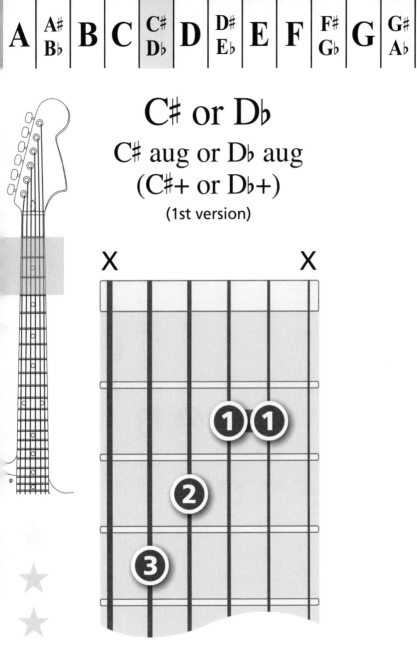

Notes in the chord:
5: C# (root); 4: E# (third); 3: A (aug fifth); 2: C#

The best fingering for a lower-pitched augmented chord of C# or D♭.

C♯ or D♭

C♯ aug or D♭ aug
(C♯+ or D♭+)
(2nd version)

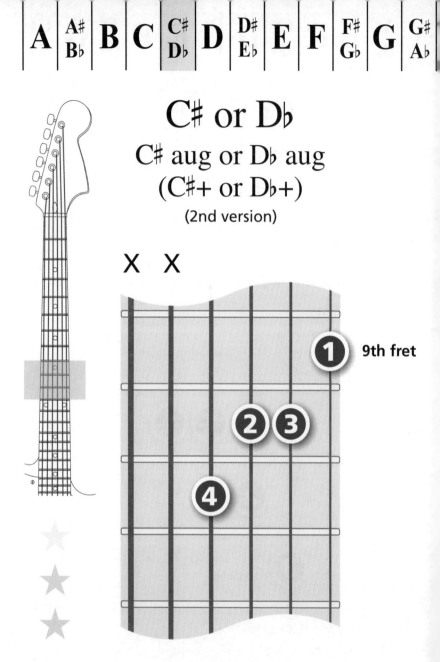

9th fret

Notes in the chord:

4: C♯ (root); 3: E♯ (third); 2: A (aug fifth); 1: C♯

A higher-register C♯+ in the guitar's 9th position.

A	A#/B♭	B	C	C#/D♭	D	D#/E♭	E	F	F#/G♭	G	G#/A♭

C♯ or D♭
C♯ minor or D♭ minor
(C♯m or D♭m)
(1st version)

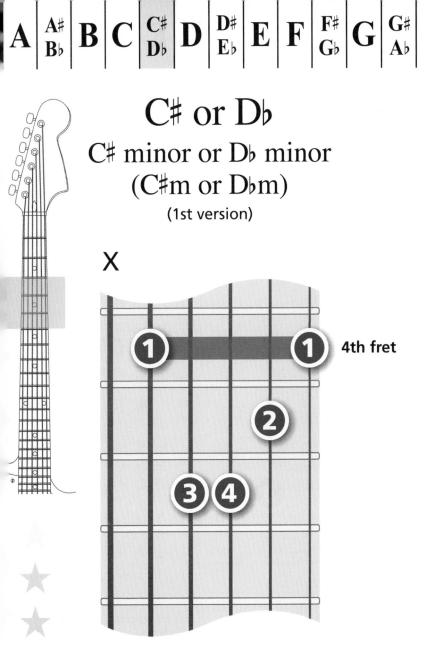

4th fret

Notes in the chord:

5: C# (root); 4: G# (fifth); 3: C#; 2: E (third); 1: G#

A second inversion is available if you hold down the 6th string at the 4th fret with your barré.

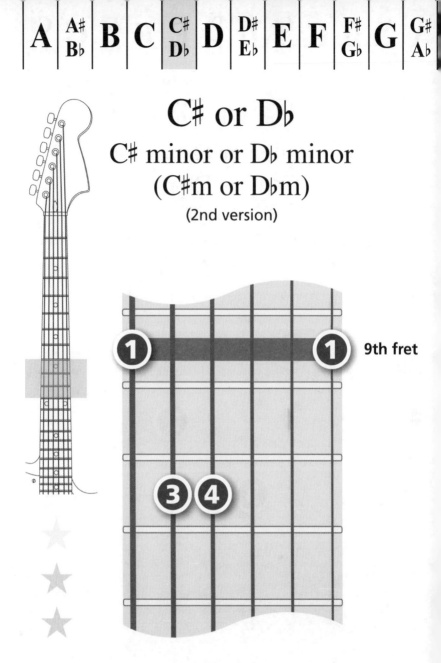

C# or Db
C# minor or Db minor
(C#m or Dbm)
(2nd version)

9th fret

Notes in the chord:
6: C# (root); 5: G# (fifth); 4: C#; 3: E (third); 2: G#; 1: C#

Play a four-string version of this chord by omitting the
two lowest strings.

C# or Db

C# minor or Db minor
(C#m or Dbm)
(3rd version)

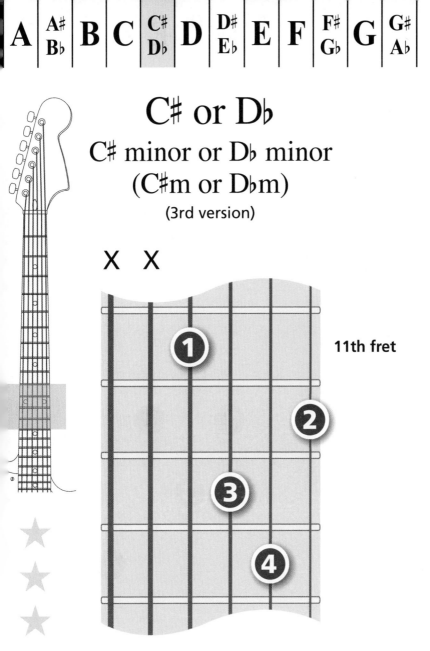

X   X

11th fret

Notes in the chord:

4: C# (root); 3: G# (fifth); 2: C#; 1: E (third)

An effective voicing, though placed quite high on the fingerboard.

A	A# B♭	B	C	C# D♭	D	D# E♭	E	F	F# G♭	G	G# A♭

C♯ or D♭
C♯m6 or D♭m6
(1st version)

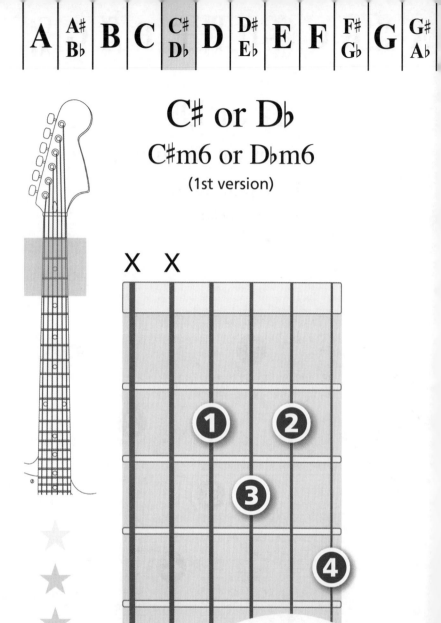

Notes in the chord:
4: E (third); 3: A# (sixth); 2: C#; 1: G# (fifth)

A first-inversion voicing, with E as its lowest note.

C# or D♭

C#m6 or D♭m6

(2nd version)

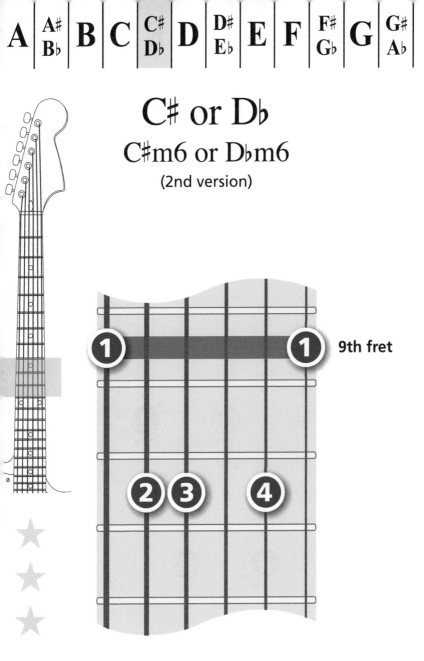

9th fret

Notes in the chord:

6: C# (root); 5: G# (fifth); 4: C#; 3: E (third); 2: A# (sixth); 1: C#

A six-string, root position example of the chord.

C# or Db

C#m7 or Dbm7

(1st version)

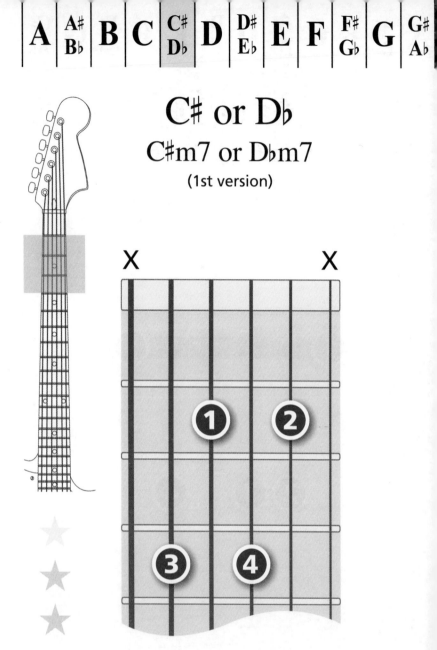

Notes in the chord:

4: C# (root); 3: E (third); 2: B (dom seventh); 1: C#

For an alternative fingering, use your index in a barré across the 2nd fret.

A	A# Bb	B	C	C# Db	D	D# Eb	E	F	F# Gb	G	G# Ab

C# or Db

C#m7 or Dbm7

(2nd version)

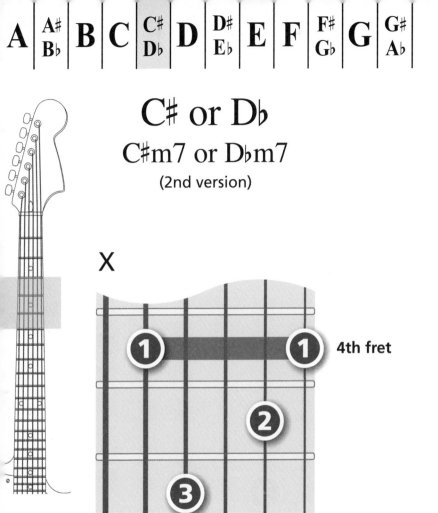

X

4th fret

Notes in the chord:

5: C# (root); 4: G# (fifth); 3: B (dom seventh); 2: E (third); 1: G#

Make sure the 3rd string doesn't buzz beneath your
barré here.

A	A# Bb	B	C	C# Db	D	D# Eb	E	F	F# Gb	G	G# Ab

C# or Db
C#m7 or Dbm7
(3rd version)

9th fret

Notes in the chord:
6: C# (root); 5: G# (fifth); 4: B (dom seventh); 3 E (third); 2: G#; 1: C#

Play this as a broken chord (one note after the other) to
produce a striking musical effect.

C♯ or D♭
C♯m9 or D♭m9

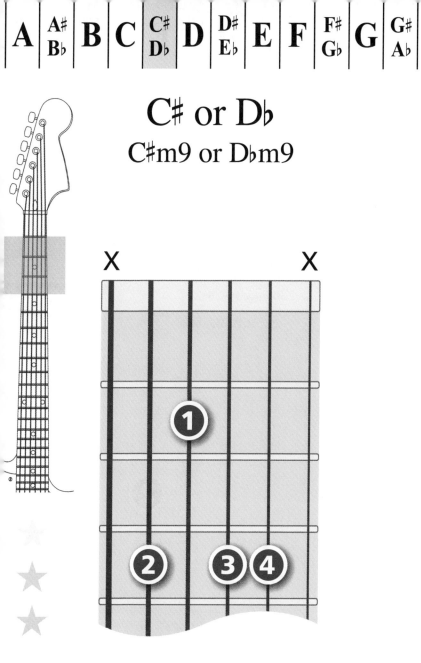

Notes in the chord:
5: C# (root); 4: E (third); 3: B (dom seventh); 2: D# (ninth)

A lower-register chord from the inner strings.

D
'Bare' D (D5)

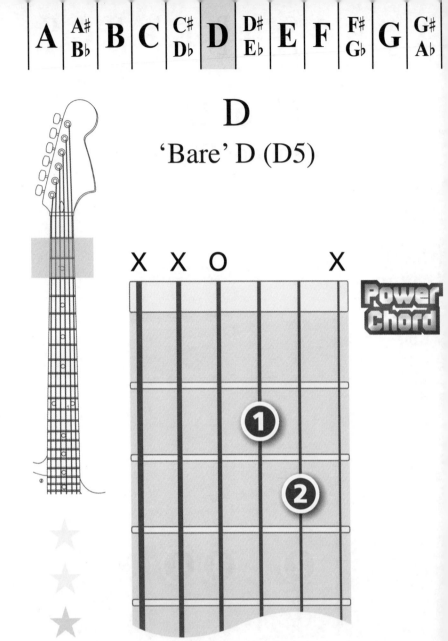

Power Chord

Notes in the chord:
4: D (root); 3: A (fifth); 2: D

This chord contains no third, and is therefore neither major nor minor. The 6th, 5th and 1st strings aren't played.

D

D major

(1st version)

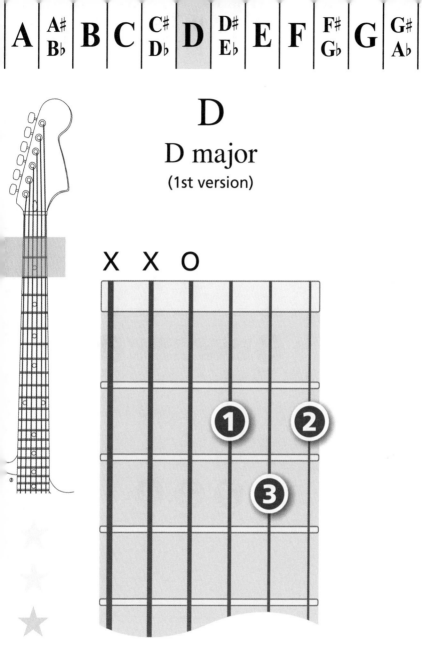

X   X   O

Notes in the chord:

4: D (root); 3: A (fifth); 2: D; 1: F# (third)

Sounding the open 5th string here produces a bass A, and changes this chord (which normally has D as its root) into a second inversion.

163

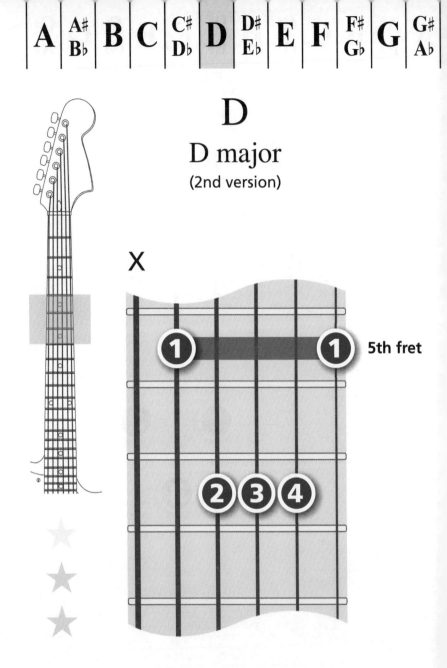

D
D major
(2nd version)

Notes in the chord:
5: D (root); 4: A (fifth); 3: D; 2: F# (third); 1: A

A good chord to 'slide up' to.

D

D major
(3rd version)

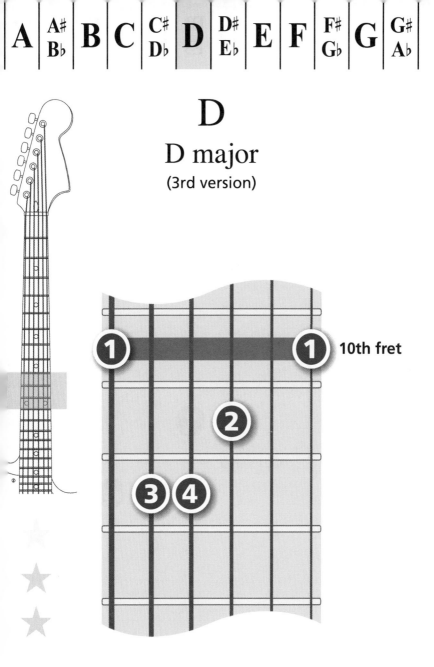

10th fret

Notes in the chord:
6: D (root); 5: A (fifth); 4: D; 3: F# (third); 2: A; 1: D

A nice higher-register chord, though it will be tricky to
finger on guitars with only 12 frets easily accessible.

D
D sus4

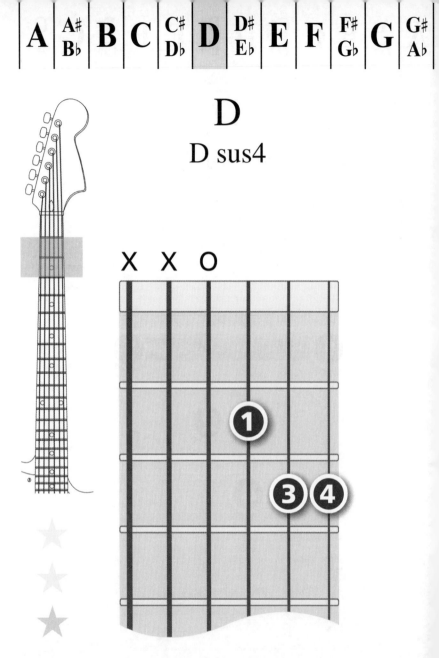

Notes in the chord:
4: D (root); 3: A (fifth); 2: D; 1: G (sus fourth)

This 'suspended fourth' chord is especially easy to resolve to the standard D major shown on page 163, or the D minor on page 183.

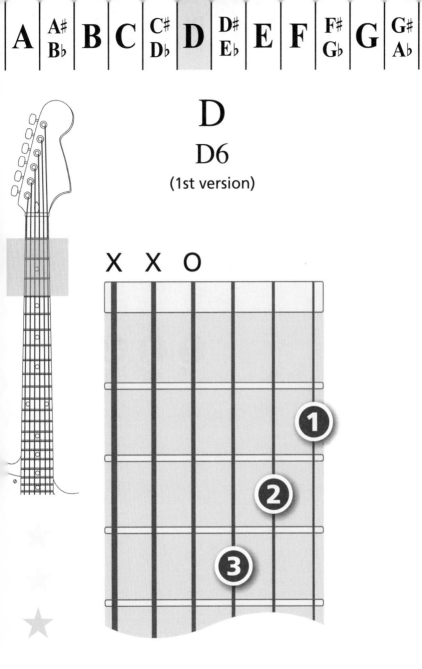

| A | A#
Bb | B | C | C#
Db | D | D#
Eb | E | F | F#
Gb | G | G#
Ab |

D
D6
(1st version)

Notes in the chord:

4: D (root); 3: B (added sixth); 2: D; 1: F# (third)

The notes in this straightforward chord are particularly
easy to adapt to your specific musical needs.

A	A# Bb	B	C	C# Db	D	D# Eb	E	F	F# Gb	G	G# Ab

D
D6
(2nd version)

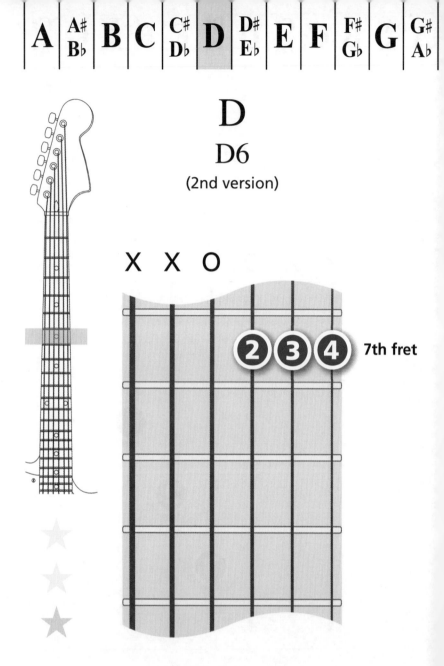

X X O

② ③ ④ **7th fret**

Notes in the chord:
4: D (root); 3: D; 2: F# (third); 1: B (added sixth)

This shape can, of course, also be played with a
first-finger barré.

D
D6/9

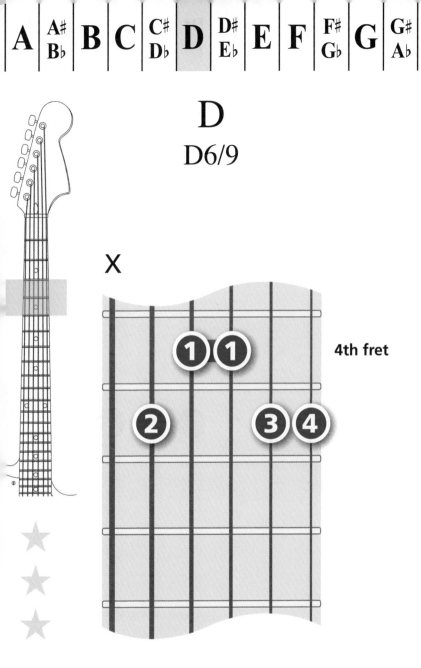

4th fret

Notes in the chord:
5: D (root); 4: F# (third); 3: B (sixth); 2: E (ninth); 1: A (fifth)

A jazzy chord that's sometimes used to conclude a number.

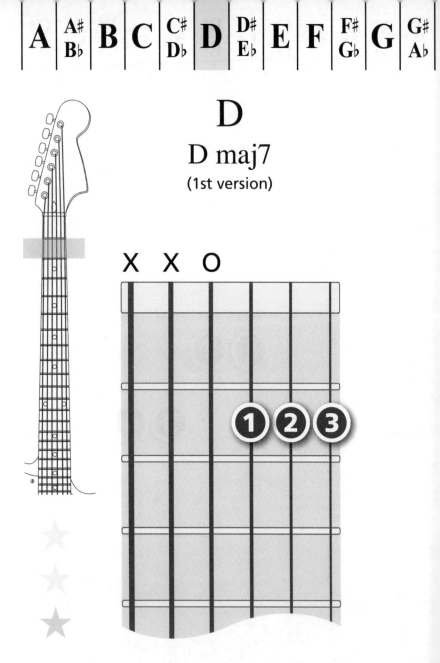

A	A# B♭	B	C	C# D♭	D	D# E♭	E	F	F# G♭	G	G# A♭

D
D maj7
(1st version)

X   X   O

①②③

Notes in the chord:
4: D (root); 3: A (fifth); 2: C# (maj seventh); 1: F# (third)

Another very simple fingering that can also be played with a barré.

170

A	A# Bb	B	C	C# Db	D	D# Eb	E	F	F# Gb	G	G# Ab

D

D maj7
(2nd version)

X X O

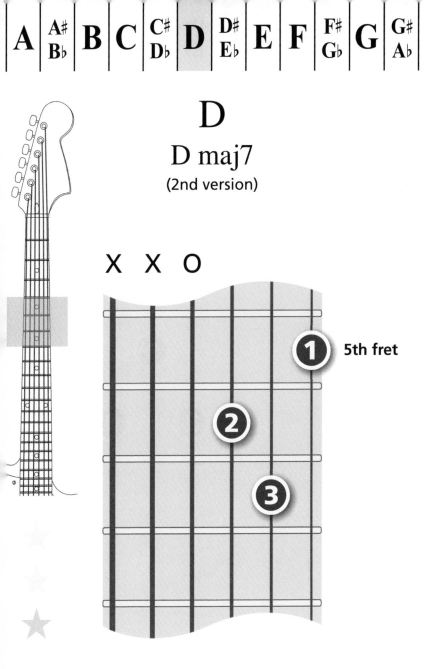

5th fret

Notes in the chord:
4: D (root); 3: C# (maj seventh); 2: F# (third); 1: A (fifth)

Higher voicings of chords like the major seventh pose few
problems in D, as its root note is frequently available on
the open 4th string.

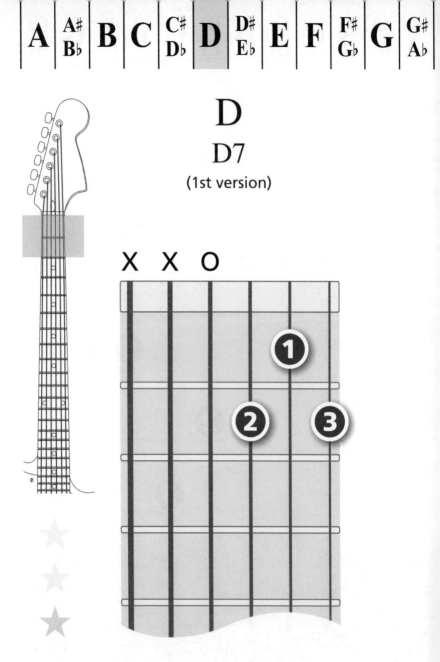

| A | A#/Bb | B | C | C#/Db | D | D#/Eb | E | F | F#/Gb | G | G#/Ab |

D
D7
(1st version)

X   X   O

Notes in the chord:

4: D (root); 3: A (fifth); 2: C (dom seventh); 1: F# (third)

A guitarists' staple!

172

| A | A#/Bb | B | C | C#/Db | D | D#/Eb | E | F | F#/Gb | G | G#/Ab |

D
D7
(2nd version)

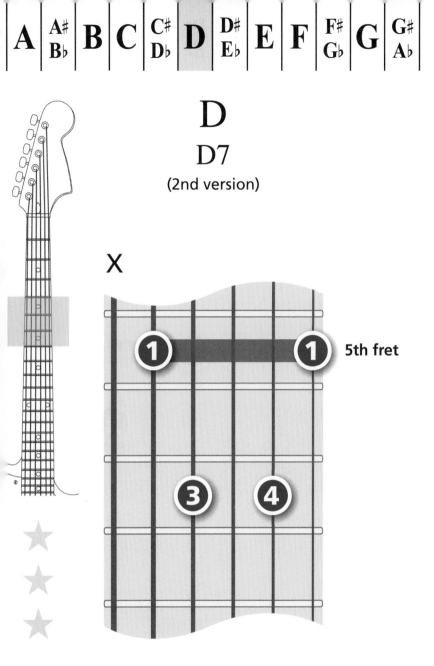

X

5th fret

Notes in the chord:

5: D (root); 4: A (fifth); 3: C (dom seventh); 2: F# (third); 1: A

Though higher-position D7s often don't require a barré,
many players prefer this fingering, because the left hand
controls all the strings' sustain.

A	A# Bb	B	C	C# Db	D	D# Eb	E	F	F# Gb	G	G# Ab

D
D7
(3rd version)

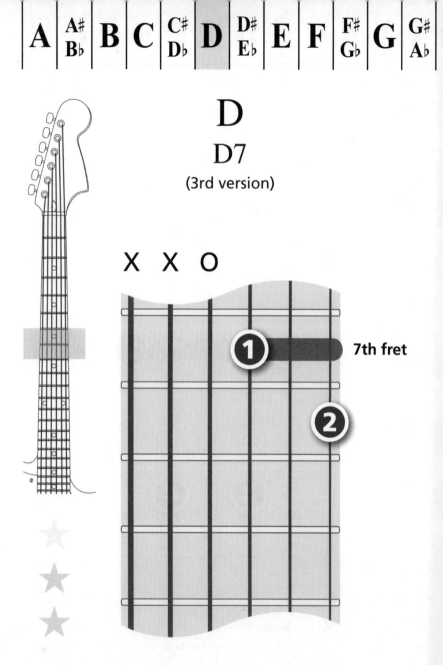

X   X   O

1 ⸺ **7th fret**

2

Notes in the chord:
4: D (root); 3: D; 2: F# (third); 1: C (dom seventh)

You could substitute individual fingers for the barré here –
but there's little advantage in doing so.

D
D7+9

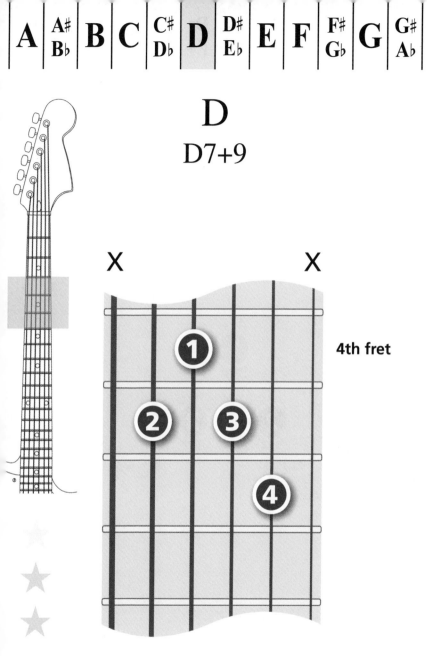

X   X

4th fret

Notes in the chord:
5: D (root); 4: F# (third); 3: C (dom seventh); 2: E# (aug ninth)

This chord has a pleasing sound, thanks to the guitar's
inner strings.

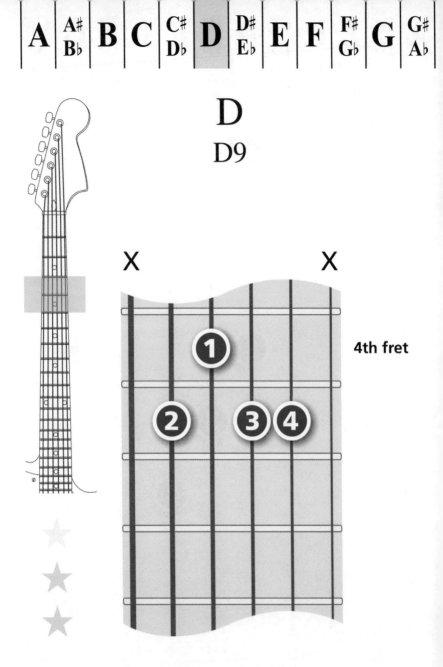

D
D9

4th fret

Notes in the chord:
5: D (root); 4: F# (third); 3: C (dom seventh); 2: E (ninth)

Another gutsy harmony from the instrument's middle register.

D
D11

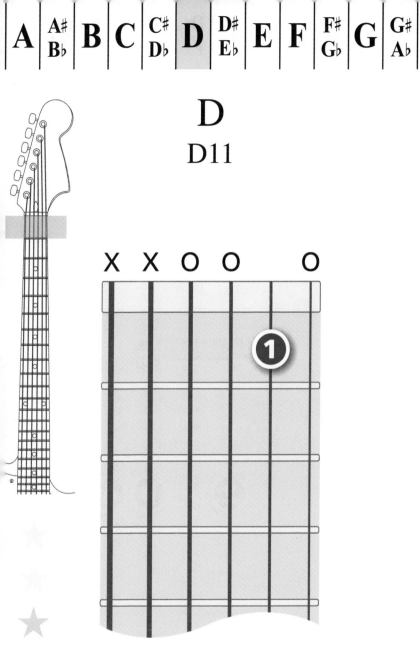

X X O O   O

Notes in the chord:

4: D (root); 3: G (eleventh); 2: C (dom seventh); 1: E (ninth)

A simple fingering for a harmony that sometimes replaces
D7 when heading towards a key chord of G.

| A | A#
Bb | B | C | C#
Db | D | D#
Eb | E | F | F#
Gb | G | G#
Ab |

D
D13

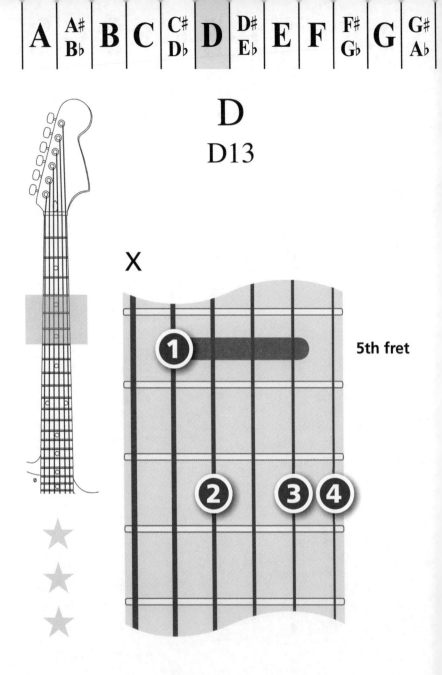

X

5th fret

Notes in the chord:

5: D (root); 4: A (fifth); 3: C (dom 7); 2: F# (third); 1: B (thirteenth)

To include the ninth (E) of the chord instead of its third (F#)
here, release your third finger from the 2nd string.

D

D diminished (D dim, D°)

(1st version)

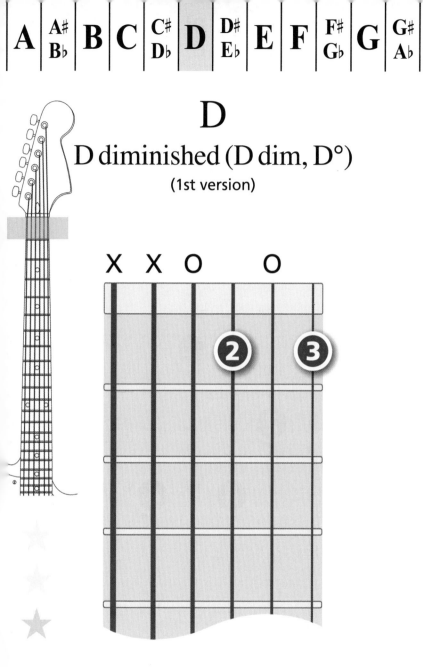

Notes in the chord:

4: D (root); 3: G# (dim fifth); 2: B (dim seventh); 1: F (minor third)

Two open strings in a diminished chord is something
of a luxury!

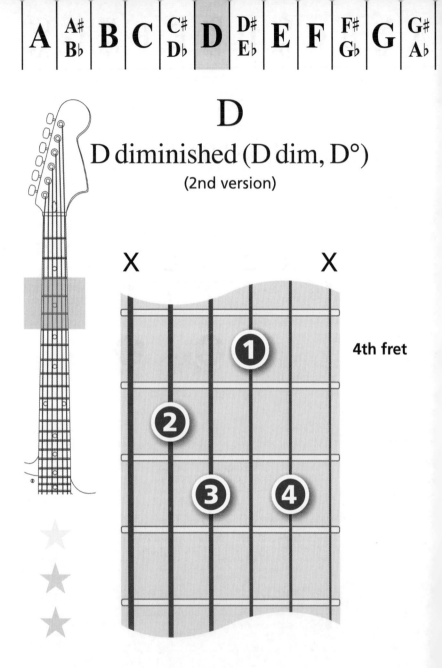

D

D diminished (D dim, D°)

(2nd version)

X   X

4th fret

Notes in the chord:

5: D (root); 4: G# (dim fifth); 3: B (dim seventh); 2: F (minor third)

Another fingering, a little higher up the neck, to produce
the same notes as the shape on page 179.

D

D augmented (D aug, D+)

(1st version)

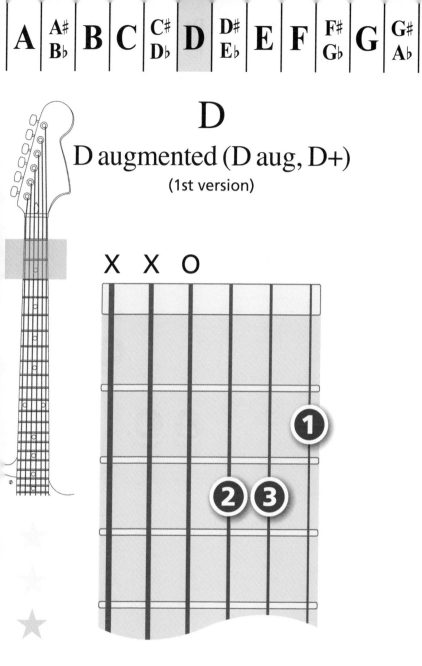

X   X   O

Notes in the chord:

4: D (root); 3: A# (aug fifth); 2: D; 1: F# (third)

This augmented shape, like many others in the present key, features a root note from the open D string.

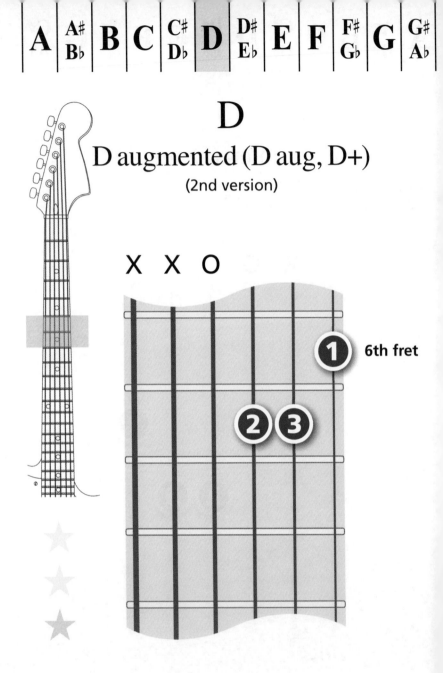

| A | A#
B♭ | B | C | C#
D♭ | D | D#
E♭ | E | F | F#
G♭ | G | G#
A♭ |

D
D augmented (D aug, D+)
(2nd version)

X   X   O

1 6th fret

2 **3**

Notes in the chord:
4: D (root); 3: D; 2: F# (third); 1: A# (aug fifth)

An attractive higher voicing of 'D aug'.

182

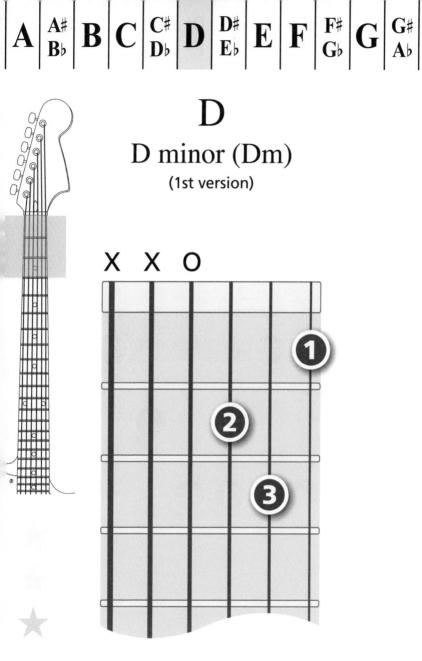

| A | A# Bb | B | C | C# Db | D | D# Eb | E | F | F# Gb | G | G# Ab |

D

D minor (Dm)

(1st version)

Notes in the chord:

4: D (root); 3: A (fifth); 2: D; 1: F (third)

One of the first minor chords that guitarists learn – and it's
perennially useful.

D
D minor (Dm)
(2nd version)

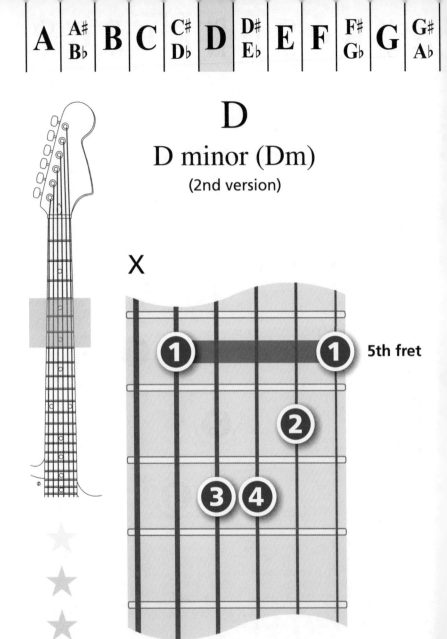

X

5th fret

Notes in the chord:

5: D (root); 4: A (fifth); 3: D; 2: F (third); 1: A

An essential 'middle register' shape.

A	A# Bb	B	C	C# Db	D	D# Eb	E	F	F# Gb	G	G# Ab

D
D minor (Dm)
(3rd version)

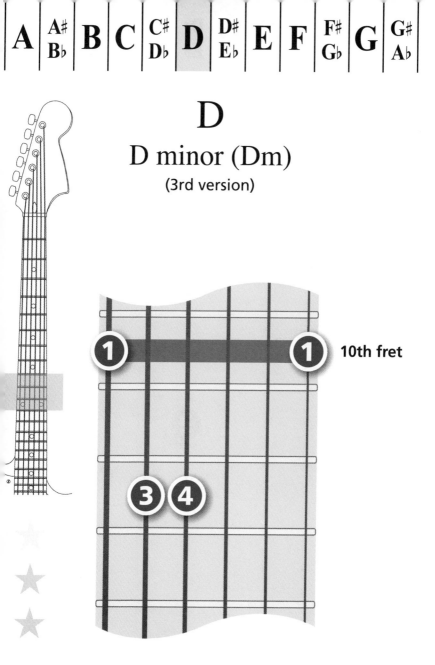

10th fret

Notes in the chord:
6: D (root); 5: A (fifth); 4: D; 3: F (third); 2: A; 1: D

This one will be hard to manage if your instrument has only 12 easily accessible frets. However, there's no problem on a guitar with a cutaway.

D
Dm6
(1st version)

Notes in the chord:

4: D (root); 3: A (fifth); 2: B (sixth); 1: F (third)

A simple shape to learn and remember.

D
Dm6
(2nd version)

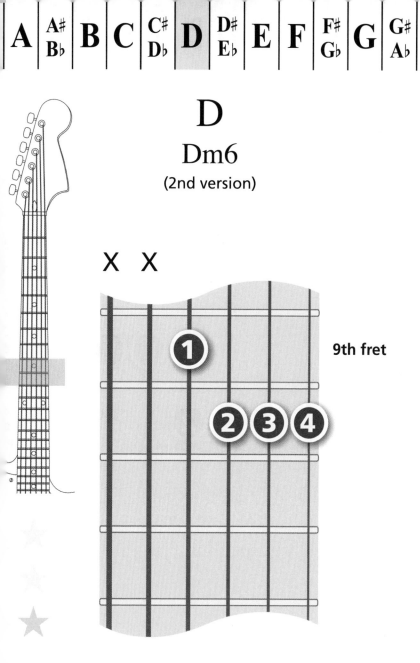

9th fret

Notes in the chord:
4: B (sixth); 3: F (third); 2: A (fifth); 1: D

An attractive voicing of Dm6, even though it doesn't have D at its root.

A	A# Bb	B	C	C# Db	D	D# Eb	E	F	F# Gb	G	G# Ab

D
Dm7
(1st version)

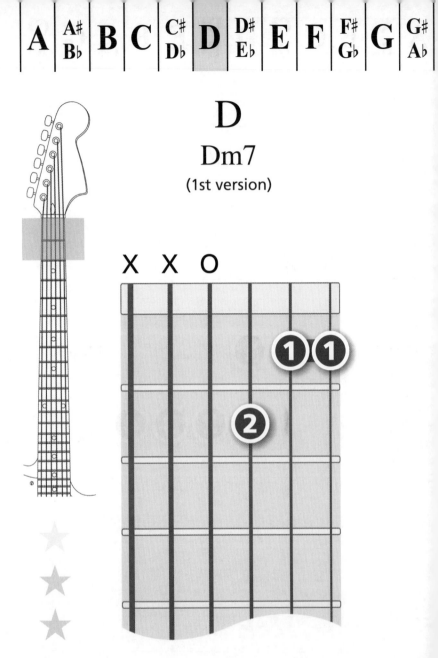

X X O

Notes in the chord:

4: D (root); 3: A (fifth); 2: C (dom seventh); 1: F (third)

The most basic Dm7 shape.

D
Dm7
(2nd version)

X X O

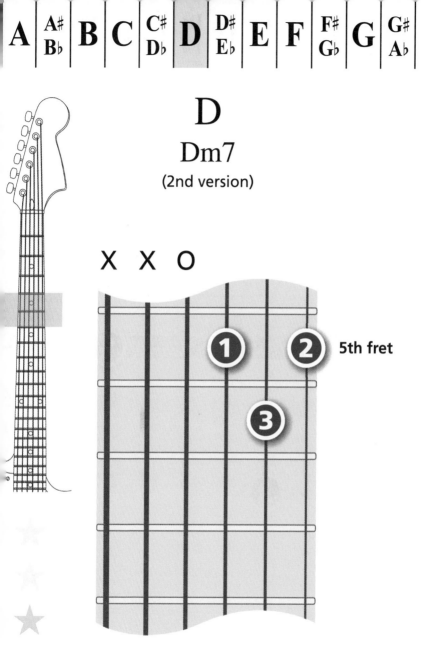

5th fret

Notes in the chord:

4: D (root); 3: C (dom seventh); 2: F (third); 1: A (fifth)

This 5th position chord is combined with an open
bass string.

D
Dm7
(3rd version)

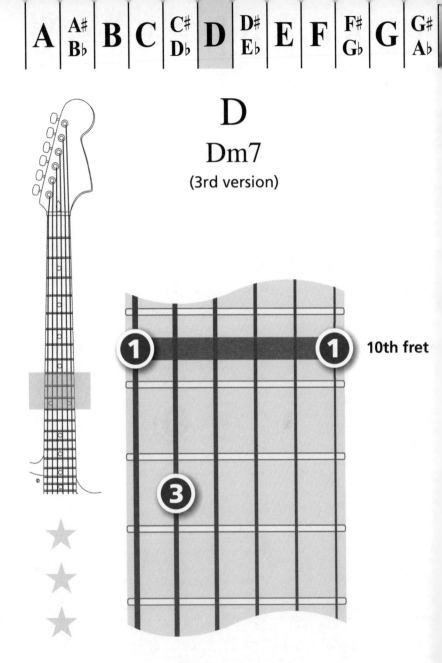

10th fret

Notes in the chord:
6: D (root); 5: A (fifth); 4: C (dom seventh); 3; F (third); 2: A; 1: D

A firm barré is essential to ensure that the 2nd, 3rd and
4th strings don't buzz.

D
Dm9

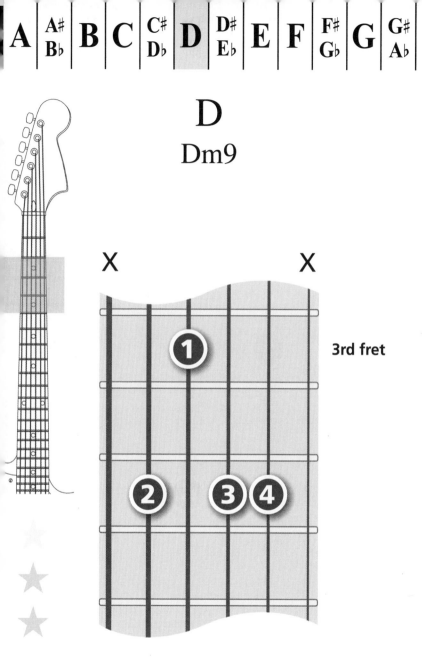

X   X

①

3rd fret

②   ③④

Notes in the chord:

5: D (root); 4: F (third); 3: C (dom seventh); 2: E (ninth)

A convenient shape, although it omits the fifth of
the chord (A).

D# or Eb

'Bare' D# or 'bare' Eb
(D#5 or Eb5)

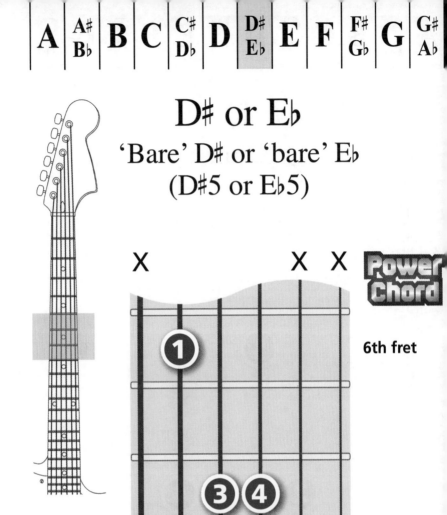

6th fret

Power Chord

Notes in the chord:
5: Eb (root); 4: Bb (fifth); 3: Eb

As usual with this 'power chord' fingering, the 1st, 2nd
and 6th strings aren't played.

A	A# Bb	B	C	C# Db	D	D# Eb	E	F	F# Gb	G	G# Ab

D# or Eb

D# major or Eb major
(1st version)

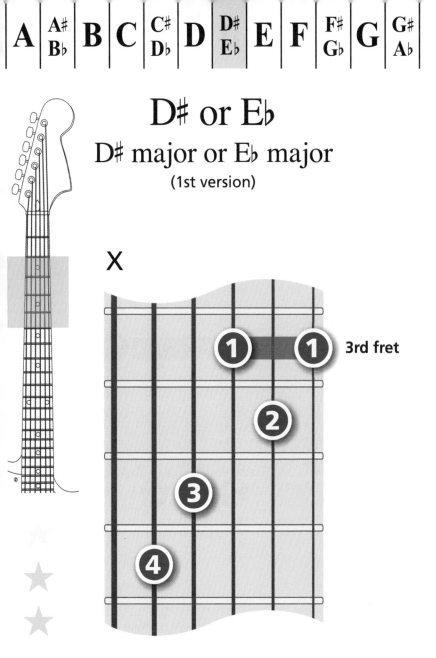

3rd fret

Notes in the chord:
5: Eb (root); 4: G (third); 3: Bb (fifth); 2: Eb; 1: G

The more flats there are in a key, the harder it gets for guitarists… and in Eb even a simple major chord requires some effort!

193

A	A# Bb	B	C	C# Db	D	D# Eb	E	F	F# Gb	G	G# Ab

D# or Eb
D# major or Eb major
(2nd version)

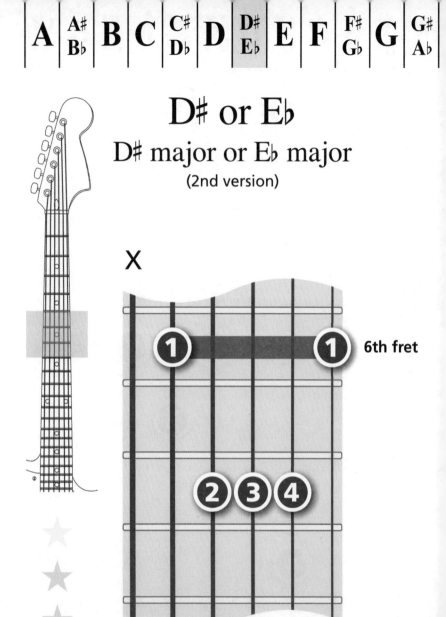

6th fret

Notes in the chord:

5; Eb (root); 4: Bb (fifth); 3: Eb; 2: G (third); 1: Bb

This standard barréd shape produces a mid-register chord of Eb.

A	A#/B♭	B	C	C#/D♭	D	D#/E♭	E	F	F#/G♭	G	G#/A♭

D# or E♭

D# major or E♭ major

(3rd version)

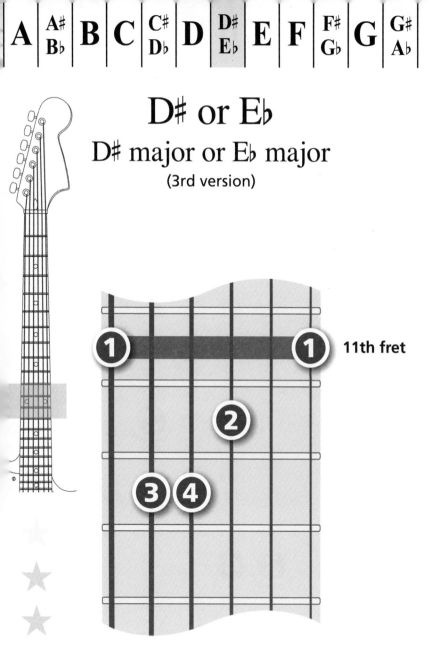

11th fret

Notes in the chord:

6: E♭ (root); 5: B♭ (fifth); 4: E♭; 3: G (third); 2: B♭ (fifth); 1: E♭

Such a high chord may be hard to manage on some guitars.

195

D♯ or E♭
D♯ sus4 or E♭ sus4

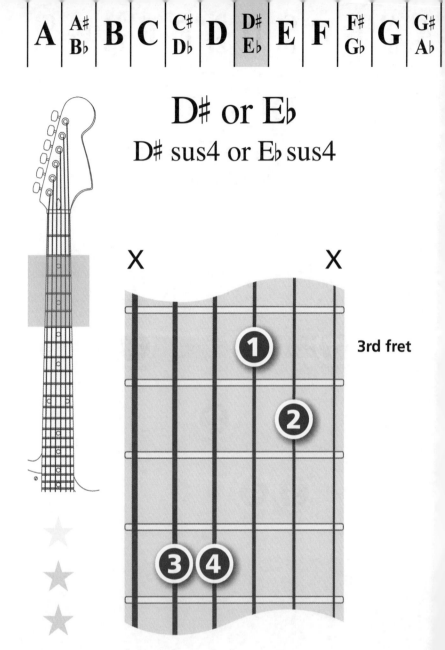

X   X

3rd fret

Notes in the chord:
5: E♭ (root); 4: A♭ (sus fourth); 3: B♭ (fifth); 2: E♭

The fingering here is based on the movable shape shown on page 193, but with an A♭ replacing the G on the 4th string.

A	A# B♭	B	C	C# D♭	D	D# E♭	E	F	F# G♭	G	G# A♭

D♯ or E♭
D♯6 or E♭6
(1st version)

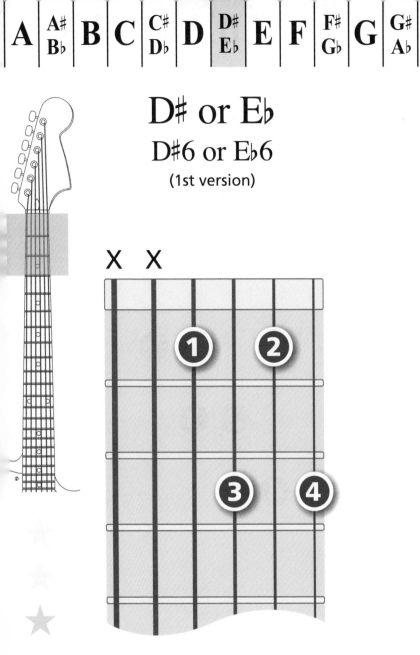

X X

Notes in the chord:
4: E♭ (root); 3: B♭ (fifth); 2: C (added sixth); 1: G (third)

You could finger the notes on the first fret with a barré
if it feels more comfortable.

A	A# B♭	B	C	C# D♭	D	D# E♭	E	F	F# G♭	G	G# A♭

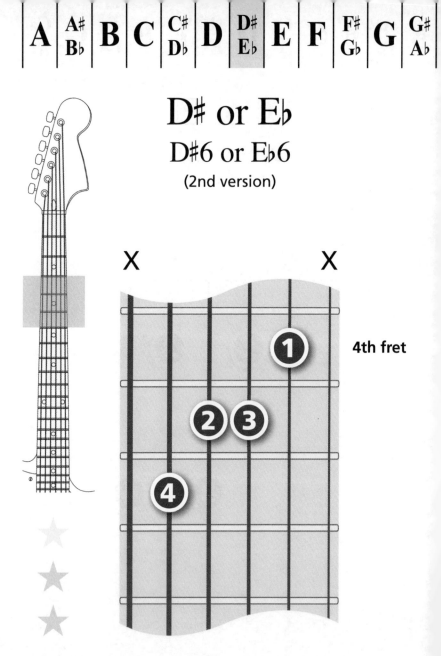

D♯ or E♭
D♯6 or E♭6
(2nd version)

4th fret

Notes in the chord:
5: E♭ (root); 4: G (third); 3: C (added sixth); 2: E♭

The inner strings supply the notes for this added sixth chord.

D# or Eb
D#6/9 or Eb6/9

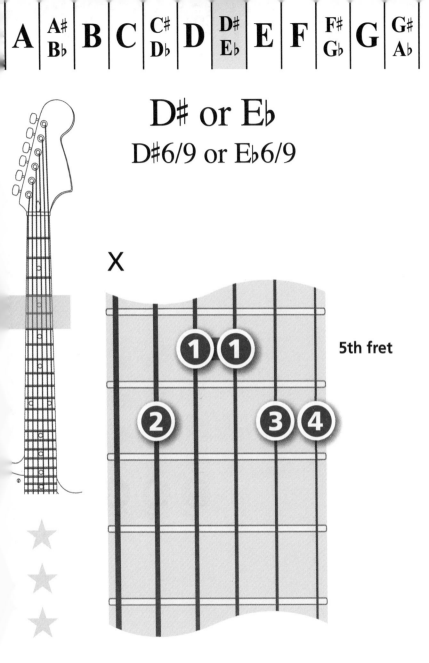

X

5th fret

Notes in the chord:
5: Eb (root); 4: G (third); 3: C (sixth); 2: F (ninth); 1: Bb (fifth)

A fifth-position Eb6/9.

D# or Eb
D# maj7 or Eb maj7
(1st version)

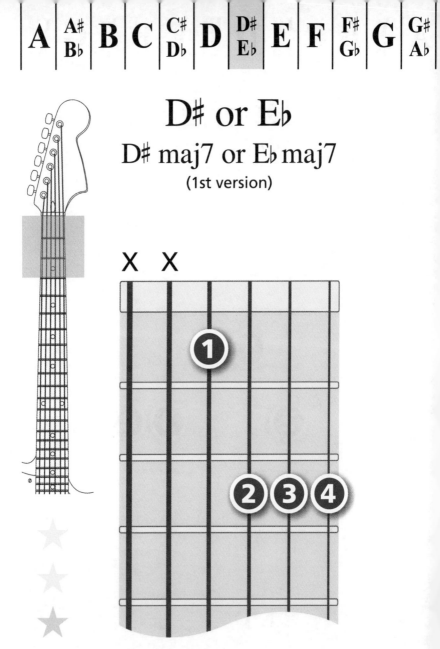

Notes in the chord:

4: Eb (root); 3: Bb (fifth); 2: D (maj seventh); 1: G (third)

The Eb on the 4th string is the lowest key note available on the guitar.

D♯ or E♭

D♯ maj7 or E♭ maj7
(2nd version)

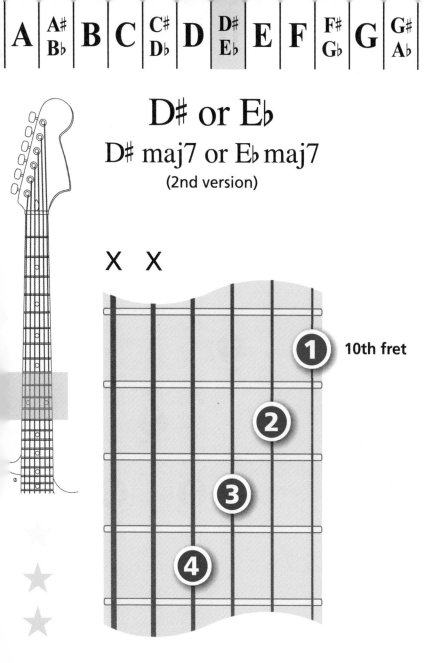

X X

① **10th fret**

②

③

④

Notes in the chord:
4: E♭ (root); 3: G (third); 2: B♭ (fifth); 1: D (maj seventh)

This very high voicing takes your little finger all the way up to the 13th fret!

A	A#/B♭	B	C	C#/D♭	D	**D#/E♭**	E	F	F#/G♭	G	G#/A♭

D# or E♭
D#7 or E♭7
(1st version)

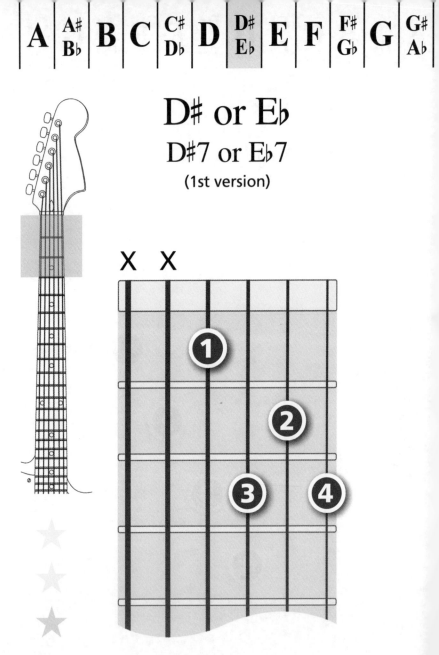

X X

Notes in the chord:
4: E♭ (root); 3: B♭ (fifth); 2: D♭ (dom seventh); 1: G (third)

A variant of the basic D7 shape (page 172) – raised by one fret, and with the index finger providing the appropriate bass note.

D# or E♭

D#7 or E♭7

(2nd version)

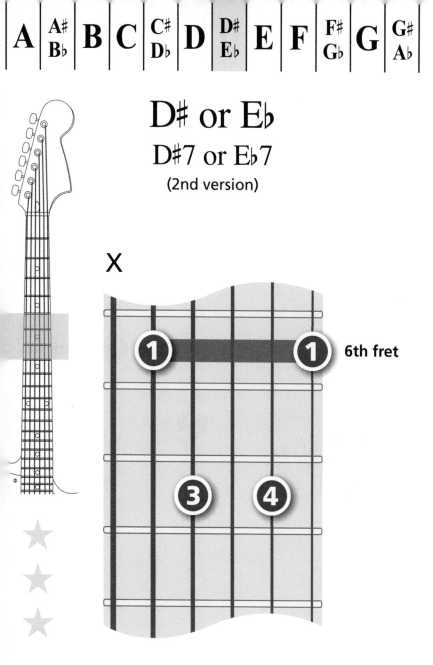

Notes in the chord:

5: E♭ (root); 4: B♭ (fifth); 3: D♭ (dom seventh); 2: G (third); 1: B♭

An always useful, if not especially easy, movable shape
seen here in the 6th position.

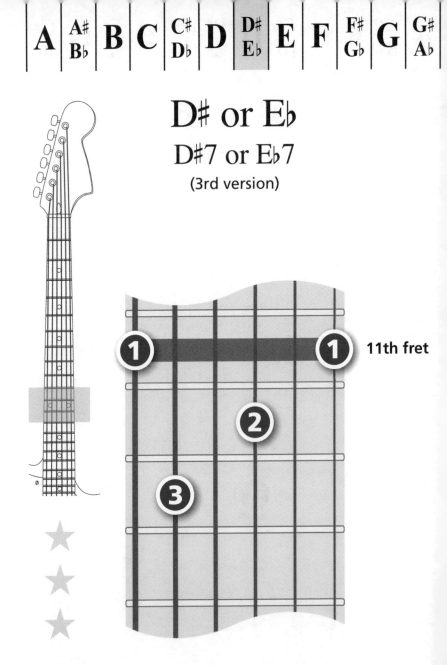

A	A#\nBb	B	C	C#\nDb	D	D#\nEb	E	F	F#\nGb	G	G#\nAb

D♯ or E♭
D♯7 or E♭7
(3rd version)

11th fret

Notes in the chord:
6: E♭ (root); 5: B♭ (fifth); 4: D♭ (dom seventh); 3: G (third); 2: B♭; 1: E♭

Another very high neck position – but it's the only place
where there's a reachable E♭ root on the 6th string.

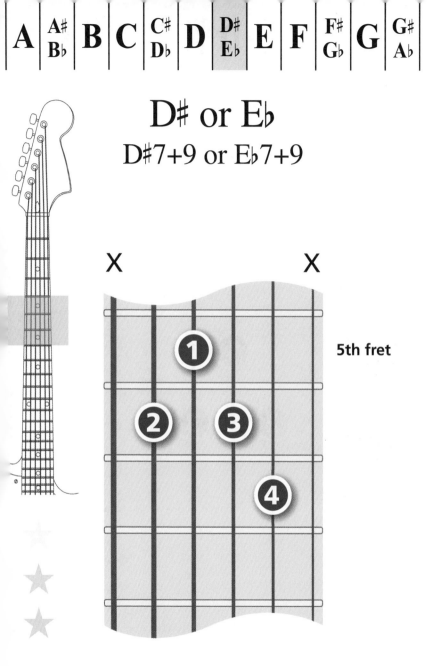

| A | A# Bb | B | C | C# Db | D | D# Eb | E | F | F# Gb | G | G# Ab |

D♯ or E♭
D♯7+9 or E♭7+9

X   X

5th fret

① ② ③ ④

Notes in the chord:
5: E♭ (root); 4: G (third); 3: D♭ (dom seventh); 2: F# (aug ninth)

A chord that can pack a punch, especially on an electric guitar.

D# or Eb
D#9 or Eb9

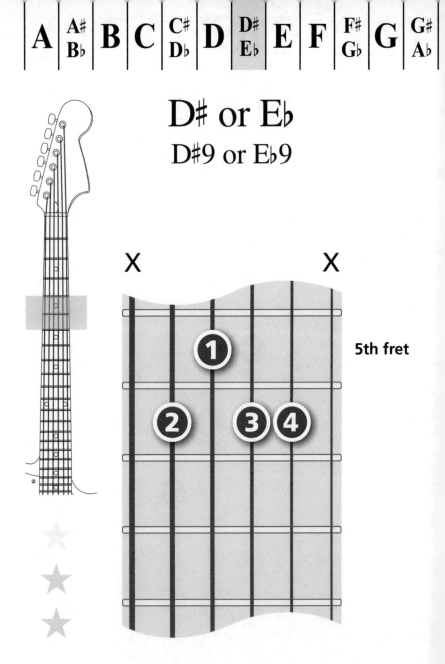

X   X

5th fret

Notes in the chord:
5: Eb (root); 4: G (third); 3: Db (dom seventh); 2: F (ninth)

A jazzy chord that's also suitable for many other
musical styles.

D# or Eb
D#11 or Eb11

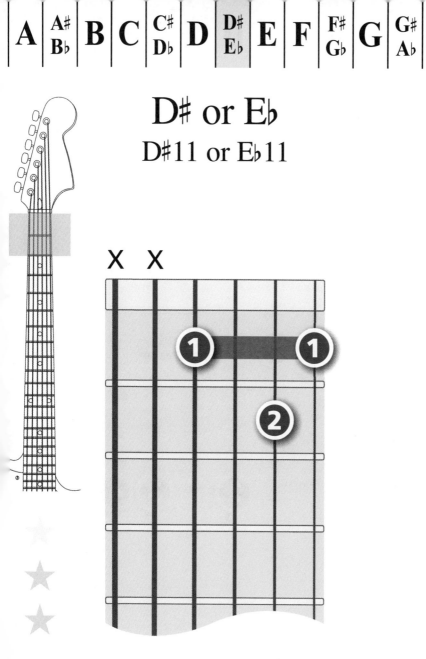

Notes in the chord:
4: Eb (root); 3: Ab (eleventh); 2: Db (dom seventh); 4: F (ninth)

For a satisfying progression, try moving from this chord to
the D#/Eb7 on page 202.

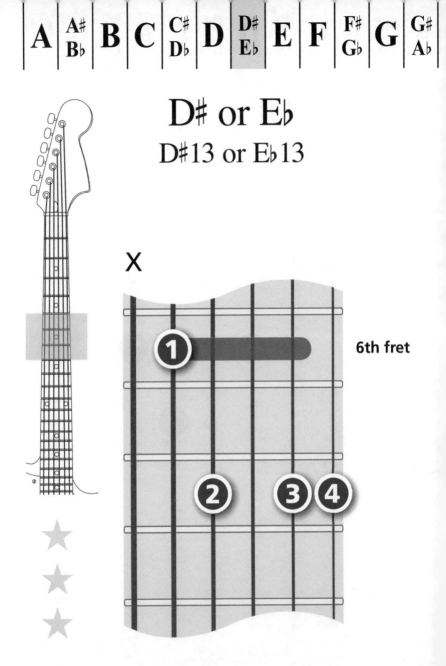

| A | A♯ B♭ | B | C | C♯ D♭ | D | D♯ E♭ | E | F | F♯ G♭ | G | G♯ A♭ |

D♯ or E♭
D♯13 or E♭13

X

6th fret

Notes in the chord:
5: E♭ (root); 4: B♭ (fifth); 3: D♭ (dom seventh); 2: G (third); 1: C (thirteenth)

Strictly speaking, a thirteenth chord should also contain a
ninth and eleventh – but this shape features the essential
notes, and sounds good on the guitar.

D♯ or E♭
D♯ dim or E♭ dim
(D♯° or E♭°)
(1st version)

X X

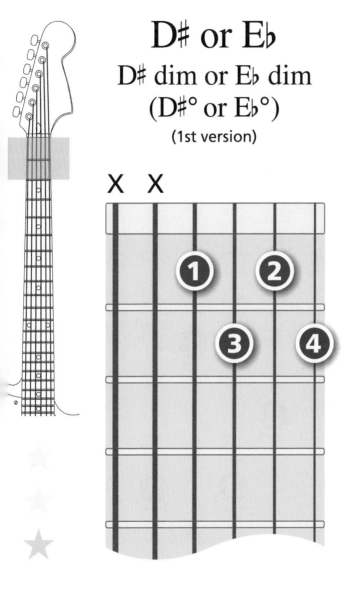

Notes in the chord:

4: E♭ (root); 3: A (dim fifth); 2: C (dim seventh); 1: G♭ (minor third)

This diminished chord is one of the easier shapes in the key of E♭!

| A | A#
Bb | B | C | C#
Db | D | D#
Eb | E | F | F#
Gb | G | G#
Ab |

D♯ or E♭
D♯ dim or E♭ dim
(D♯° or E♭°)
(2nd version)

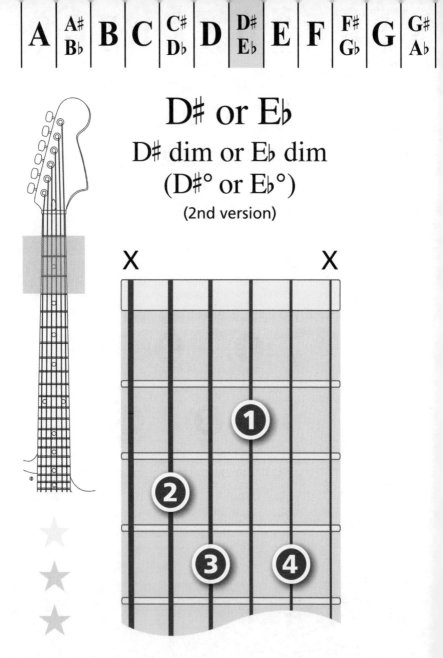

Notes in the chord:

4: C (dim seventh); 3: G♭ (minor third); 2: A (dim fifth); 1: E♭ (keynote)

This 'reshuffling' of the diminished chord's notes places
E♭ at the top of the chord.

D# or Eb
D# aug or Eb aug
(D#+ or Eb+)
(1st version)

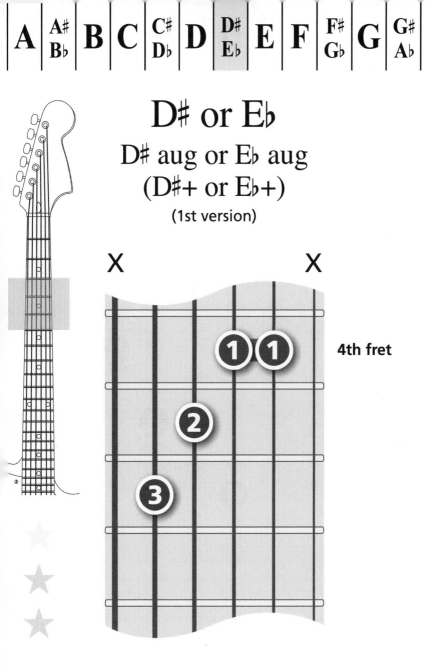

4th fret

Notes in the chord:

5: Eb (root); 4: G (third); 3: B (aug fifth); 1: Eb

A standard augmented shape, placed here in the 4th position on the fingerboard.

D♯ or E♭
D♯ aug or E♭ aug
(D♯+ or E♭+)
(2nd version)

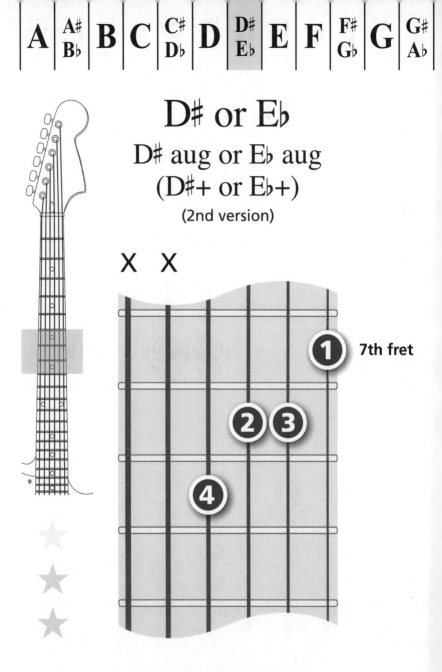

X   X

7th fret

Notes in the chord:
4: B (aug fifth); 3: E♭ (keynote); 2: G (third); 1: B

Another standard shape for an augmented chord,
raised here to the 7th position. B now displaces E♭ as
the bass note.

D♯ or E♭
D♯ minor or E♭ minor
(D♯m or E♭m)
(1st version)

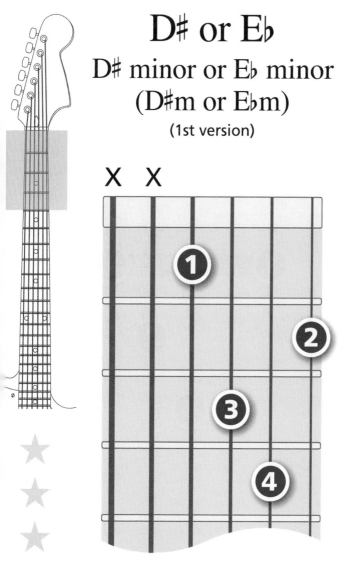

X X

Notes in the chord:
4: E♭ (root); 3: B♭ (fifth); 2: E♭; 1: G♭ (third)

The guitar's most basic four-note E♭ minor chord.

A	A# / B♭	B	C	C# / D♭	D	D# / E♭	E	F	F# / G♭	G	G# / A♭

D♯ or E♭
D♯ minor or E♭ minor
(D♯m or E♭m)
(2nd version)

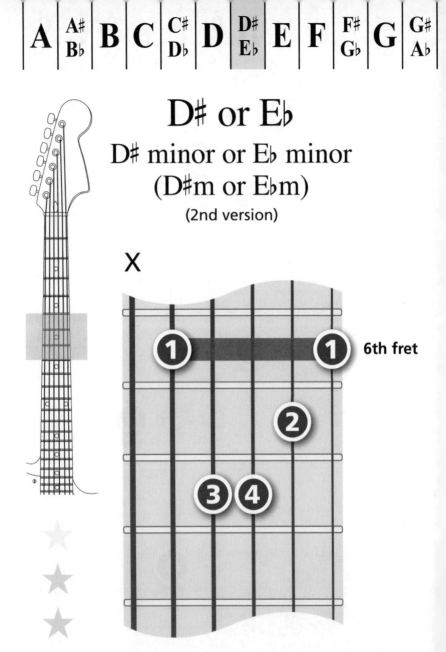

6th fret

Notes in the chord:
5: E♭ (root); 4: B♭ (fifth); 4: E♭; 3: G♭ (third); 1: B♭

A richer-sounding voicing.

214

A	A♯ B♭	B	C	C♯ D♭	D	D♯ E♭	E	F	F♯ G♭	G	G♯ A♭

D♯ or E♭
D♯ minor or E♭ minor
(D♯m or E♭m)
(3rd version)

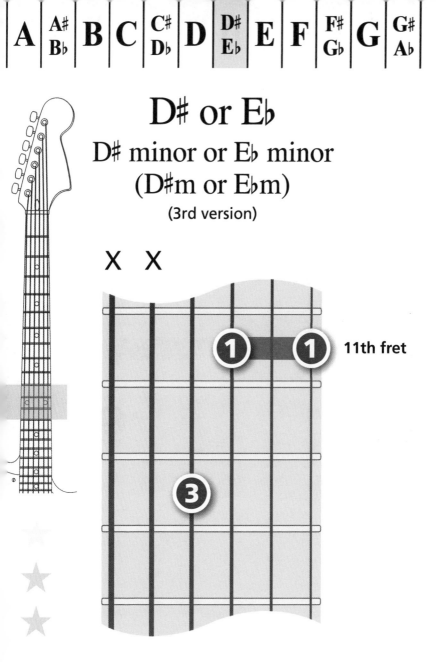

X X

11th fret

Notes in the chord:
4: E♭ (root); 3: G♭ (third); 2: B♭ (fifth); 1: E♭

This shape, displayed as a 'four-noter', can be extended across all six strings by barréing, and holding down the 5th string at the 13th fret.

215

A	A# Bb	B	C	C# Db	D	D# Eb	E	F	F# Gb	G	G# Ab

D♯ or E♭
D♯m6 or E♭m6
(1st version)

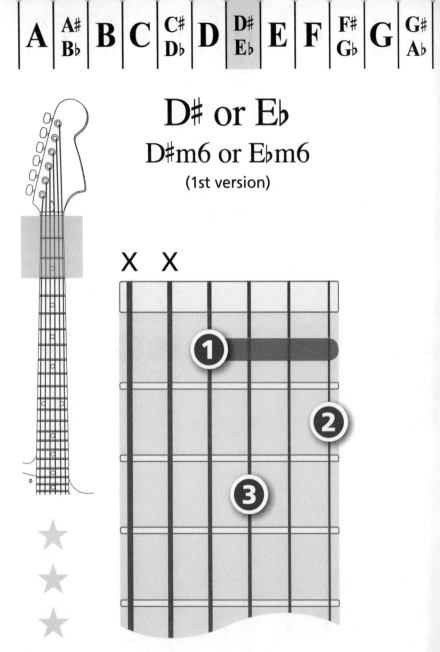

Notes in the chord:

4: E♭ (root); 3: B♭ (fifth); 2: C (sixth); 1: G♭ (third)

A pleasing minor sixth chord.

216

D# or Eb

D#m6 or Ebm6

(2nd version)

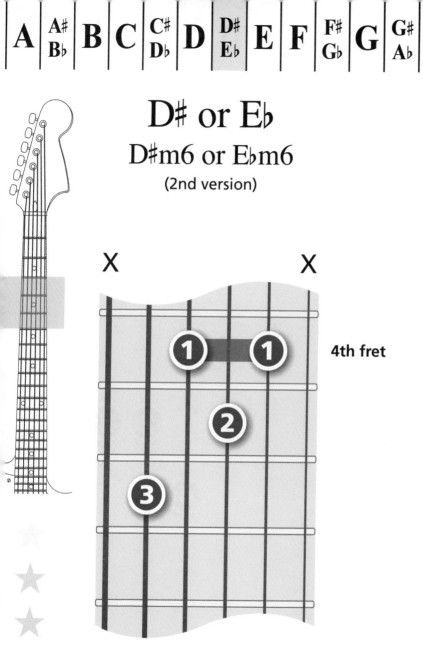

4th fret

Notes in the chord:
5: Eb (root); 4: Gb (third); 3: C (sixth); 2: Eb

An effective alternative to the chord on page 216, even though this voicing leaves out the fifth (Bb).

D# or Eb
D#m7 or Ebm7
(1st version)

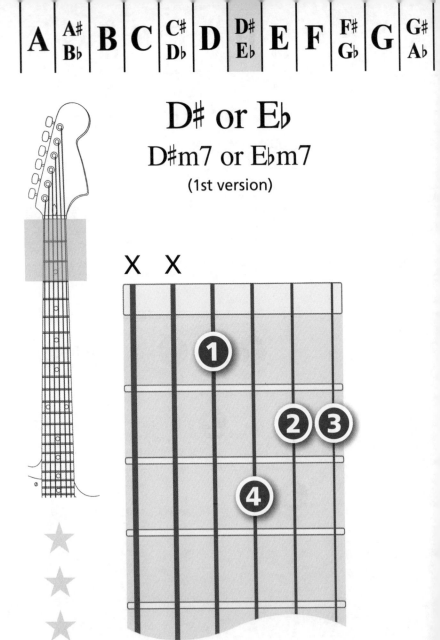

Notes in the chord:

4: Eb (root); 3: Bb (fifth); 2: Db (dom seventh); 1: Gb (third)

Quite a lightweight Ebm7.

D# or Eb

D#m7 or Ebm7
(2nd version)

X

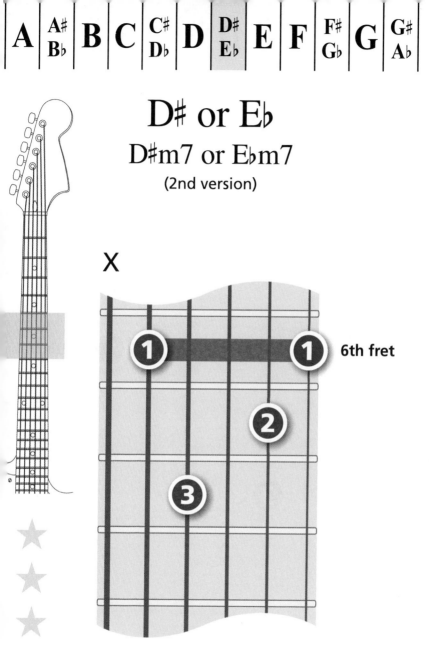

6th fret

Notes in the chord:

5: Eb (root); 4: Bb (fifth); 3: Db (dom seventh); 2: Gb (third); 1: Bb (fifth)

A more powerful, five-string voicing.

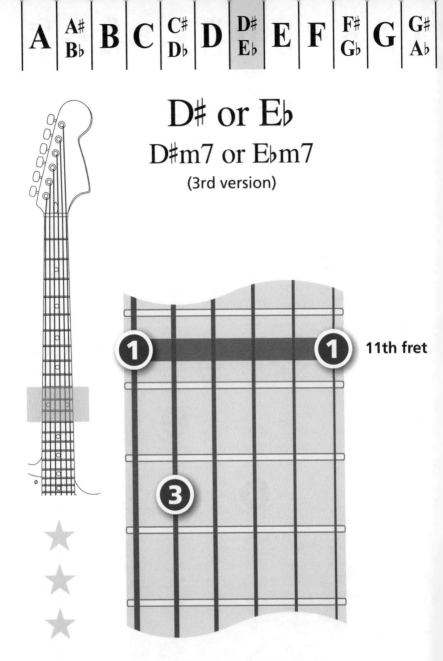

D♯ or E♭
D♯m7 or E♭m7
(3rd version)

11th fret

Notes in the chord:

6: E♭ (root); 5: B♭ (fifth); 4: D♭ (dom seventh); 3: G♭ (third); 2: B♭ (fifth); 1: E♭

A six-string chord – but its high register gives it an unexpected lightness.

220

D♯ or E♭
D♯m9 or E♭m9

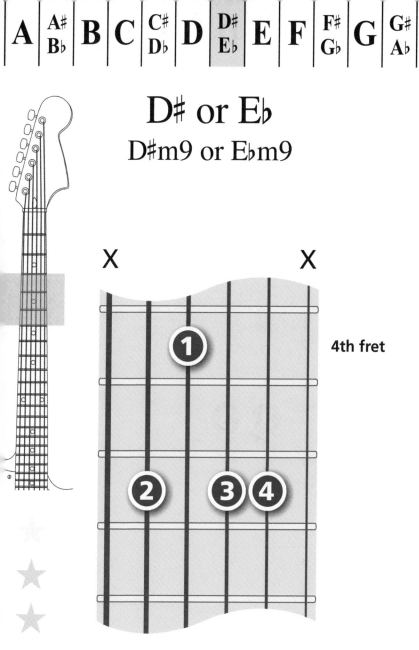

X   X

①

4th fret

②   **③④**

Notes in the chord:
5: E♭ (root); 4: G♭ (third); 3: D♭ (dom seventh); 2: F (ninth)

Avoid the outer strings here – their open Es would be a
horribly discordant addition to this chord!

A	A#/Bb	B	C	C#/Db	D	D#/Eb	E	F	F#/Gb	G	G#/Ab

E
'Bare' E (E5)

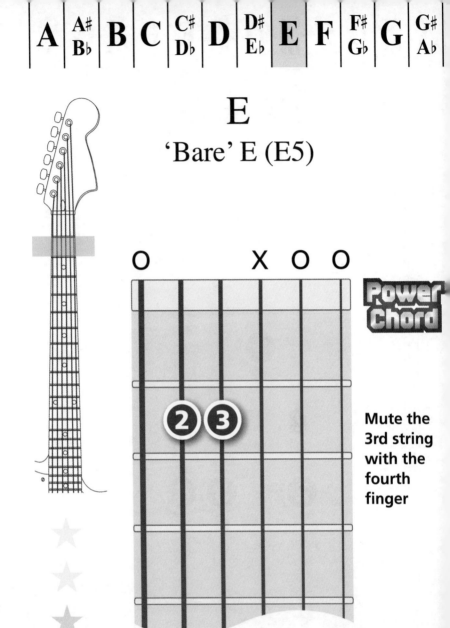

Mute the 3rd string with the fourth finger

Notes in the chord:
6: E (root); 5: B (fifth); 4: E; 2: B; 1: E

By muting the 3rd string, you can strike across all the strings, and produce an effective 'power chord'.

E

E major

(1st version)

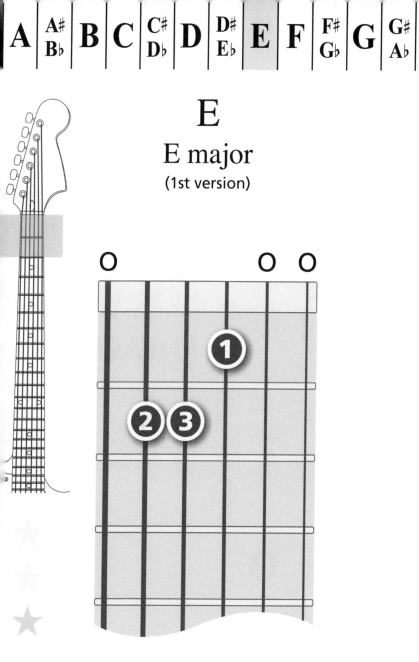

Notes in the chord:

6: E (root); 5: B (fifth); 4: E; 3: G# (third); 2: B; 1: E

The standard E shape for many guitarists.

E
E major
(2nd version)

O

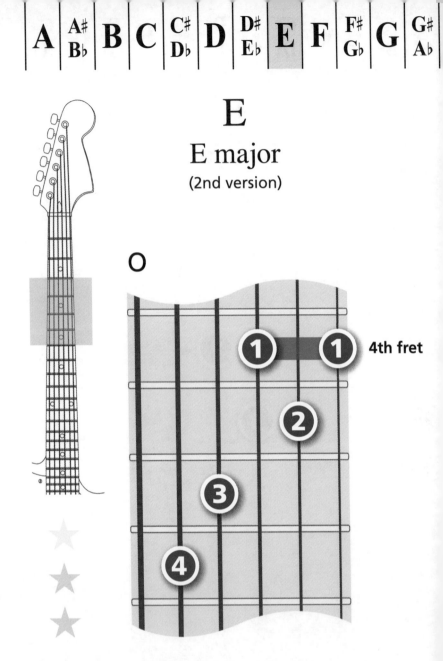

4th fret

Notes in the chord:
6: E (root); 5: E; 4: G# (third); 3: B (fifth); 2: E; 1: G#

This fingering produces major chords all over the
fingerboard; here, the open 6th string supplies an
additional low E in the bass.

E
E major
(3rd version)

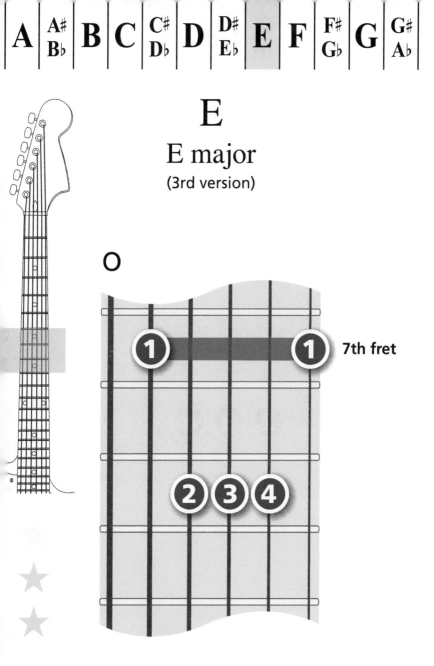

7th fret

Notes in the chord:
5: E (root); 4: B (fifth); 3: E; 2: G# (third); 1: B

The bottom string, which provides a low E,
can be omitted.

E

E sus4

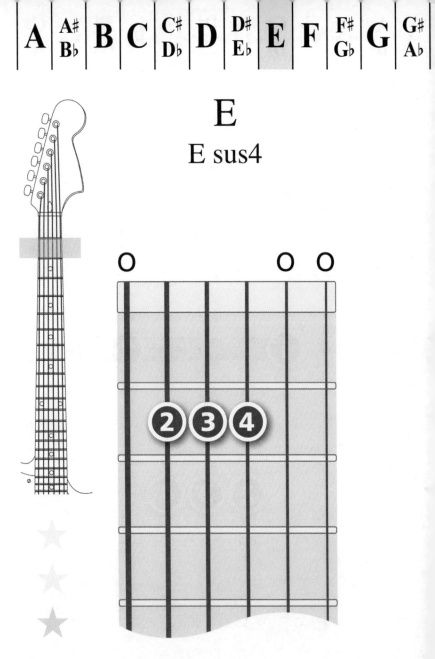

O   O   O

② ③ ④

Notes in the chord:

6: E (root); 5: B (fifth); 4: E; 3: A (sus fourth); 2: B; 1: E

Resolve this suspended chord to a standard E by raising your 4th finger, and replacing it with your index on the 3rd string, 1st fret.

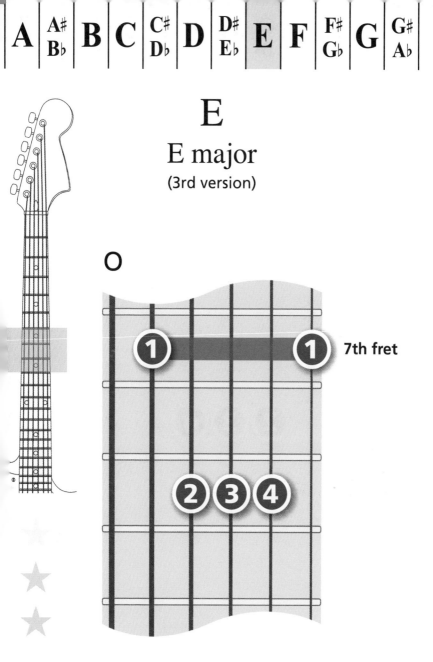

E
E major
(3rd version)

O

1   1   **7th fret**

2 3 4

Notes in the chord:
5: E (root); 4: B (fifth); 3: E; 2: G# (third); 1: B

The bottom string, which provides a low E,
can be omitted.

A | A# Bb | B | C | C# Db | D | D# Eb | E | F | F# Gb | G | G# Ab

225

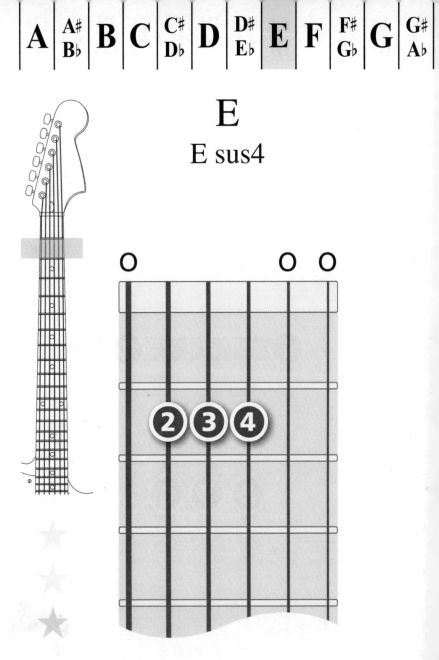

A	A# Bb	B	C	C# Db	D	D# Eb	E	F	F# Gb	G	G# Ab

E
E sus4

Notes in the chord:

6: E (root); 5: B (fifth); 4: E; 3: A (sus fourth); 2: B; 1: E

Resolve this suspended chord to a standard E by raising
your 4th finger, and replacing it with your index on the
3rd string, 1st fret.

E

E6

(1st version)

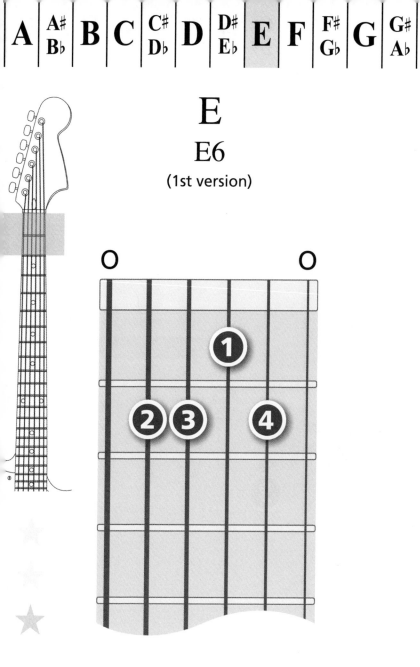

Notes in the chord:

6: E (root); 5: B (fifth); 4: E; 3: G# (third); 2: C# (added sixth); 1: E

A tasty added sixth chord that's simple to play with this fingering.

A	A#/B♭	B	C	C#/D♭	D	D#/E♭	E	F	F#/G♭	G	G#/A♭

E
E6
(2nd version)

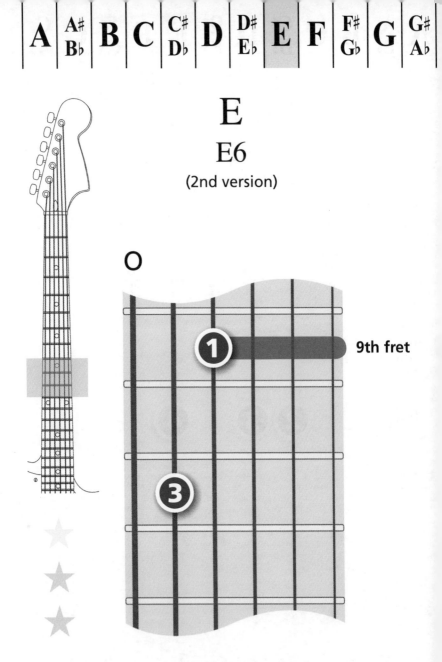

Notes in the chord:
6: E (root); 5: G# (third); 4: B (fifth); 3: E; 2: G# (third); 1: C# (added sixth)

There's a pleasingly wide range of notes here – from the open bass E to the higher notes at the 9th fret.

E
E6/9

O

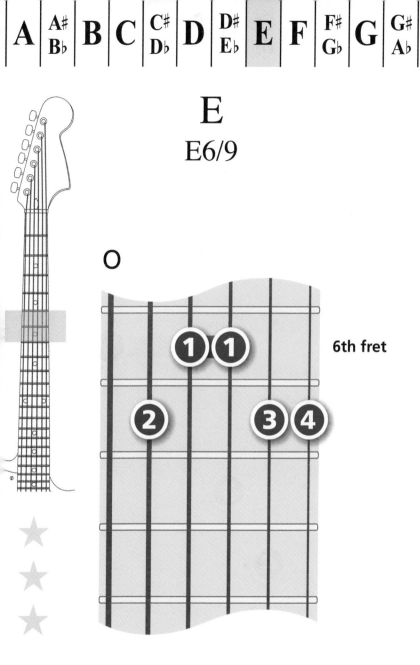

6th fret

Notes in the chord:
6: E (root); 5: E; 4: G# (third); 3: C# (sixth); 2: F# (ninth); 1: B (fifth)

This shape will be familiar – but it's a bonus to be able to combine it with an open string in the bass.

E
E maj7
(1st version)

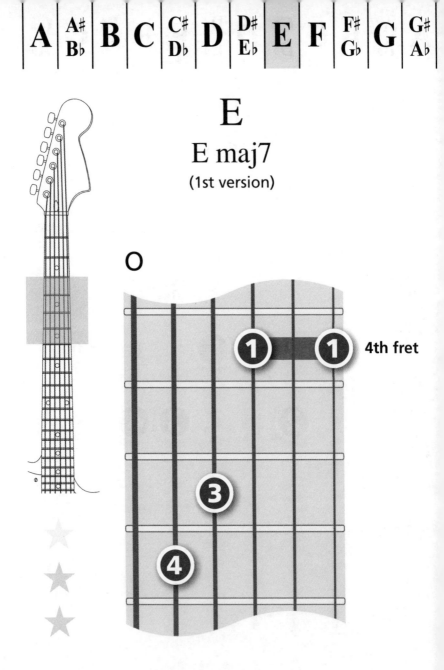

4th fret

Notes in the chord:

6: E (root); 5: E; 4: G# (third); 3: B (fifth); 2: D# (maj seventh); 1: G#

A simple modification of the E shape on page 224,
producing a major seventh chord.

230

E
E maj7
(2nd version)

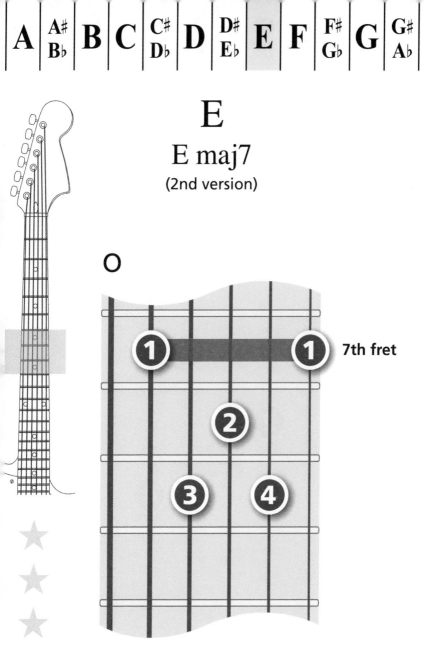

O

7th fret

Notes in the chord:

6: E (root); 5: E; 4: B (fifth); 3: D# (maj seventh); 2: G# (third); 1: B

It may take a little practice to position your index finger
barré clear of the 6th string, so that the open bass E
can sound.

E
E7
(1st version)

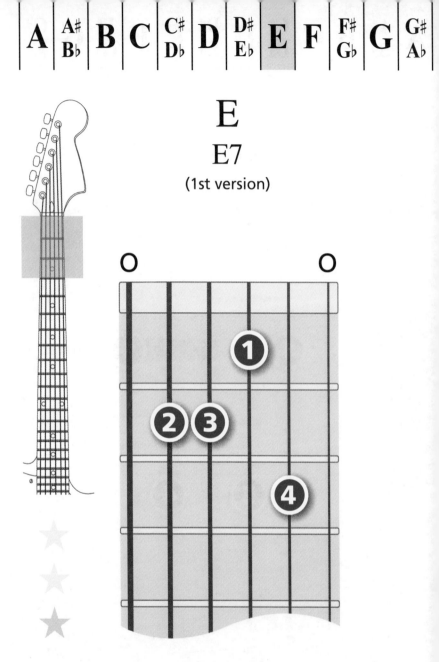

Notes in the chord:

6: E (root); 5: B (fifth); 4: E; 3: G# (third); 2: D (dom seventh); 1: E

A simple fingering that 'does the trick', especially when you're pounding out a rhythm part.

232

E
E7
(2nd version)

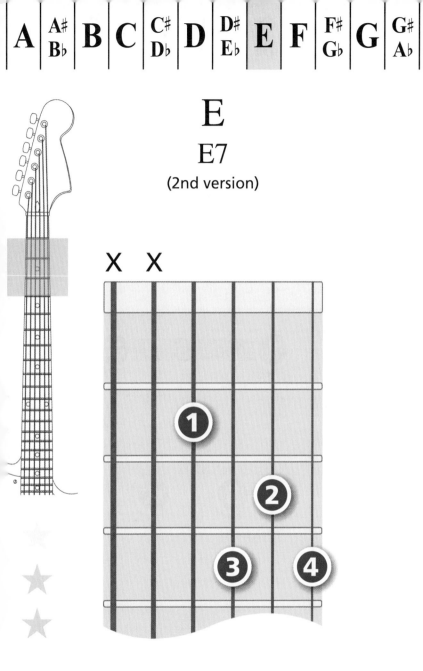

X X

Notes in the chord:
4: E (root); 3: B (fifth); 2: D (dom seventh); 1: G# (third)

A lighter-textured E7.

E
E7
(3rd version)

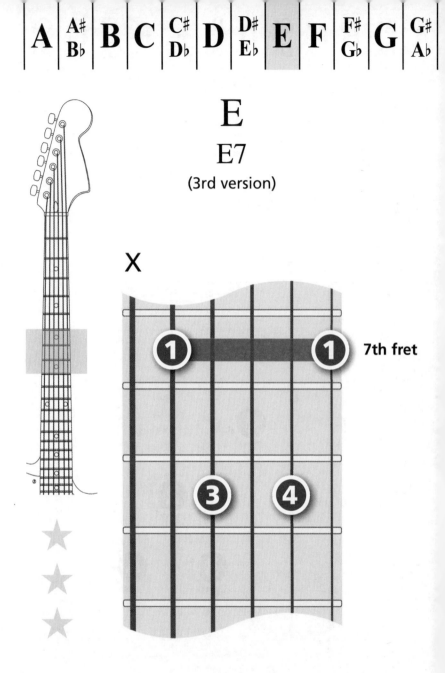

X

7th fret

Notes in the chord:
5: E (root); 4: B (fifth); 3: D (dom seventh); 2: G# (third); 1: B (fifth)

A firm barré is needed here to ensure that the
3rd string sounds properly.

E
E7+9

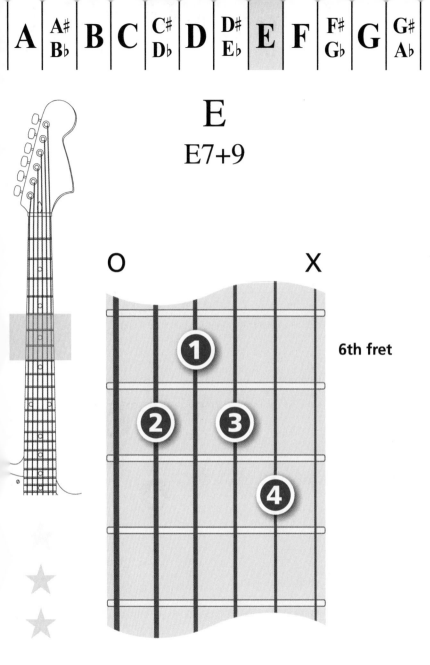

O   X

6th fret

Notes in the chord:

6: E (root); 5: E; 4: G# (third); 3: D (dom seventh);
2: F double sharp (=G) (aug ninth)

Yet another chord that benefits from the extra bass note
supplied by the 6th string.

235

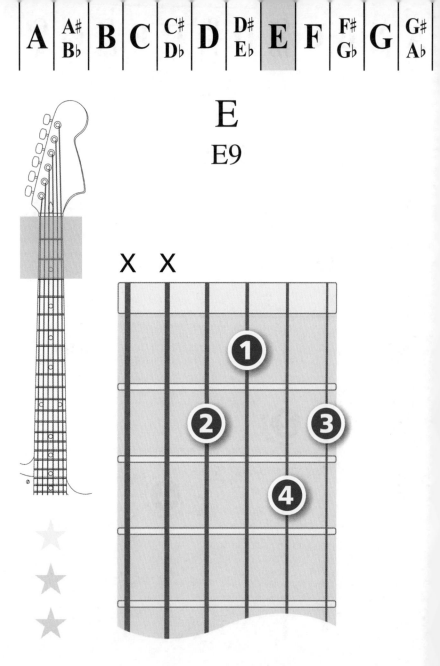

E
E9

Notes in the chord:

4: E (root); 3: G# (third); 2: D (dom seventh); 1: F# (ninth)

The left-hand fingers don't naturally 'fall into place' on this shape, but it's worth persevering with it.

E

E11

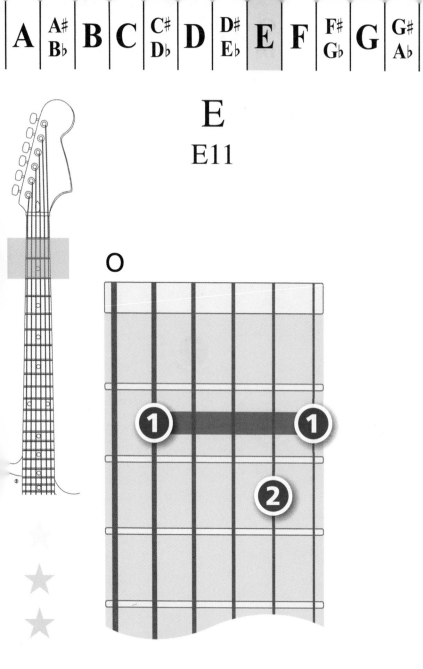

O

Notes in the chord:

6: E (root); 5: B (fifth); 4: E; 3: A (eleventh); 2: D (dom seventh); 1: F# (ninth)

A modified version of the fingering for D#/E♭11
(page 207), taking advantage of the open 6th string E.

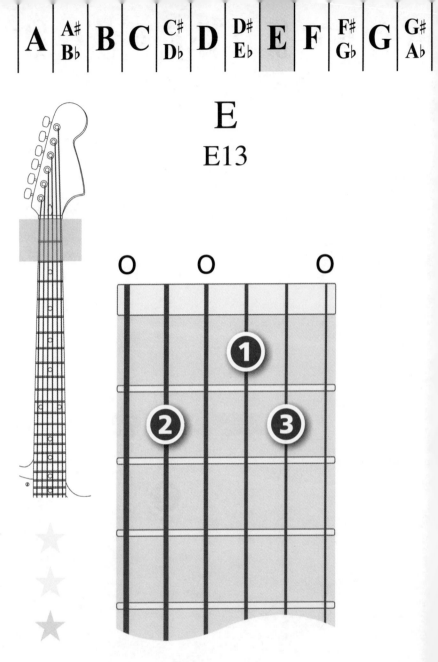

E
E13

Notes in the chord:

6: E (root); 5: B (fifth); 4: D (dom seventh); 3: G# (third); 2: C# (thirteenth); 1: E

Musically, this is quite a subtle, advanced chord; but in E,
it's very easy for guitarists to play.

238

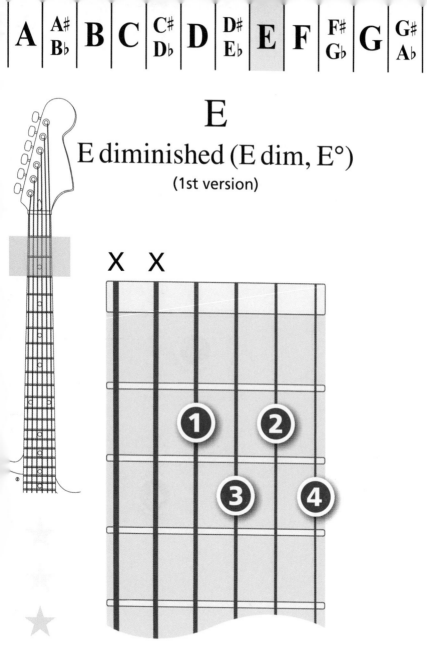

| A | A#/Bb | B | C | C#/Db | D | D#/Eb | E | F | F#/Gb | G | G#/Ab |

E
E diminished (E dim, E°)
(1st version)

X X

Notes in the chord:

4: E (root); 3: A# (dim fifth); 2: C# (dim seventh); 1: G (minor third)

A straightforward diminished shape.

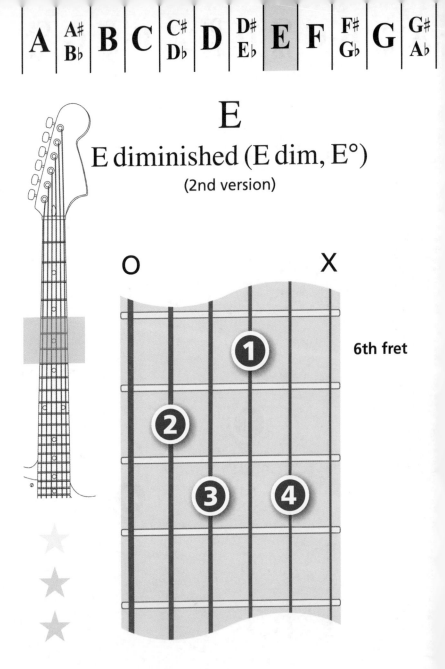

E

E diminished (E dim, E°)
(2nd version)

6th fret

Notes in the chord:

6: E (root); 5: E; 4: A# (dim fifth); 3:C# (dim seventh); 2: G (minor third)

Essentially the same chord as the one on page 239 –
but in a higher position, and enhanced with an E from
the 6th string.

A	A#\nBb	B	C	C#\nDb	D	D#\nEb	E	F	F#\nGb	G	G#\nAb

E

E augmented (E aug, E+)

(1st version)

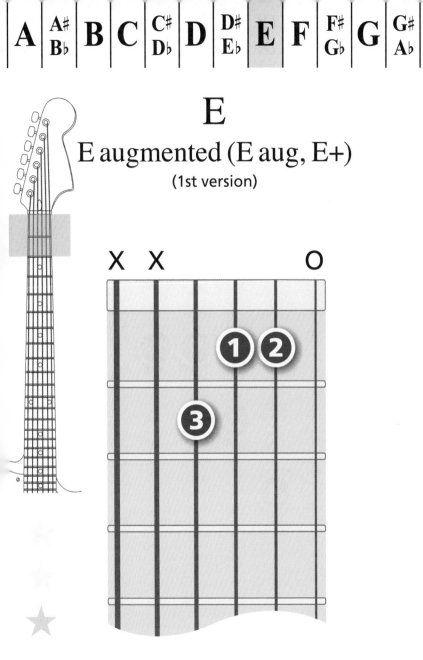

Notes in the chord:

4: E (root); 3: G# (third); 2: C (aug fifth); 1: E

Make sure your middle finger is well clear of the open
1st string here.

A	A#/Bb	B	C	C#/Db	D	D#/Eb	E	F	F#/Gb	G	G#/Ab

E
E augmented (E aug, E+)
(2nd version)

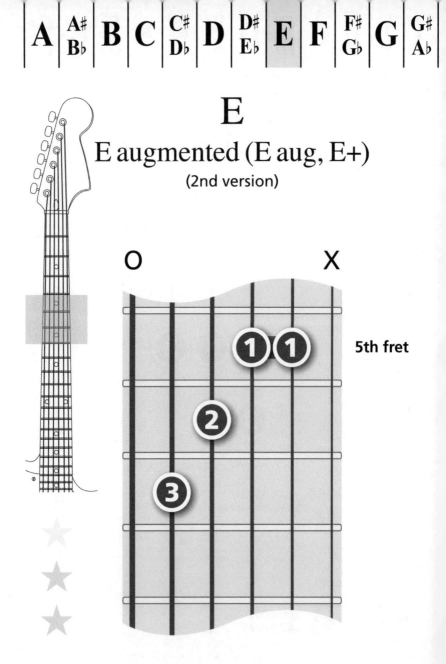

O   X

5th fret

Notes in the chord:

6: E (root); 5: E; 4: G# (third); 3: C (aug fifth); 2: E

A richer-sounding 'E aug'.

242

E

E minor (Em)

(1st version)

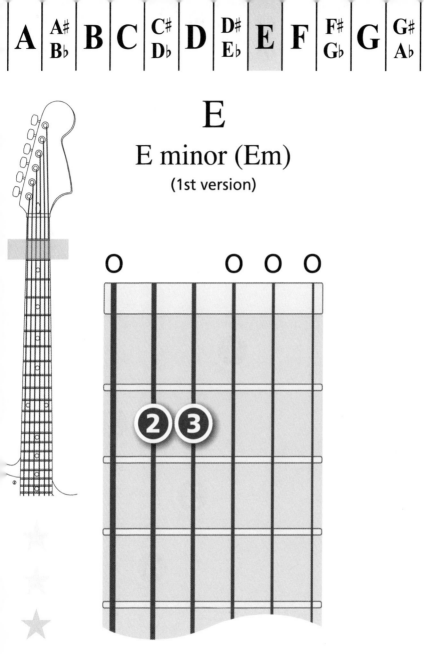

Notes in the chord:

6: E (root); 5: B (fifth); 4: E; 3: G (third); 2: B; 1: E

The first full chord many guitarists master. With no less than four open strings, it resonates pleasingly!

243

E

E minor (Em)
(2nd version)

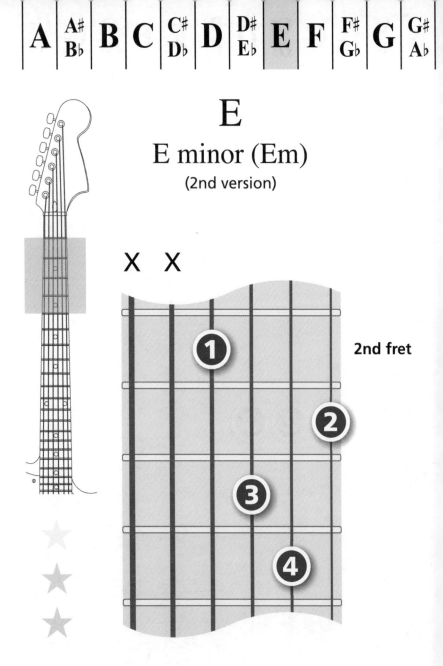

X   X

2nd fret

Notes in the chord:
4: E (root); 3: B (fifth); 2: E; 1: G (third)

A light and clear voicing, with the G that makes the chord
minor as its top note.

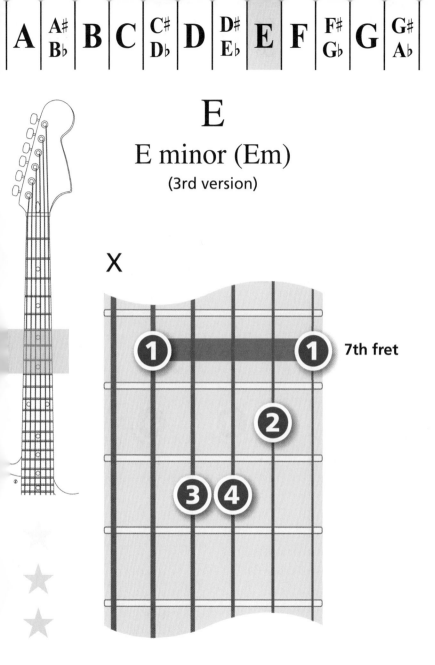

E
E minor (Em)
(3rd version)

X

7th fret

Notes in the chord:
5: E (root); 4: B (fifth); 3: E; 2: G (third); 1: B

By sounding the normally silent 6th string (fretted with your barré), you can create a second inversion of this chord, with B as its bass.

245

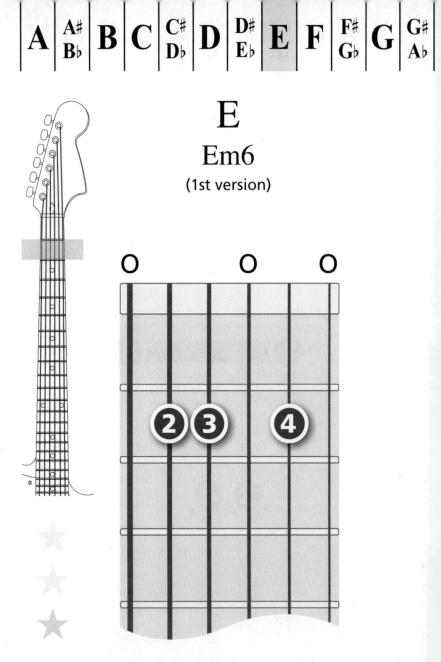

E
Em6
(1st version)

Notes in the chord:

6: E (root); 5: B (fifth); 4: E; 3: G (third); 2: C# (sixth); 1: E

A beefy chord when struck vigorously.

E

Em6

(2nd version)

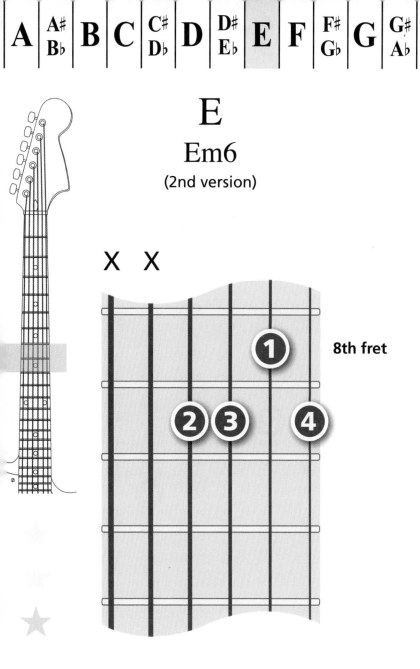

X   X

1 8th fret

2 **3** **4**

Notes in the chord:

4: B (fifth); 3: E; 2: G (third); 1: C# (sixth)

This shape gives a more delicate sound than the one on
the previous page. It's a second inversion, with B, not E,
as its bass.

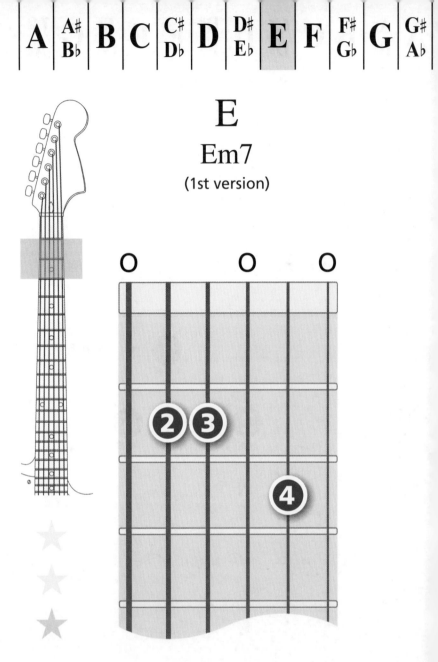

E
Em7
(1st version)

Notes in the chord:

6: E (root); 5: B (fifth); 4: E; 3: G (third); 2: D (dom seventh); 1: E

A beginner's favourite.

E

Em7

(2nd version)

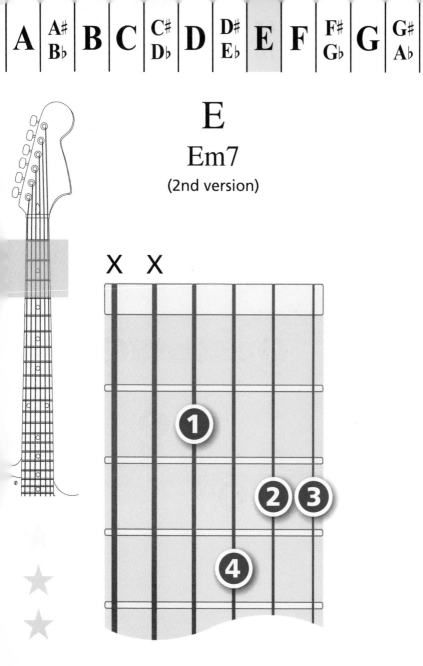

X   X

Notes in the chord:

4: E (root); 3: B (fifth); 2: D (dom seventh); 1: G (third)

A good chord for softer songs, due to its 'bass-light'
texture.

E

Em7

(3rd version)

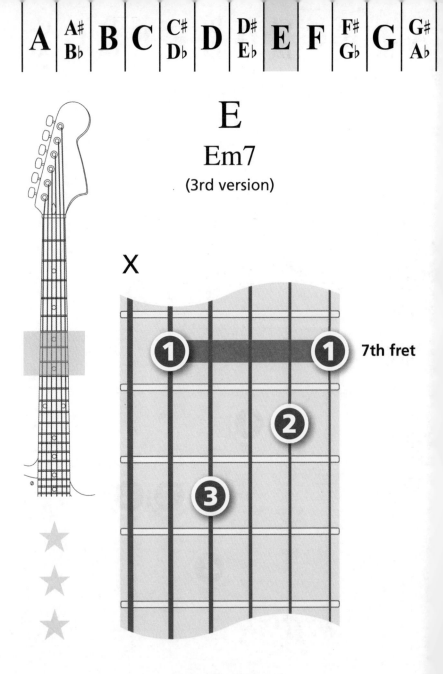

X

7th fret

Notes in the chord:

5: E (root); 4: B (fifth); 3: D (dom seventh); 2: G (third); 1: B

As with the shape on page 245, this chord can be made
into a second inversion by playing the normally silent,
barréd 6th string.

E
Em9

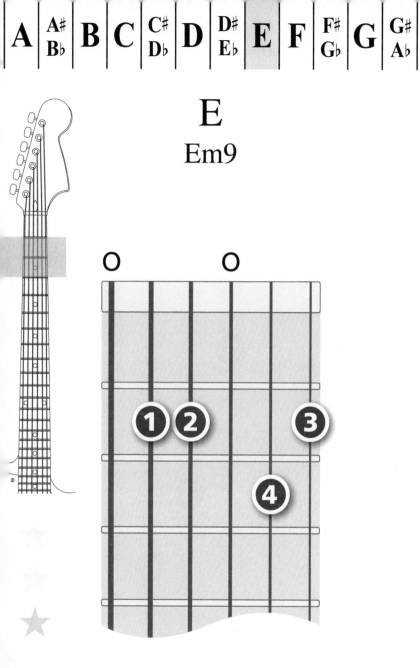

Notes in the chord:

6: E (root); 5: B (fifth); 4: E; 3: G (third); 2: D (dom seventh); 1: F# (ninth)

Don't strike the lower strings too heavily here, or the ninth
note (on the top string) won't be heard clearly.

F
'Bare' F (F5)

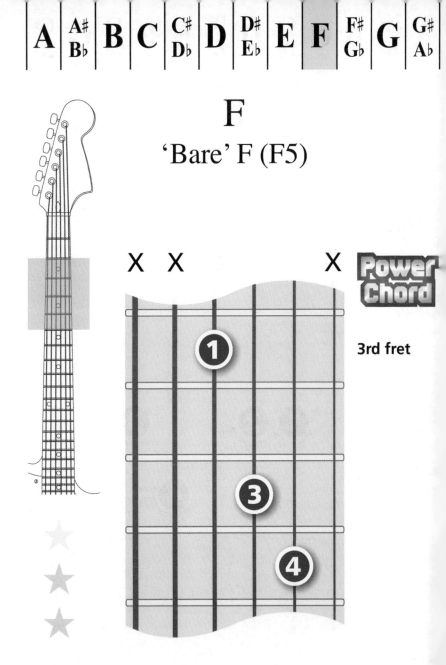

3rd fret

Notes in the chord:
4: F (root); 3: C (fifth); 2: F

Only inner strings (4th, 3rd and 2nd) are struck for this 'power chord'.

A	**A♯** **B♭**	**B**	**C**	**C♯** **D♭**	**D**	**D♯** **E♭**	**E**	**F**	**F♯** **G♭**	**G**	**G♯** **A♭**

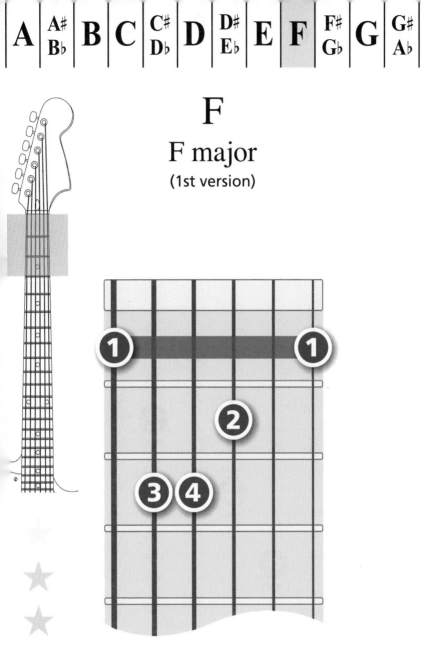

F
F major
(1st version)

Notes in the chord:

6: F (root); 5: C (fifth); 4: F; 3: A (third); 2: C; 1: F

F isn't the simplest key on the guitar: even this low-position F major requires a full barré.

253

F

F major
(2nd version)

X

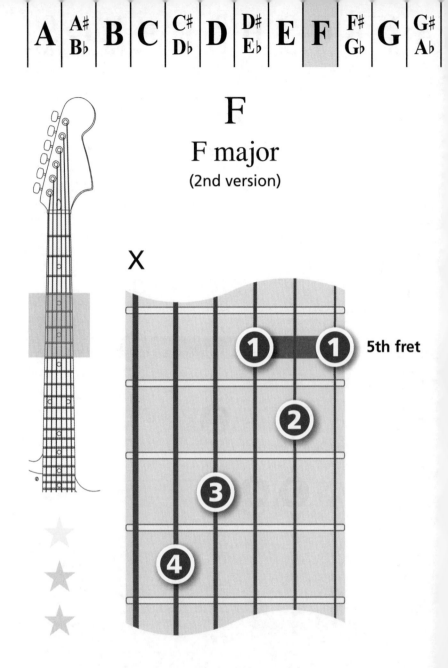

5th fret

Notes in the chord:
5: F (root); 4: A (third); 3: C (fifth); 2: F; 1: A

A very useful 5th position F chord – though it lacks a
deep bass note.

F

F major
(3rd version)

X

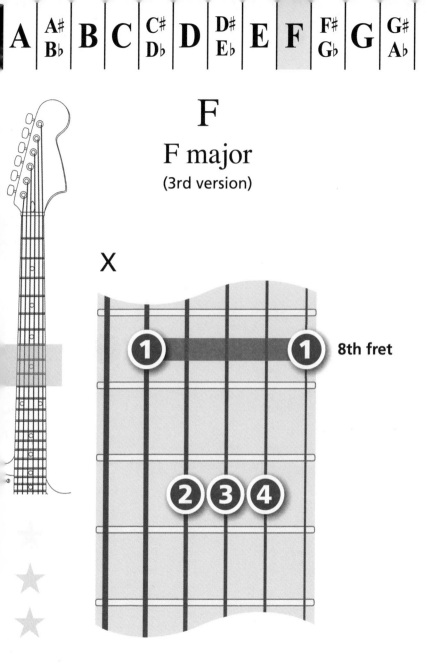

8th fret

Notes in the chord:
5: F (root); 4: C (fifth); 3: F; 2: A (third); 1: C

A good chord to 'slide up' to.

F
F sus4

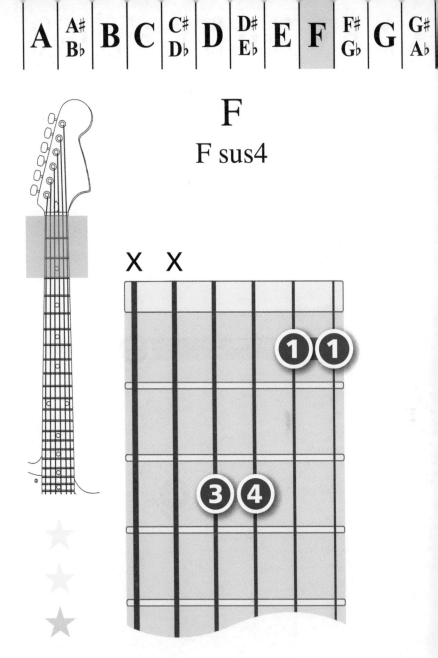

X   X

Notes in the chord:

4: F (root); 3: B♭ (sus fourth); 2: C (fifth); 1: F

Lifting your fourth finger, and replacing it with your second finger at the 3rd string's 2nd fret, resolves the suspension by producing a four-string F.

F

F6

(1st version)

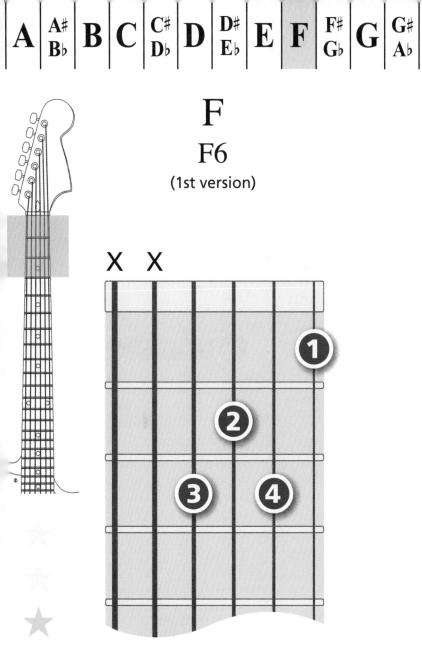

Notes in the chord:

4: F (root); 3: A (third); 2: D (added sixth); 1: F

Another attractive chord that's just a digit away from the
four-string F major described on the previous page.

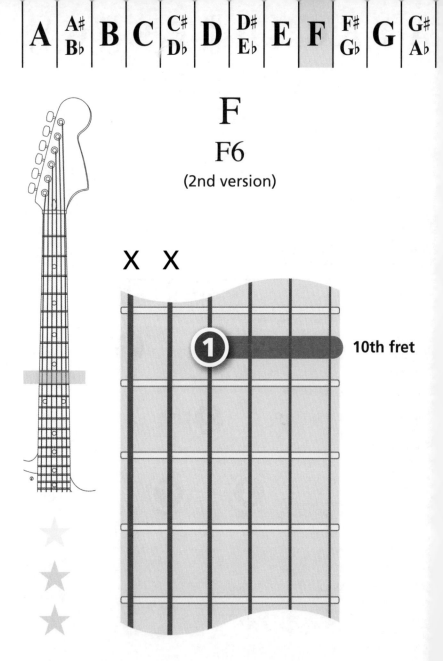

F
F6
(2nd version)

X X

① 10th fret

Notes in the chord:
4: C: (fifth); 3: F; 2: A (third); 1: D (added sixth)

Make it easy on yourself with this second-inversion added
sixth; you could, of course, hold down its notes with
individual fingers rather than a barré.

A	A# B♭	B	C	C# D♭	D	D# E♭	E	F	F# G♭	G	G# A♭

F
F6/9

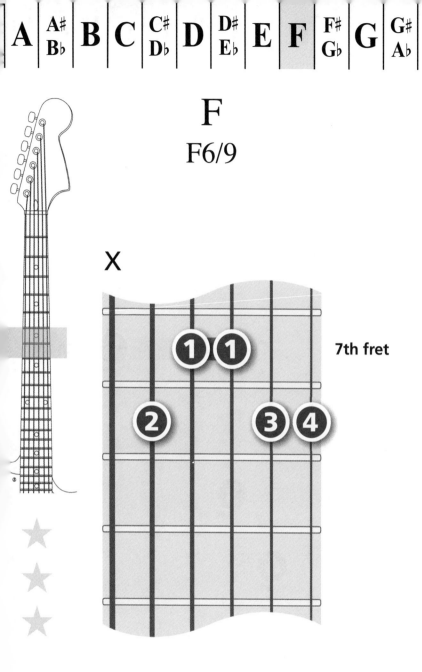

X

7th fret

Notes in the chord:
5: F (root); 4: A (third); 3: D (sixth); 2: G (ninth); 1: C (fifth)

A familiar shape, appearing here in the 7th position, where
no low bass F is available.

F

F maj7

(1st version)

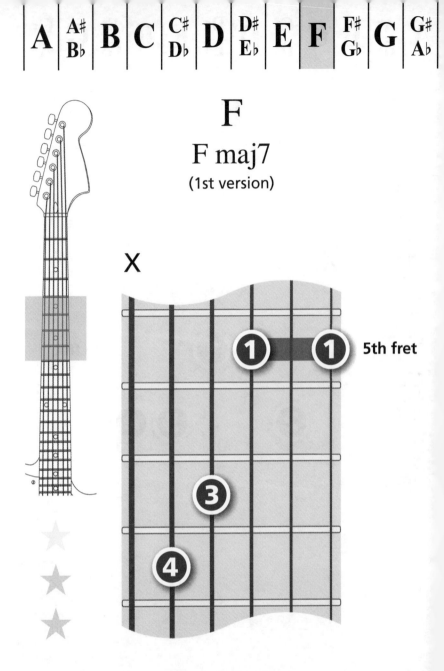

X

5th fret

Notes in the chord:

5: F (root); 4: A (third); 3: C (fifth); 2: E (maj seventh); 1: A

Placing your second finger on the 2nd string at the 6th fret
will convert this 'major seventh' to a regular F major.

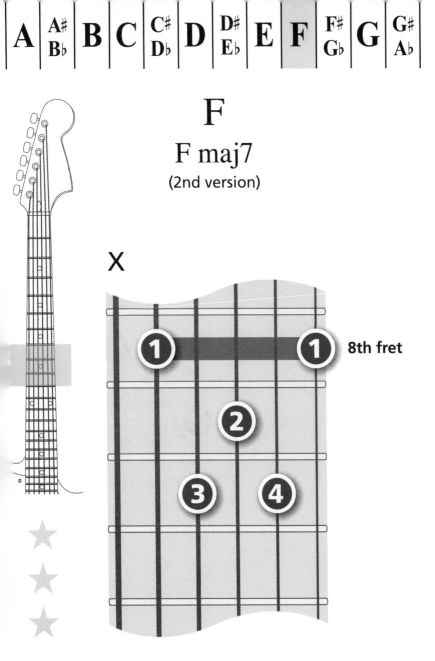

F
F maj7
(2nd version)

Notes in the chord:
5: F (root); 4: C (fifth); 3: E (maj seventh); 2: A (third); 1: C

A nice higher voicing of F major seventh.

F
F7
(1st version)

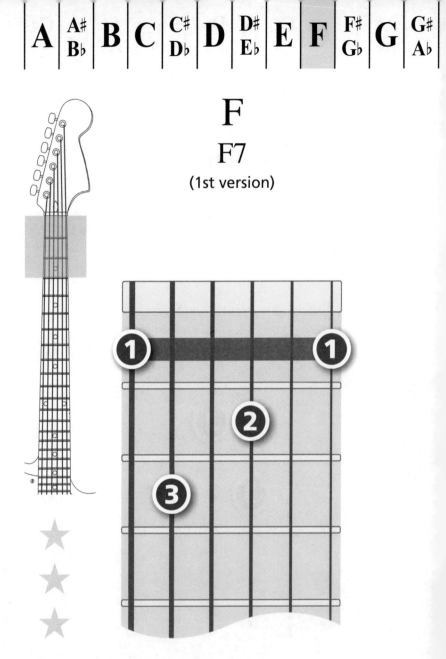

Notes in the chord:

6: F (root); 5: C (fifth); 4: Eb (dom seventh); 3: A (third); 2: C; 1: F

Depending on your guitar's action, and/or the strength
of your index finger, you may find it hard to sound the
4th string cleanly.

F

F7

(2nd version)

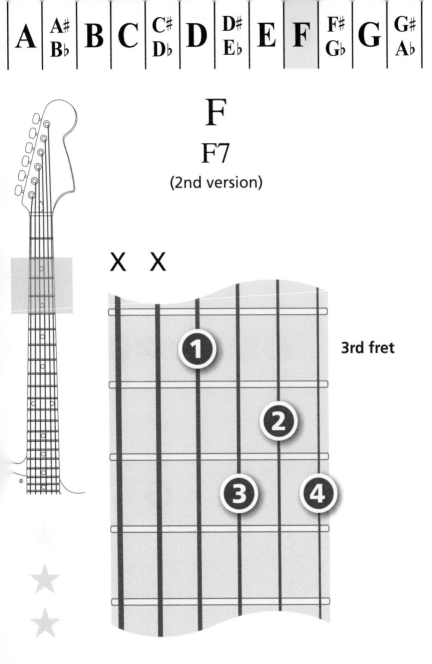

3rd fret

Notes in the chord:

4: F (root); 3: C (fifth); 2: E♭ (dom seventh); 1: A (third)

A light-sounding F7 that can sound funky if you strike it hard and staccato on an electric guitar.

| A | A#
B♭ | B | C | C#
D♭ | D | D#
E♭ | E | F | F#
G♭ | G | G#
A♭ |

F
F7
(3rd version)

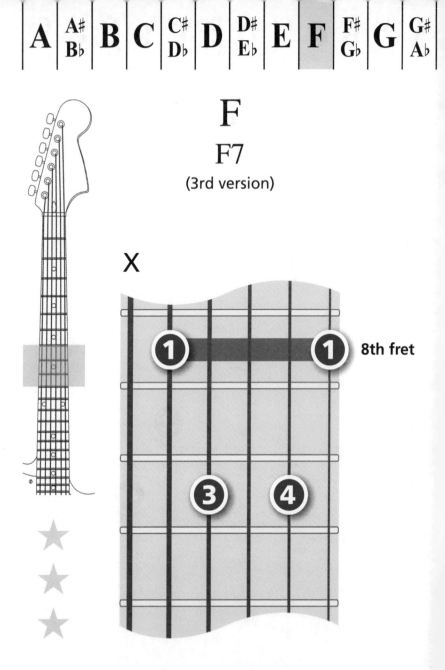

X

8th fret

Notes in the chord:

5: F (root); 4: C (fifth); 3:E♭ (dom seventh); 2: A (third); 1: C

As always with this important but difficult shape, getting the 3rd string not to buzz can be a challenge.

F
F7+9

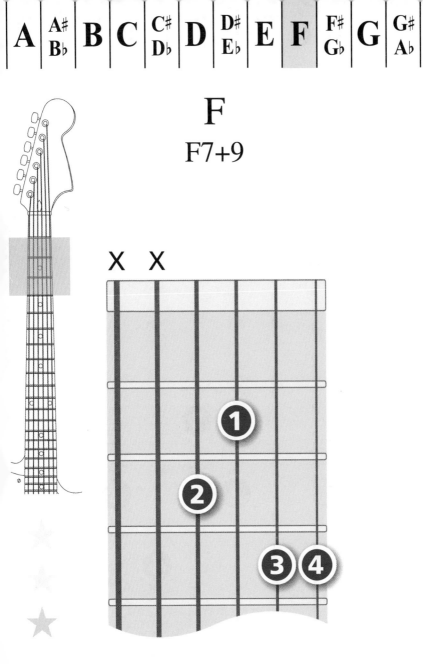

X X

Notes in the chord:
4: F (root); 3: A (third); 2: E♭ (dom seventh); 1:G# (aug ninth)

A piquant chord that will serve you well in many
musical contexts.

F
F9

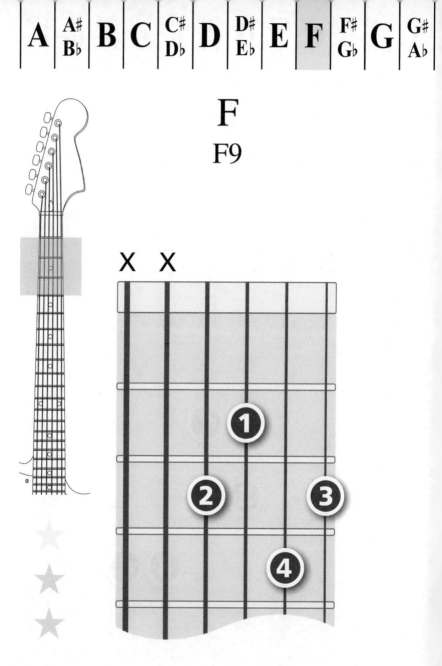

Notes in the chord:

4: F (root); 3: A (third); 2: E♭ (dom seventh); 1: G (ninth)

Not a heavy-sounding chord – but a very effective one.

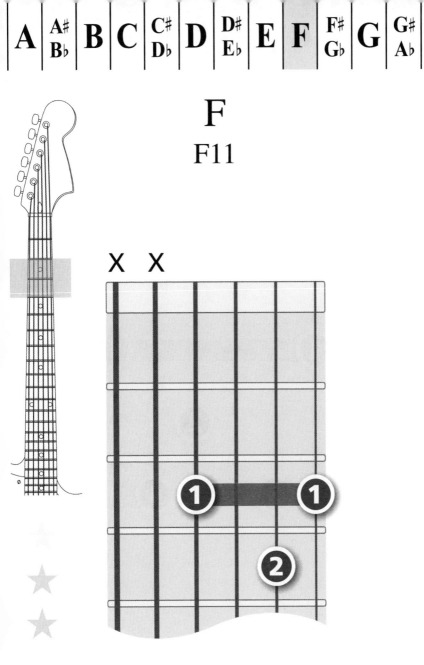

| A | A#/Bb | B | C | C#/Db | D | D#/Eb | E | F | F#/Gb | G | G#/Ab |

F
F11

X X

Notes in the chord:

4: F (root); 3: B♭ (eleventh); 2: E♭ (dom seventh); 1: G (ninth)

A standard four-string eleventh shape, used here in
the 3rd position.

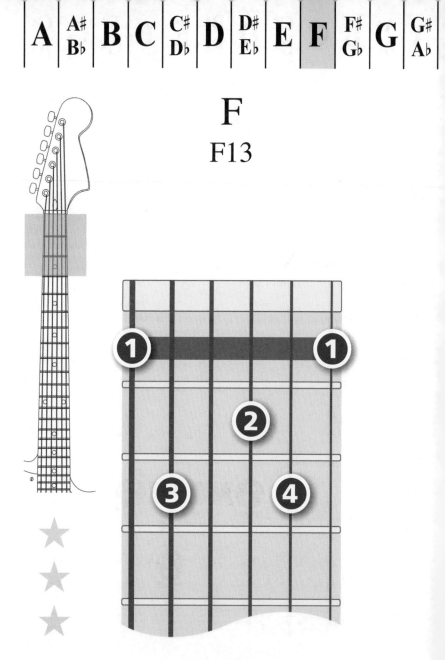

F
F13

Notes in the chord:

6: F (root); 5: C (fifth); 4: E♭ (dom seventh); 3: A (third); 2: D (thirteenth); 1: F

A shape with a quite a weighty bass end, thanks to the
low F and C on the 6th and 5th strings.

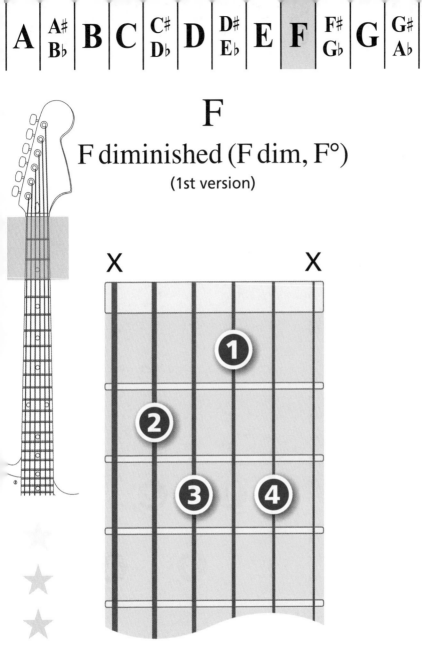

F
F diminished (F dim, F°)
(1st version)

Notes in the chord:
5: B (dim fifth); 4: F (keynote); 3: A♭ (minor third); 2: D (dim seventh)

A five-string version of F diminished; it doesn't have the
key note at its root.

F

F diminished (F dim, F°)

(2nd version)

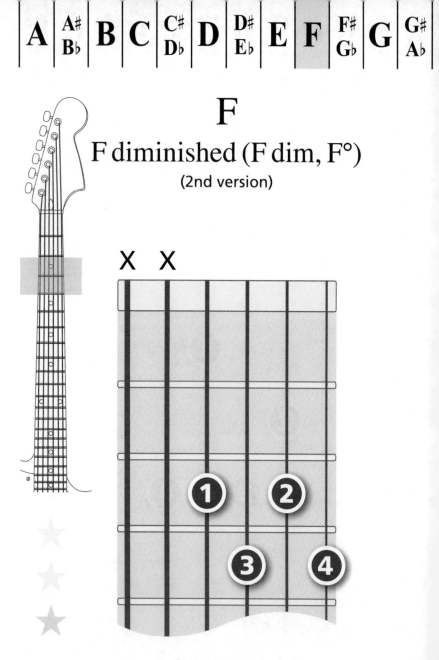

Notes in the chord:

4: F (root); 3: B (dim fifth); 2: D (dim seventh); 1: Ab (minor third)

The standard fingering for a four-string diminished.

F

F augmented (F aug, F+)

(1st version)

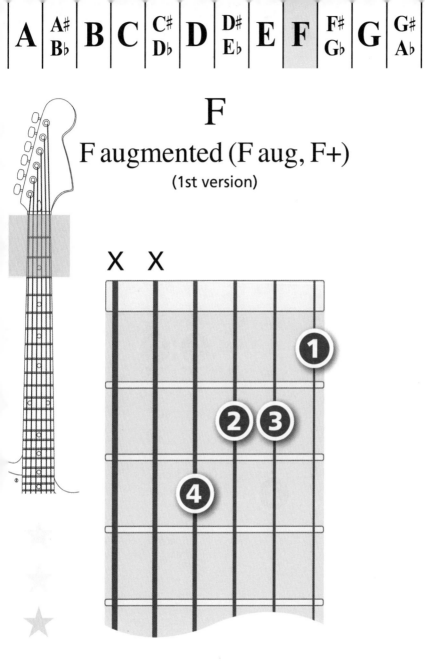

Notes in the chord:

4: F (root); 3: A (third); 2: C# (aug fifth); 1: F

The simplest fingering for an augmented F chord.

| A | A# Bb | B | C | C# Db | D | D# Eb | E | F | F# Gb | G | G# Ab |

F

F augmented (F aug, F+)

(2nd version)

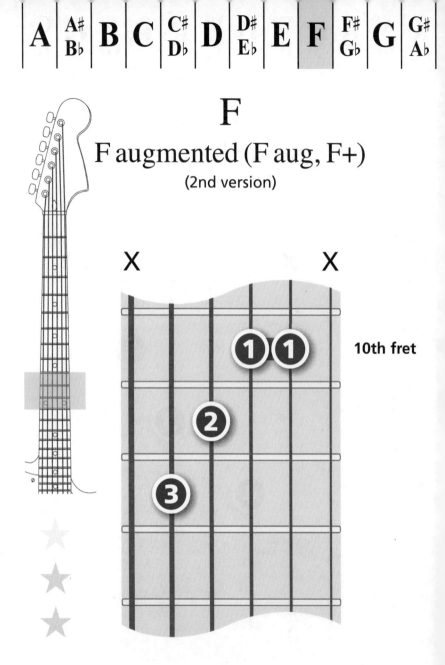

X   X

10th fret

Notes in the chord:

5: A (third); 4: C# (aug fifth); 3: F (keynote); 2: A

A much higher voicing of this augmented chord.

272

A	A# Bb	B	C	C# Db	D	D# Eb	E	F	F# Gb	G	G# Ab

F
F minor (Fm)
(1st version)

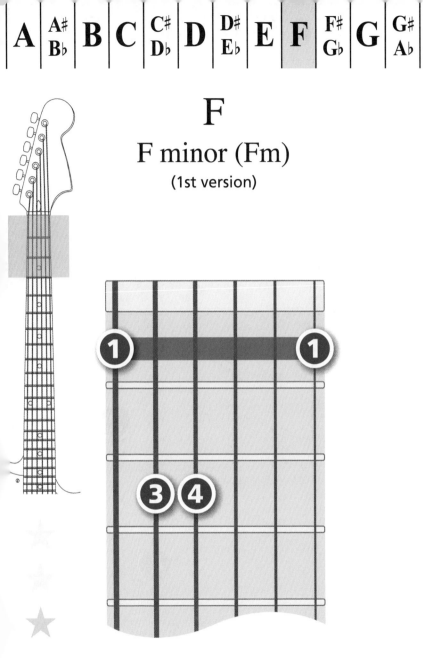

Notes in the chord:

6: F (root); 5: C (fifth); 4: F; 3: Ab (third); 2: C; 1: F

If you get tired of having to make a full barré here, you can omit the 6th and 5th strings.

273

F

F minor (Fm)

(2nd version)

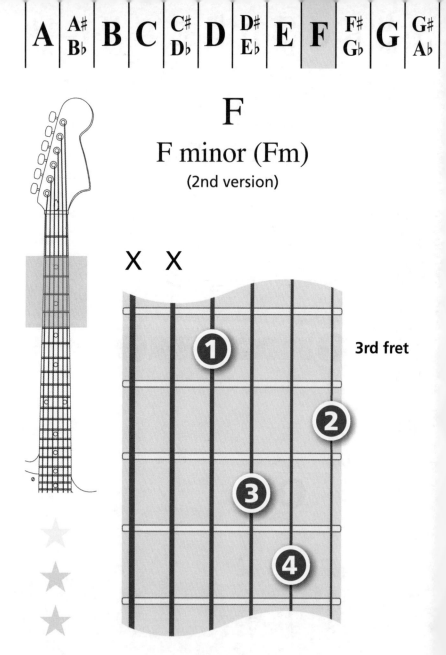

X   X

3rd fret

Notes in the chord:

4: F (root); 3: C (fifth); 2: F: 1: Ab (third)

This four-string shape has the chord's minor third
at its highest note.

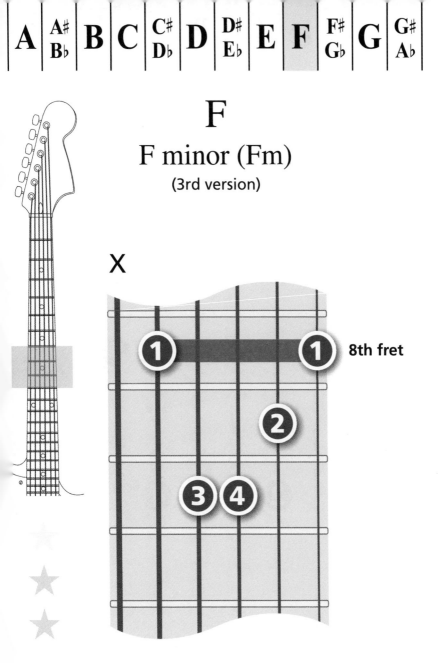

F

F minor (Fm)

(3rd version)

Notes in the chord:

5: F (root); 4: C (fifth); 3: F; 2: Ab (third); 1: C

By sounding the normally silent 6th string (fretted with your barré), you can create a second inversion of this chord, with C as its bass.

F
Fm6
(1st version)

Notes in the chord:

6: F (root); 5: C (fifth); 4; F; 3: Ab (third); 2: D (sixth); 1: F

Lift off your 4th finger, and this Fm6 becomes a standard F minor.

A	A# Bb	B	C	C# Db	D	D# Eb	E	F	F# Gb	G	G# Ab

F
Fm6
(2nd version)

X X

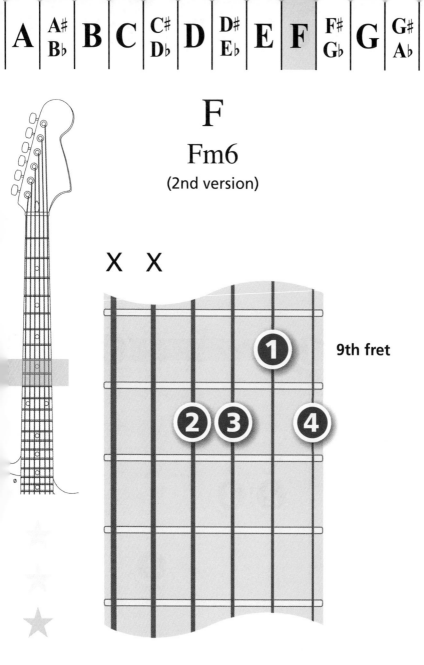

9th fret

Notes in the chord:
4: C (fifth); 3: F; 2: Ab (third); 1: D (sixth)

This chord is a second inversion, but will work well in musical contexts where a bass F isn't necessary.

F

Fm7

(1st version)

Notes in the chord:

6: F (root); 5: C (fifth); 4: F; 3: A♭ (third); 2: E♭ (dom seventh); 1: F

The 4th finger is hard to position correctly in the chord,
but the effort is worth it.

F

Fm7

(2nd version)

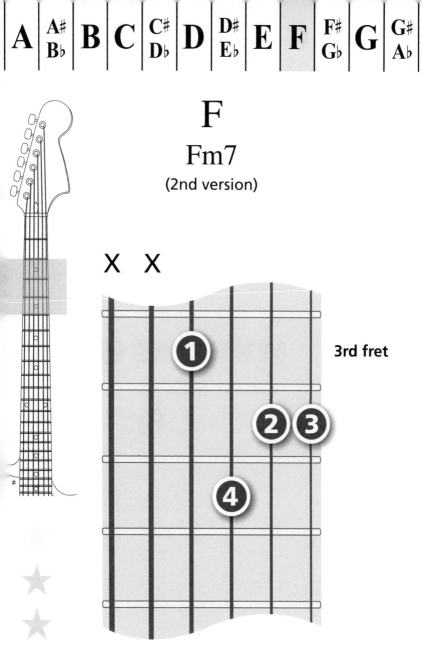

X   X

3rd fret

Notes in the chord:
4: F (root); 3: C (fifth); 2: Eb (dom seventh); 1: Ab (third)

A tasty four-string Fm7.

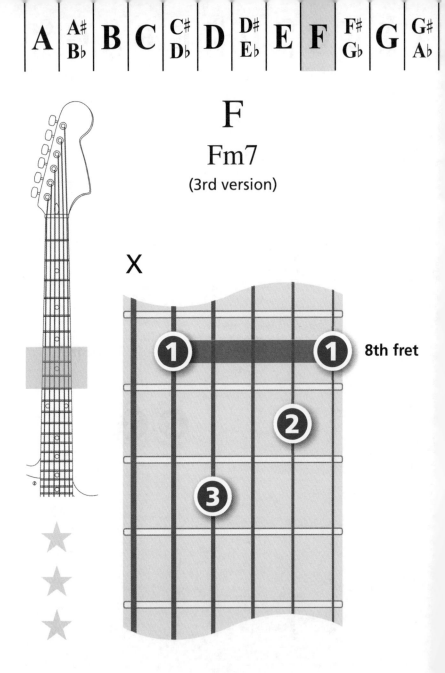

F
Fm7
(3rd version)

X

8th fret

Notes in the chord:

5: F (root); 4: C (fifth); 3: E♭ (dom seventh); 2: A♭ (third); 1: C

A higher voicing of Fm7; make sure the 3rd string
sounds properly!

280

F
Fm9

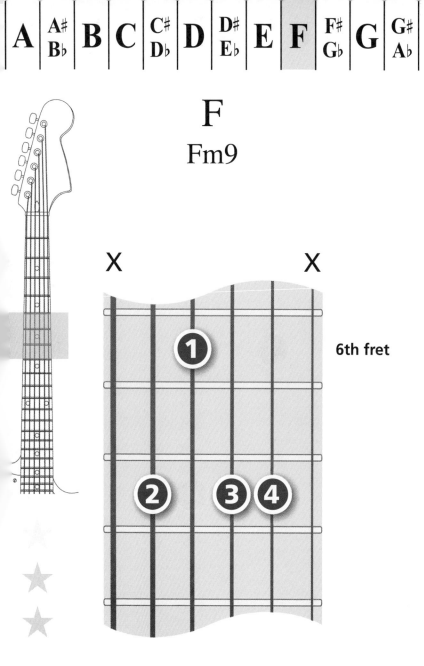

6th fret

Notes in the chord:
5: F (root); 4: Ab (third); 3: Eb (dom seventh); 2: G (ninth)

The outer strings stay silent here.

281

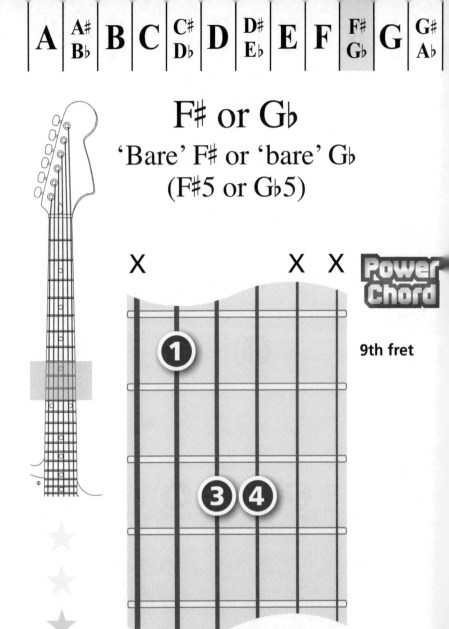

F♯ or G♭

'Bare' F♯ or 'bare' G♭
(F♯5 or G♭5)

X   X   X

Power Chord

9th fret

Notes in the chord:

5: F# (root); 4: C# (fifth); 3: F#

As usual with this chord, only three strings are needed.

F♯ or G♭
F♯ major or G♭ major
(1st version)

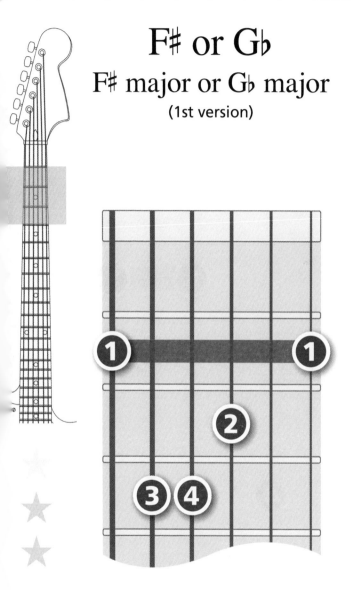

Notes in the chord:

6: F# (root); 5: C# (fifth); 4: F#; 3: A# (third); 2: C#; 1: F#

Whether we describe the current key as F# or Gb, it's equally tricky for guitarists, requiring frequent barrés, even on simple chords like this one.

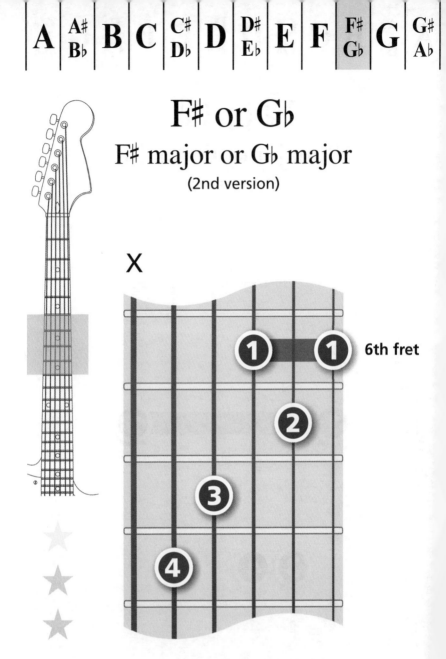

F♯ or G♭

F♯ major or G♭ major

(2nd version)

X

6th fret

Notes in the chord:

5: F# (root); 4: A# (third); 3: C# (fifth); 2: F#; 1: A#

A familiar movable shape, deployed here in the
6th position.

F♯ or G♭
F♯ major or G♭ major
(3rd version)

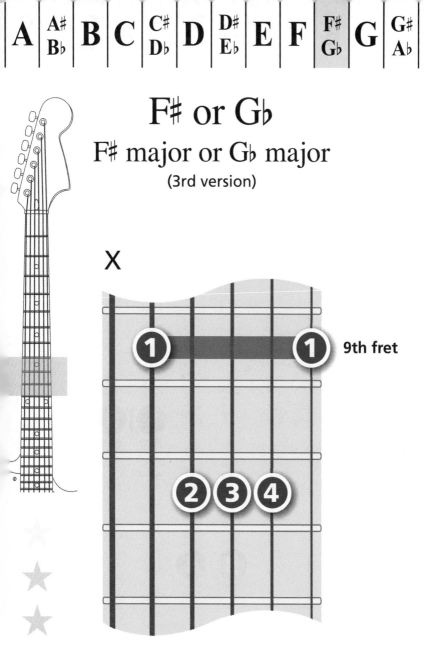

X

9th fret

Notes in the chord:
5: F# (root); 4: C# (fifth); 3: F#; 2: A# (third); 1: C#

Another standard fingering, which can supply a second-inversion chord if the barré is extended to the 6th string.

F♯ or G♭
F♯ sus4 or G♭ sus4

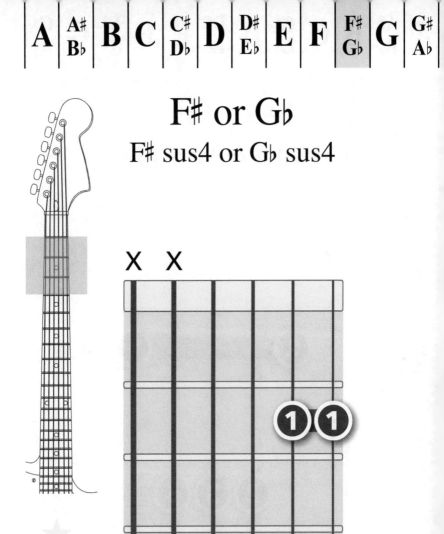

X X

Notes in the chord:

4: F# (root); 3: B (sus fourth); 2: C# (fifth); 1: F#

A simpler shape!

F# or G♭
F#6 or G♭6
(1st version)

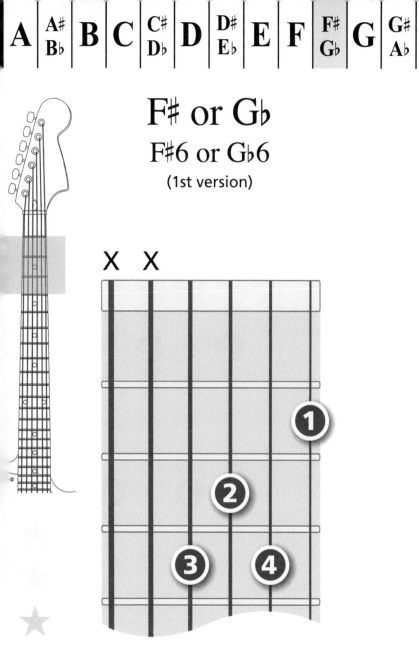

Notes in the chord:
4: F# (root); 3: A# (third); 2: D# (added sixth); 1: F#

You could add a bass F# here by fretting the 6th string at the 2nd fret with your left-hand thumb.

F♯ or G♭
F♯6 or G♭6
(2nd version)

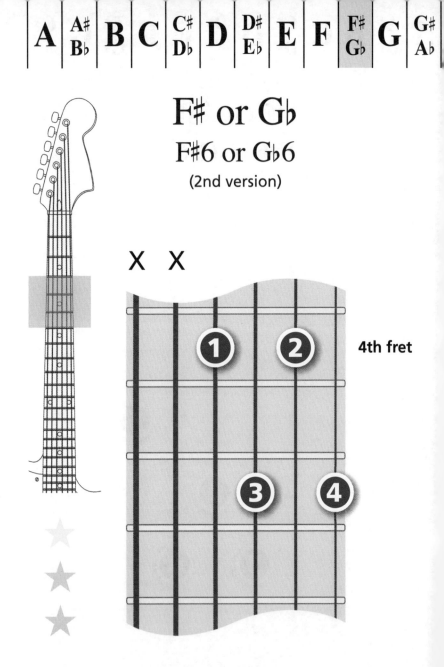

X   X

4th fret

Notes in the chord:
4: F# (root); 3: C# (fifth); 2: D# (added sixth); 1: A# (third)

As always with this fingering, a barré could replace the individual digits at the 4th fret.

F♯ or G♭
F♯6/9 or G♭6/9

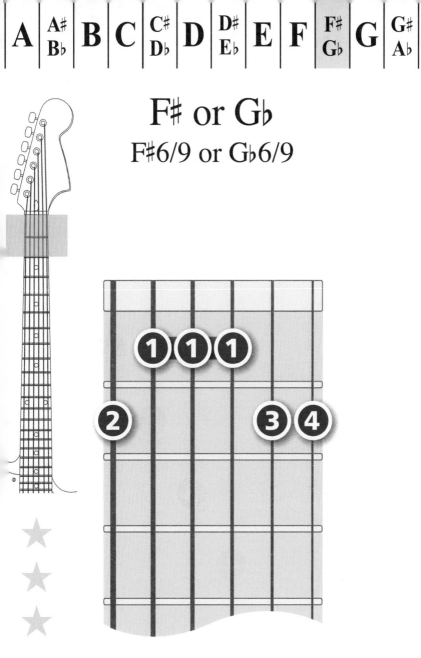

Notes in the chord:

6: F♯ (root); 5: A♯ (third); 4: D♯ (sixth); 3: G♯ (ninth); 2: C♯ (fifth); 1: F♯

A meaty-sounding 6/9 in this low fret position.

| A | A#/B♭ | B | C | C#/D♭ | D | D#/E♭ | E | F | F#/G♭ | G | G#/A♭ |

F# or G♭

F# maj7 or G♭ maj7

(1st version)

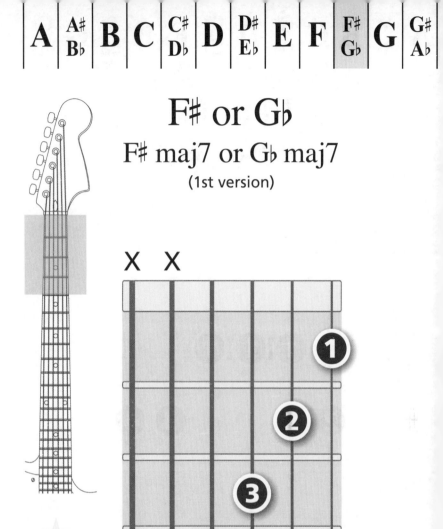

X X

Notes in the chord:

4: F# (root); 3: A# (third); 2: C# (fifth); 1: E# (maj seventh)

Simple, and fairly light in texture.

A	A# Bb	B	C	C# Db	D	D# Eb	E	F	F# Gb	G	G# Ab

F♯ or G♭

F♯ maj7 or G♭ maj7
(2nd version)

X X

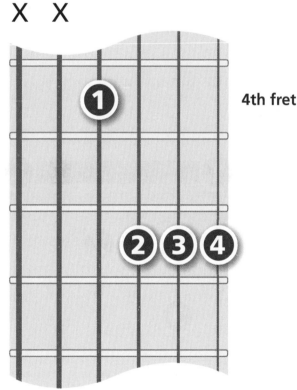

4th fret

①

②③④

Notes in the chord:
4: F# (root); 3: C# (fifth); 2: E# (maj seventh); 1: A# (third)

Effective as a broken chord as well as when vigorously strummed.

F# or Gb

F#7 or Gb7

(1st version)

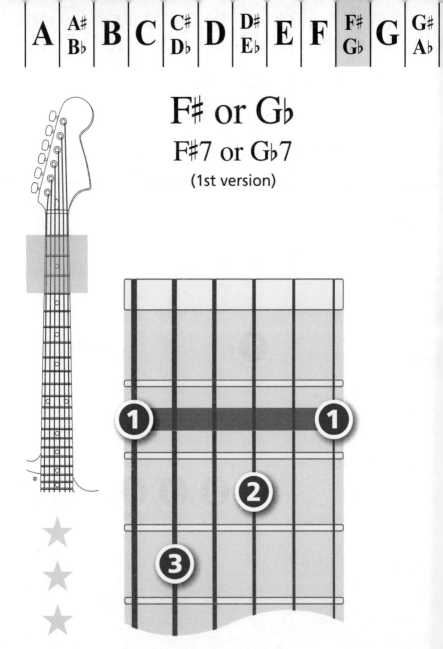

Notes in the chord:

6: F# (root); 5: C# (fifth); 4: E (dom seventh); 3: A# (third); 2: C#; 1: F#

Make sure the all-important dominant seventh note on the 4th string doesn't buzz!

A	A# Bb	B	C	C# Db	D	D# Eb	E	F	F# Gb	G	G# Ab

F♯ or G♭

F♯7 or G♭7

(2nd version)

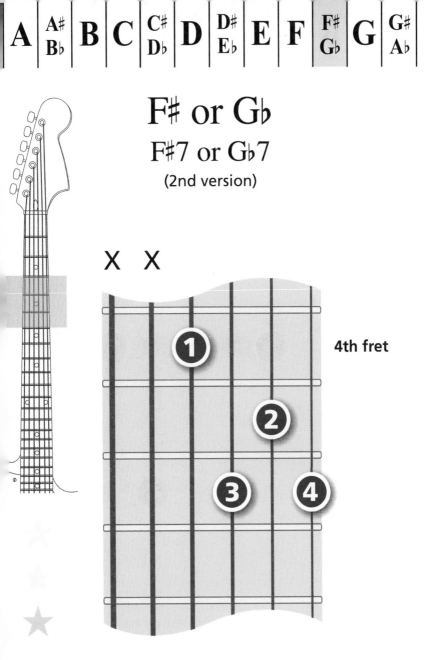

X   X

4th fret

Notes in the chord:

4: F# (root); 3: C# (fifth); 2: E (dom seventh); 1: A#

A F#/Gb7 voicing with no deep bass.

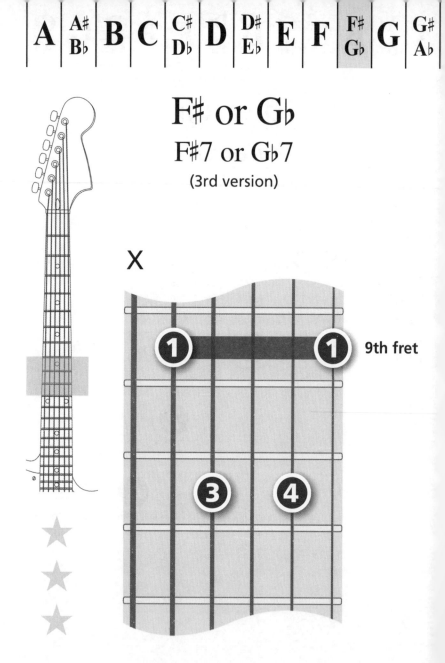

F♯ or G♭
F♯7 or G♭7
(3rd version)

X

9th fret

Notes in the chord:
5: F♯ (root); 4: C♯ (fifth); 3: E (dom seventh); 2: A♯ (third); 1: C♯

This higher-register chord can have a strident timbre.

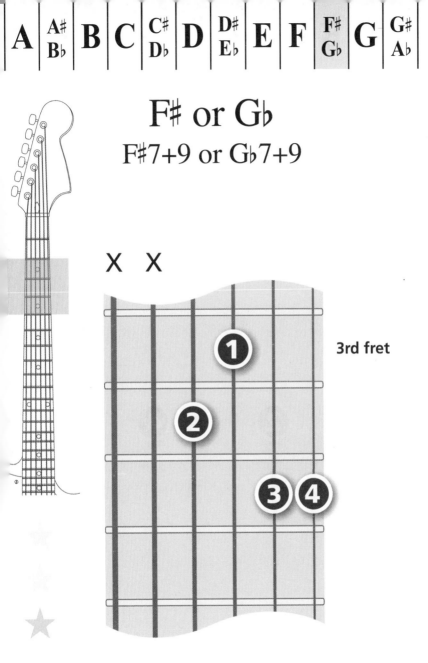

F♯ or G♭
F♯7+9 or G♭7+9

3rd fret

Notes in the chord:
4: F♯ (root); 3: A♯ (third); 2: E (dom seventh); 1: G double sharp (A) (aug ninth)

7+9s are characterized by the musical 'clash' they contain
– found here between the notes on the 1st and 3rd strings.

295

F♯ or G♭

F♯9 or G♭9

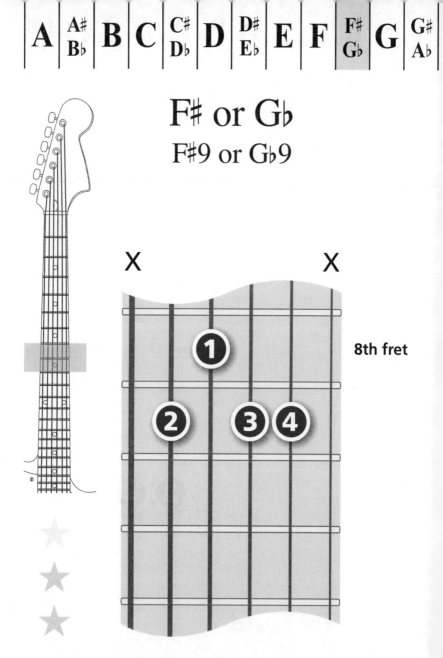

X   X

8th fret

Notes in the chord:

5: F# (root); 4: A# (third); 3: E (dom seventh); 2: G# (ninth)

Little more than an octave separates the notes in this spicy chord.

F♯ or G♭
F♯11 or G♭11

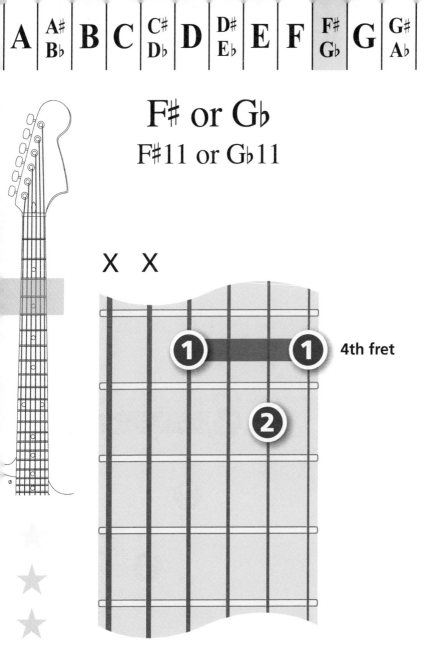

X   X

4th fret

Notes in the chord:
4: F# (root); 3: B (eleventh); 2: E (dom seventh); 1: G# (ninth)

A now familiar fingering for a four-string 11th chord.

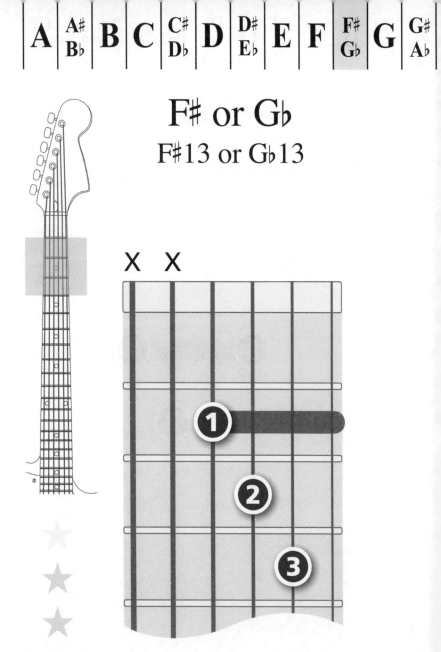

F♯ or G♭
F♯13 or G♭13

Notes in the chord:
4: E (dom seventh); 3: A# (third); 2: D# (thirteenth); 1: F#

There's no F#/G♭ in the bass here: it can be supplied
by placing the left-hand thumb on the 6th string at
the 2nd fret.

A	A#/Bb	B	C	C#/Db	D	D#/Eb	E	F	F#/Gb	G	G#/Ab

F# or Gb

F# dim or Gb dim
(F#° or Gb°)
(1st version)

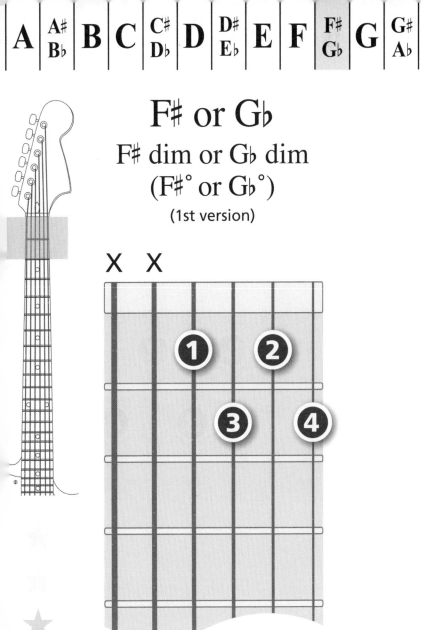

X X

Notes in the chord:
4: D# (dim seventh); 3: A (minor third); 2: C (dim fifth); 1: F# (keynote)

Once again, there's no keynote at the root of this
diminished F#/Gb – and providing one from the 6th
string would be awkward.

A	A♯ B♭	B	C	C♯ D♭	D	D♯ E♭	E	F	F♯ G♭	G	G♯ A♭

F♯ or G♭
F♯ dim or G♭ dim
(F♯° or G♭°)
(2nd version)

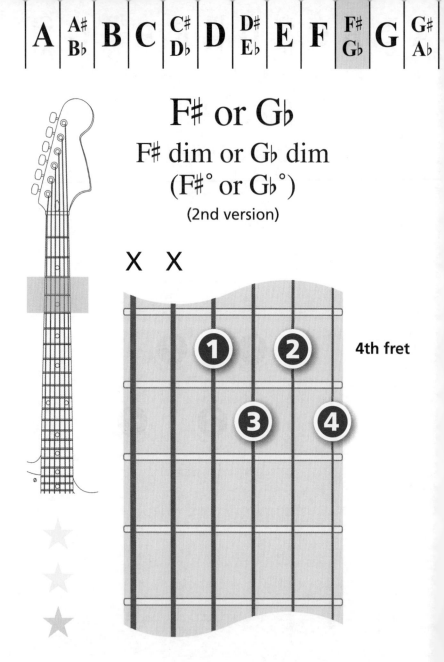

X X

4th fret

Notes in the chord:

4: F# (root); 3: C (dim fifth); 2: D# (dim seventh); 1: A (third)

This 'reshuffle' of the diminished notes places an F#/G♭ at
the bottom of the chord.

300

F# or Gb
F# aug or Gb aug
(F#+ or Gb+)
(1st version)

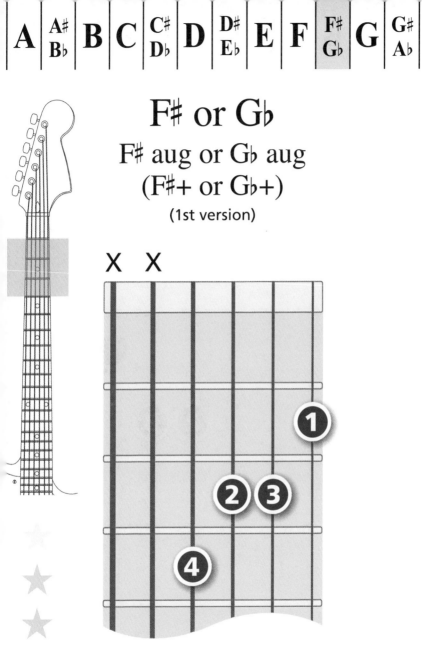

Notes in the chord:
4: F# (root); 3: A# (third); 2: D (aug fifth): 1: F#

A handy four-string augmented chord.

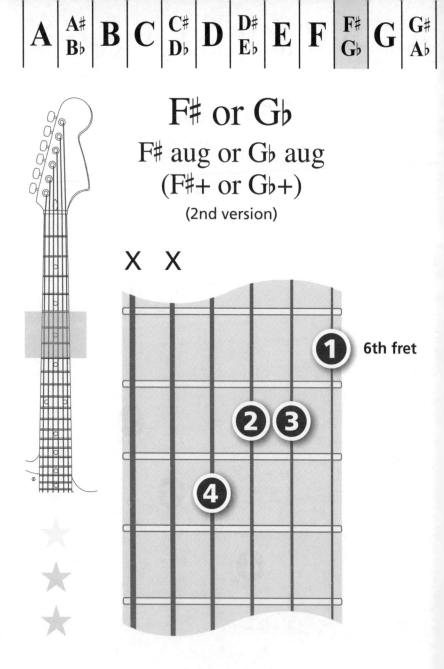

F# or Gb

F# aug or Gb aug
(F#+ or Gb+)
(2nd version)

X   X

6th fret

Notes in the chord:
4: A# (third); 3: D (aug fifth); 2: F#; 1: A# (third)

A higher voicing, with the third note of the augmented
chord now in the bass.

302

F♯ or G♭
F♯ minor or G♭ minor
(F♯m or G♭m)
(1st version)

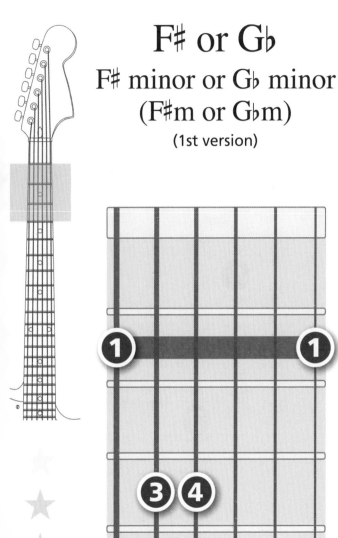

Notes in the chord:
6: F# (root); 5: C# (fifth); 4: F#; 3: A (third); 2: C#; 1: F#

Lighten and simplify this chord by playing only the top
four strings.

F♯ or G♭

F♯ minor or G♭ minor
(F♯m or G♭m)
(2nd version)

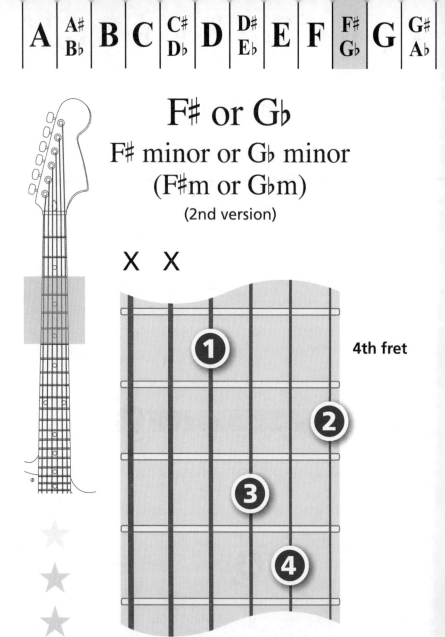

X X

4th fret

Notes in the chord:

4: F# (root); 3: C# (fifth); 2: F#; 1: A (third)

The minor third is here given prominence as the chord's
highest note.

F# or Gb
F# minor or Gb minor
(F#m or Gbm)
(3rd version)

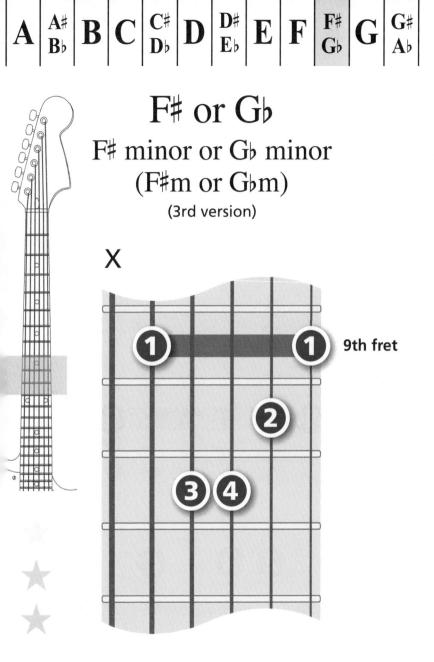

9th fret

Notes in the chord:
5: F# (root); 4: C# (fifth); 3: F#; 2: A (third); 1: C#

Extend the barré to the lowest string for a bass C# that
will create a second-inversion F#/Gb minor.

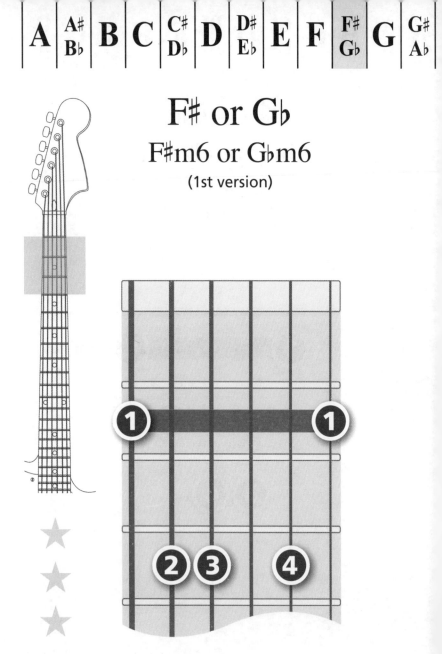

F♯ or G♭
F♯m6 or G♭m6
(1st version)

Notes in the chord:

6: F# (root); 5: C# (fifth); 4: F#; 3: A (third); 2: D# (sixth); 1: F#

This chord, like the one on page 303, can be made less of a strain if the 5th and 6th strings aren't played or fretted.

306

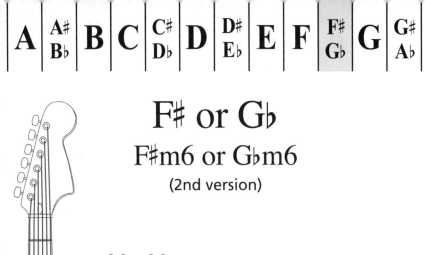

F♯ or G♭
F♯m6 or G♭m6
(2nd version)

X   X

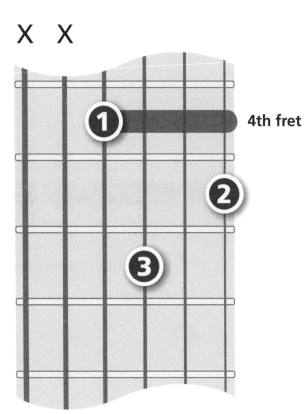

4th fret

Notes in the chord:
4: F# (root); 3: C# (fifth); 2: D# (sixth); 1: A (third)

A good shape for when no deep bass notes are necessary.

307

F# or G♭

F#m7 or G♭m7

(1st version)

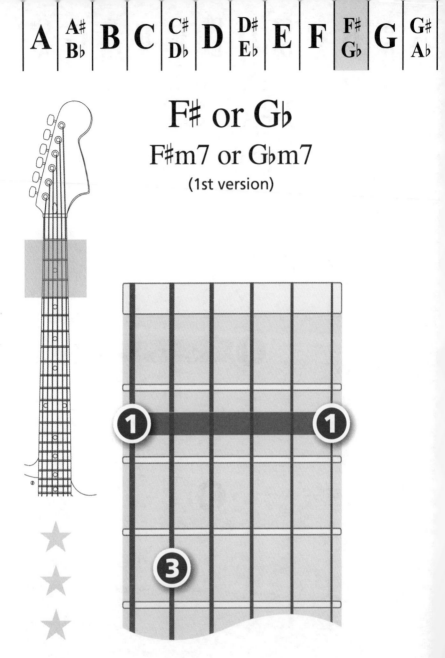

Notes in the chord:

6: F# (root); 5: C# (fifth); 4: E (dom seventh); 3: A (third); 2: C#; 1: F#

A basic six-string fingering.

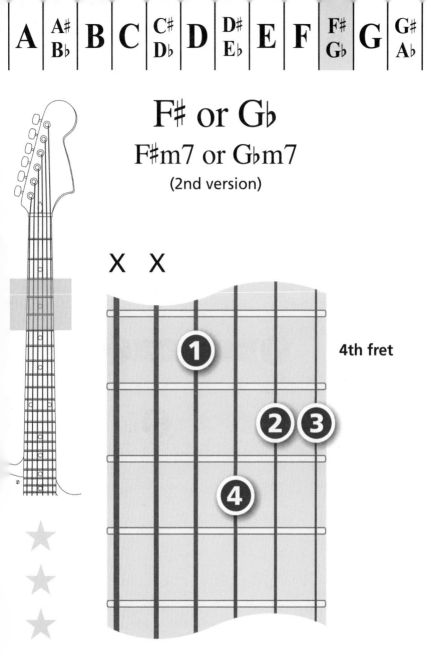

F# or Gb
F#m7 or Gbm7
(2nd version)

X   X

4th fret

Notes in the chord:
4: F# (root); 3: C# (fifth); 2: E (dom seventh); 1: A (third)

Less weighty than the 'dom 7' on the previous page.

F♯ or G♭

F♯m7 or G♭m7

(3rd version)

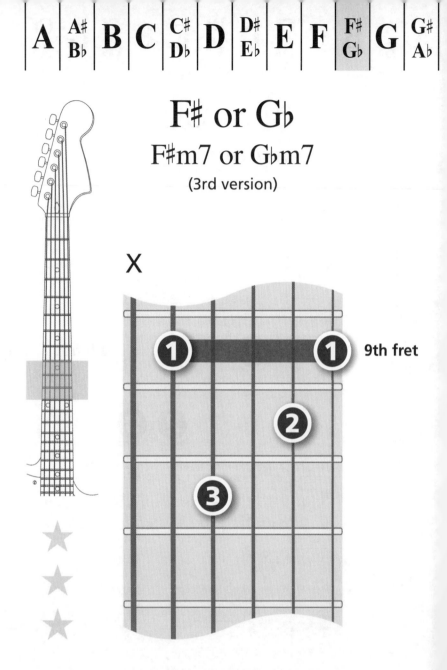

X

9th fret

Notes in the chord:

5: F# (root); 4: C# (fifth); 3: E (dom seventh); 2: A (third); 1: C#

Up to the 9th position for this voicing.

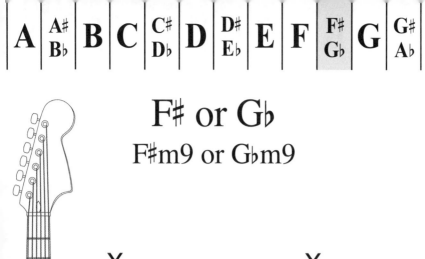

F♯ or G♭
F♯m9 or G♭m9

X   X

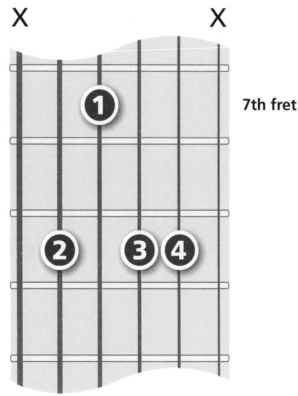

7th fret

Notes in the chord:
5: F# (root); 4: A (third); 3: E (dom seventh); 2: G# (ninth)

Inner strings only here!

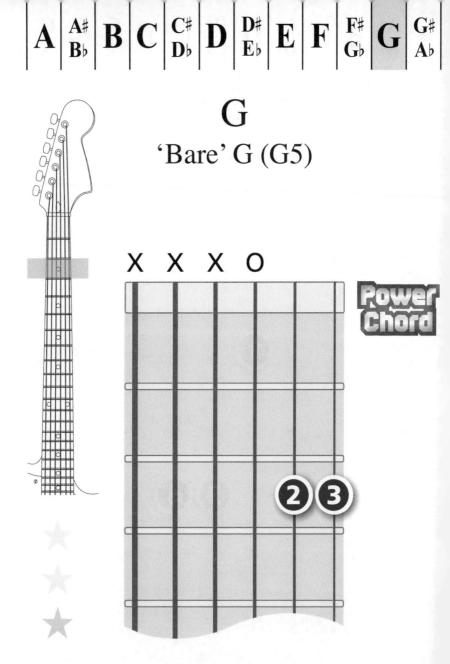

G
'Bare' G (G5)

X X X O

Power Chord

Notes in the chord:
3: G (root); 2: D (fifth); 1: G

A 'stripped-down' power chord; it has no deep bass notes, but is still effective.

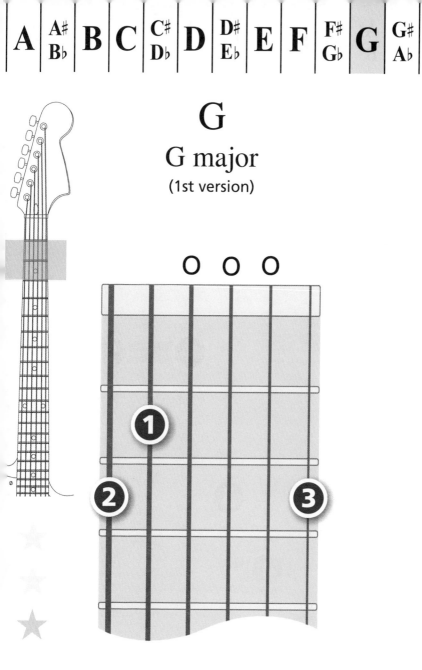

G

G major
(1st version)

O O O

Notes in the chord:

6: G (root); 5: B (third); 4: D (fifth); 3: G; 2: B; 1: G

An easy and popular fingering – though its three open strings make it a little too resonant for some musical contexts.

G

G major
(2nd version)

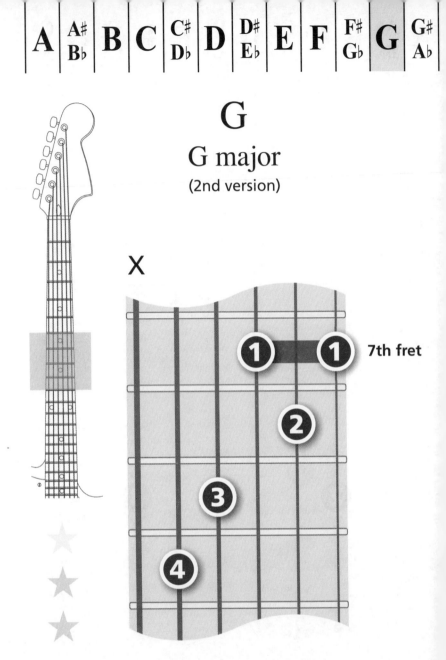

X

7th fret

Notes in the chord:

5: G (root); 4: B (third); 3: D (fifth); 2: G; 1: B

A lighter, higher voicing than the one on the previous page.

G

G major
(3rd version)

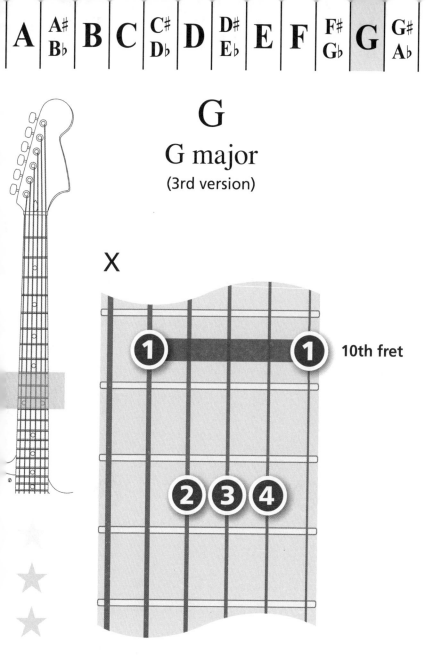

X

10th fret

Notes in the chord:

5: G (root); 4: D (fifth); 3: G; 2: B (third); 1: D

Despite its lack of a low bass note, this chord has excellent
cutting power.

G

G sus4

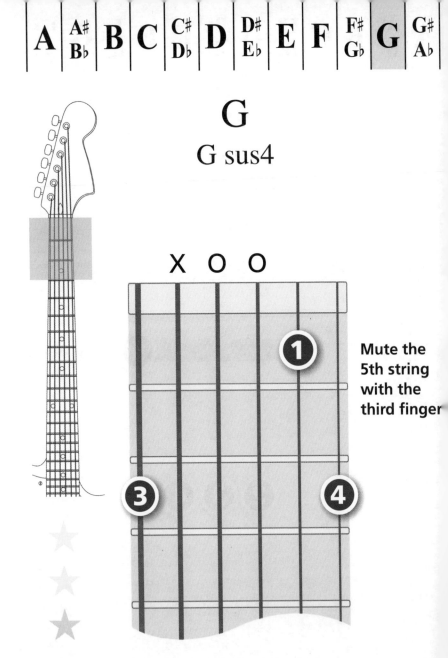

X O O

1

Mute the 5th string with the third finger

3 **4**

Notes in the chord:

6: G (root); 4: D (fifth); 3: G; 2: C (sus fourth); 1: G

The muting technique is easier than it sounds – and this 'suspended fourth' can be resolved onto a standard G major by simply lifting your index finger.

316

| A | A#
B♭ | B | C | C#
D♭ | D | D#
E♭ | E | F | F#
G♭ | G | G#
A♭ |

G
G6
(1st version)

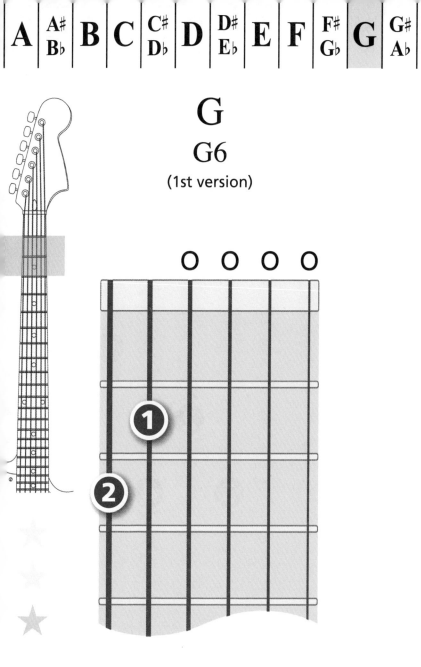

Notes in the chord:

6: G (root); 5: B (third); 4: D (fifth); 3: G; 2: B; 1: E (added sixth)

A full-bodied added sixth chord.

G

G6

(2nd version)

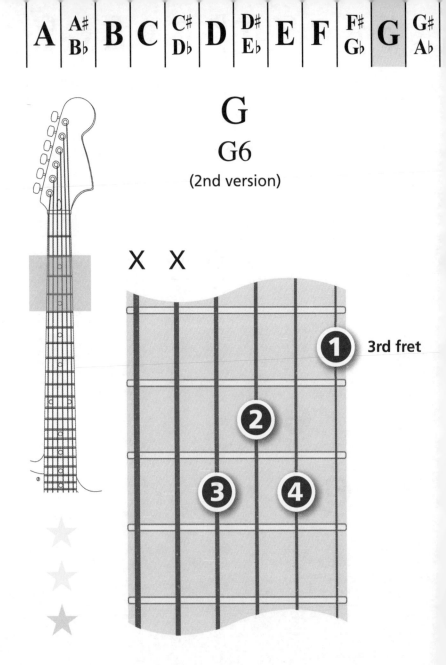

X X

1 3rd fret

2

3 **4**

Notes in the chord:

4: G (root); 3: B (third); 2: E (added sixth); 1: G

A crisper, more biting G6 than the example on page 317.

G
G6/9

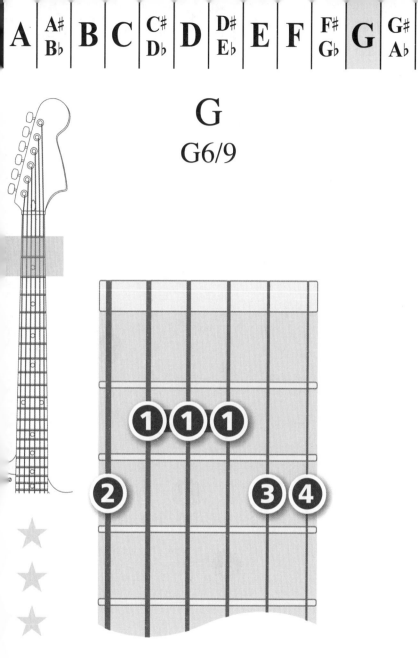

Notes in the chord:

6: G (root); 5: B (third); 4: E (sixth); 3: A (ninth); 2: D (fifth); 1: G

A classic six-string 6/9 shape that sounds good here
in its low neck position.

G

G maj7

(1st version)

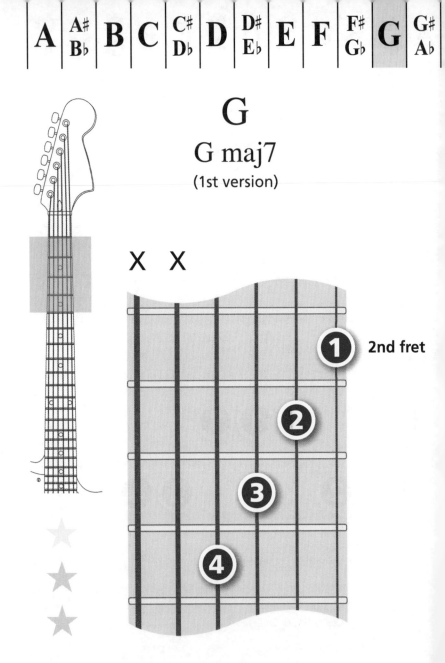

X   X

1 **2nd fret**

2

3

4

Notes in the chord:

4: G (root); 3: B (third); 2: D (fifth); 1: F# (maj seventh)

This major seventh shape works well when you play it as a 'broken chord' (one note after the other).

G

G maj7
(2nd version)

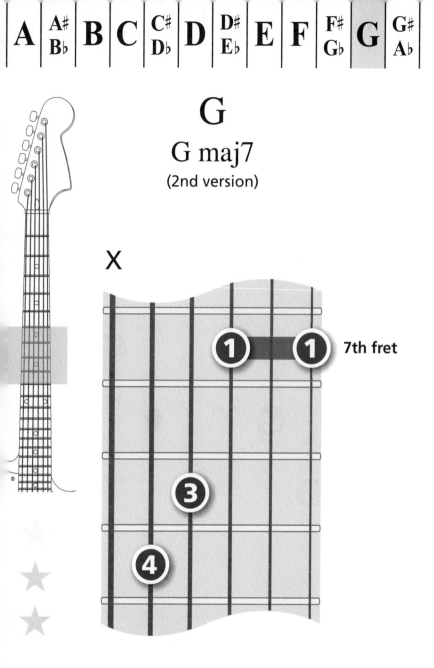

X

7th fret

Notes in the chord:

5: G (root); 4: B (third); 3: D (fifth); 2: F# (maj seventh); 1: B

A simple variant of the 7th position G chord on page 314.

G
G7
(1st version)

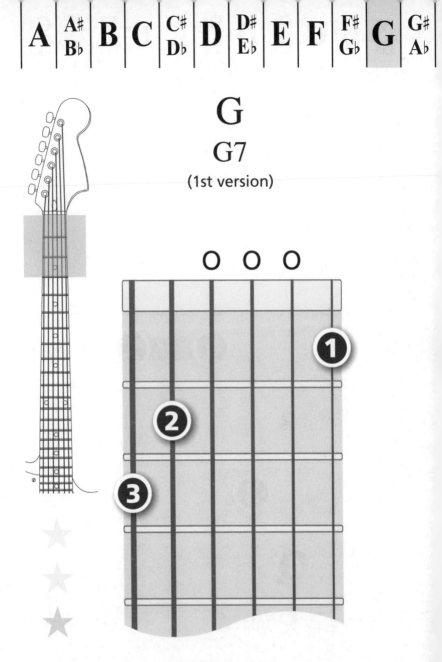

O O O

Notes in the chord:
6: G (root); 5: B (third); 4: D (fifth); 3: G; 2: B; 1: F (dom seventh)

Just about every guitarist uses this shape! Convert it to a standard G by placing your fourth finger on the 1st string, 3rd fret.

G

G7

(2nd version)

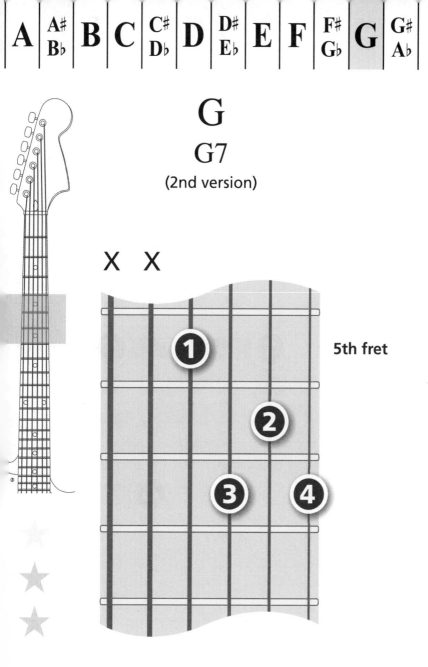

X X

5th fret

Notes in the chord:

4: G (root); 3: D (fifth); 2: F (dom seventh); 1: B (third)

A versatile chord, which sounds fine whether it's stroked or struck more vigorously.

G
G7
(3rd version)

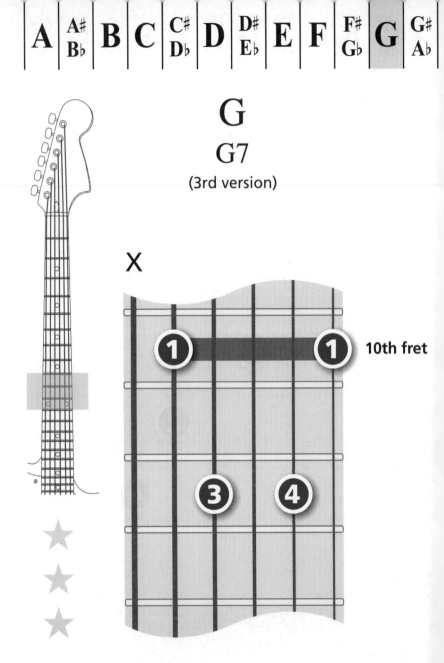

X

10th fret

Notes in the chord:

5: G (root); 4: D (fifth); 3: F (dom seventh); 2: B (third); 1: D

Potential problems with string buzzing may be exacerbated when deploying this tricky shape so far up the fingerboard.

A	A# Bb	B	C	C# Db	D	D# Eb	E	F	F# Gb	G	G# Ab

G

G7+9

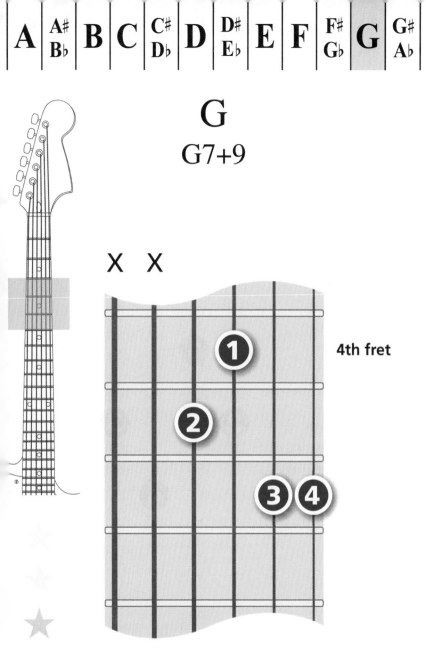

4th fret

Notes in the chord:

4: G (root); 3: B (third); 2: F (dom seventh); 1: A# (aug ninth)

A piquant chord that will serve you well in many
musical contexts.

G
G9

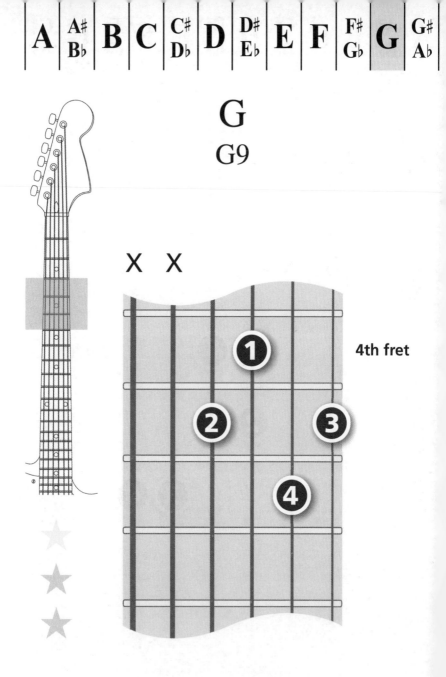

4th fret

Notes in the chord:
4: G (root); 3: B (third); 2: F (dom seventh); 1: A (ninth)

This shape is very effective when followed by the 3rd position C chord shown on page 104.

G
G11

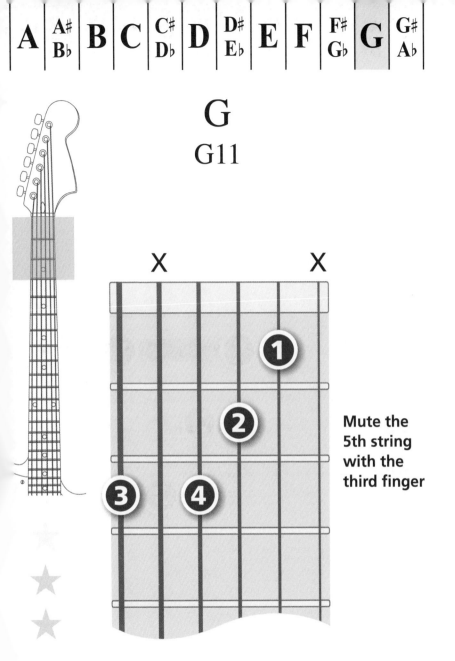

X   X

Mute the
5th string
with the
third finger

Notes in the chord:
6: G (root); 4: F (dom seventh); 3: A (ninth); 2: C (eleventh)

A mellow, tasty G11!

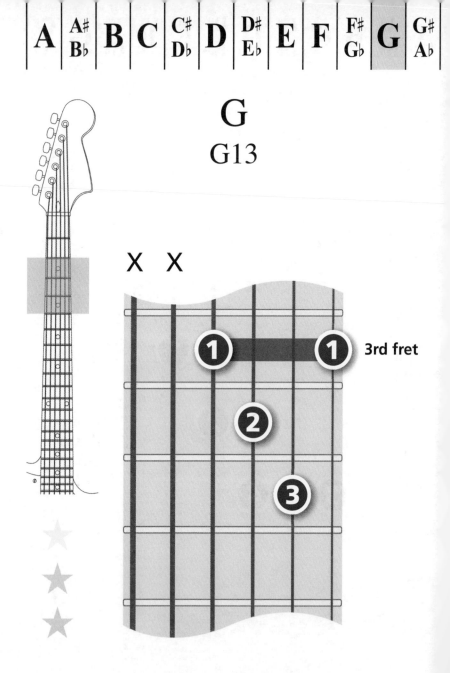

G

G13

Notes in the chord:

4: F (dom seventh); 3: B (third); 2: E (thirteenth); 1: G

If you need to add a bass G here, your left-hand thumb
could hold down the 6th string at the 3rd fret.

G

G diminished (G dim, G°)

(1st version)

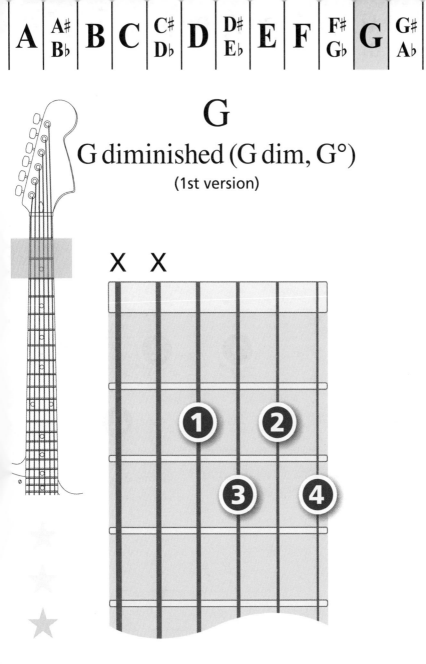

Notes in the chord:

4: E (dim seventh); 3: B♭ (minor third); 2: C# (dim fifth); 1: G (keynote)

This fingering places G at the top of the diminished chord,
not at its root.

A	A# B♭	B	C	C# D♭	D	D# E♭	E	F	F# G♭	G	G# A♭

G

G diminished (G dim, G°)
(2nd version)

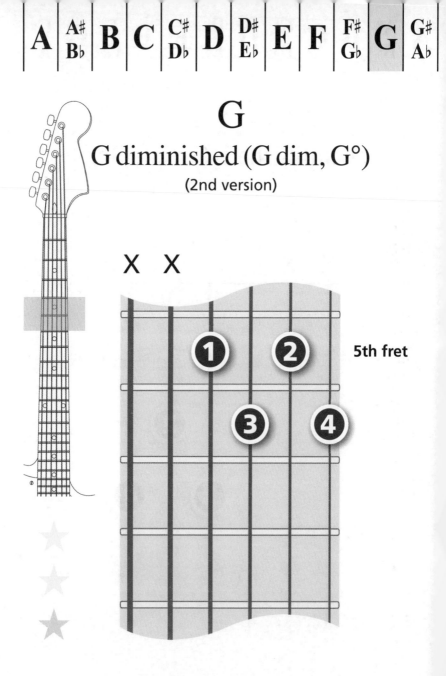

X X

5th fret

Notes in the chord:

4: G (root); 3: C# (dim fifth); 2: E (dim seventh); 1: B♭ (minor third)

The same shape, when shifted up to the 5th position,
rearranges the notes to put a G in the bass.

A	A#/B♭	B	C	C#/D♭	D	D#/E♭	E	F	F#/G♭	G	G#/A♭

G

G augmented (G aug, G+)

(1st version)

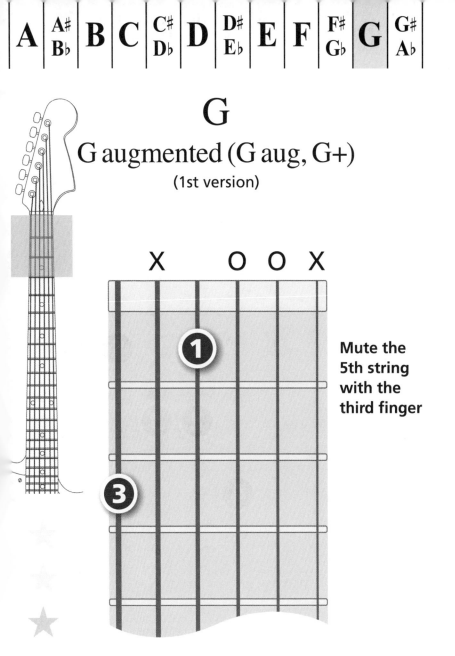

X   O   O   X

Mute the 5th string with the third finger

Notes in the chord:

6: G (root); 4: D# (aug fifth); 3: G; 2: B (third)

The best option for a lower-pitched augmented chord of G.

331

G

G augmented (G aug, G+)

(2nd version)

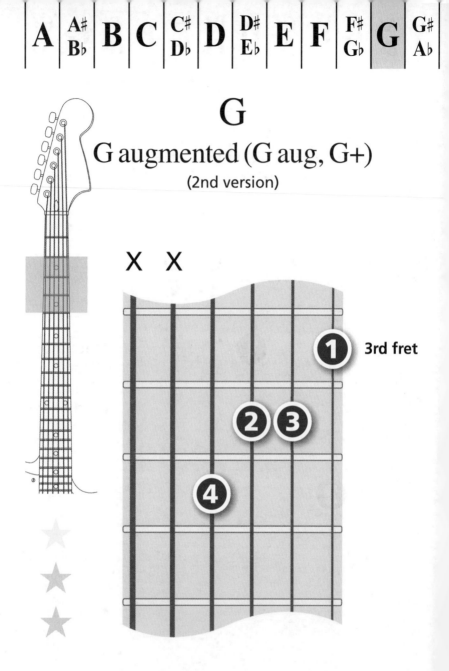

X X

1 — 3rd fret
2 3
4

Notes in the chord:

4: G (root); 3: B (third); 3: D# (aug fifth); 1: G

A higher version of an augmented G chord.

332

A	A# Bb	B	C	C# Db	D	D# Eb	E	F	F# Gb	G	G# Ab

G

G minor (Gm)

(1st version)

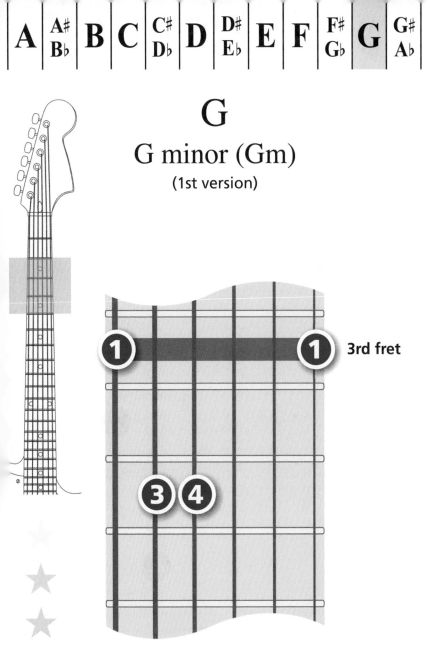

3rd fret

Notes in the chord:

6: G (root); 5: D (fifth); 4: G; 3: Bb (third); 2: D; 1: G

G minor isn't quite as 'guitar-friendly' a key as G major,
due to the Bb at its third.

333

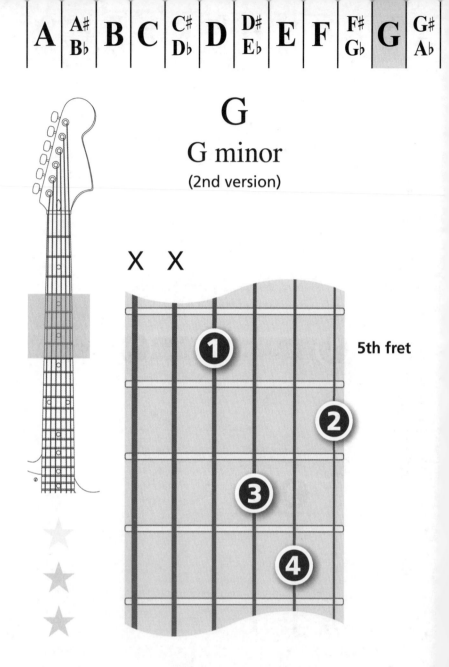

G

G minor
(2nd version)

X X

5th fret

Notes in the chord:

4: G (root); 3: D (fifth); 2: G; 1: B♭ (third)

Here, the B♭ moves to the top string, giving the chord a particularly plangent sound.

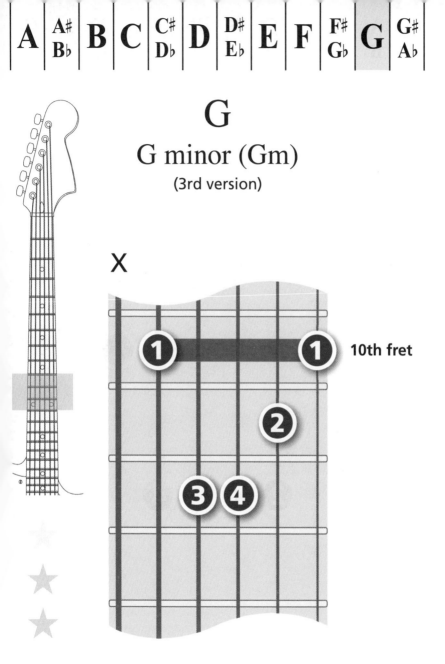

G
G minor (Gm)
(3rd version)

X

10th fret

Notes in the chord:

5: G (root); 4: D (fifth); 3: G; 2: Bb (third); 1: D

On some guitars, this chord may be a little difficult to reach.

G
Gm6
(1st version)

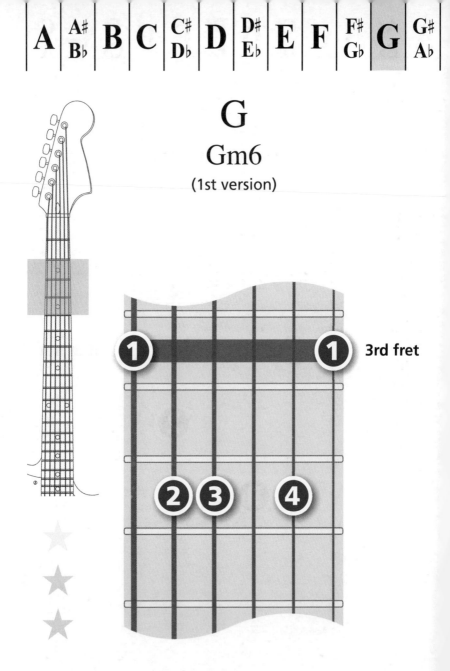

3rd fret

Notes in the chord:
6: G (root); 5: D (fifth); 4: G; 3: Bb (third); 2: E (sixth); 1: G

Quite a dense chord – to lighten it, simply omit the two
lowest strings: you'll still have a root G at the 4th.

A	A# Bb	B	C	C# Db	D	D# Eb	E	F	F# Gb	G	G# Ab

G
Gm6
(2nd version)

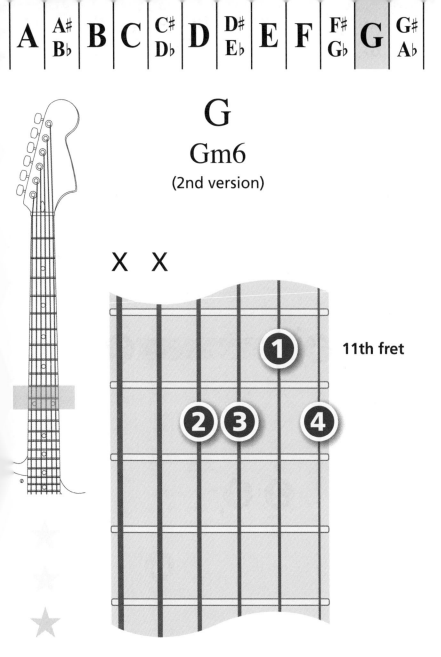

X X

1

11th fret

2 **3** **4**

Notes in the chord:
4: D (fifth); 3: G; 2: Bb (third); 1: E (sixth)

A high pitched, second-inversion Gm6.

337

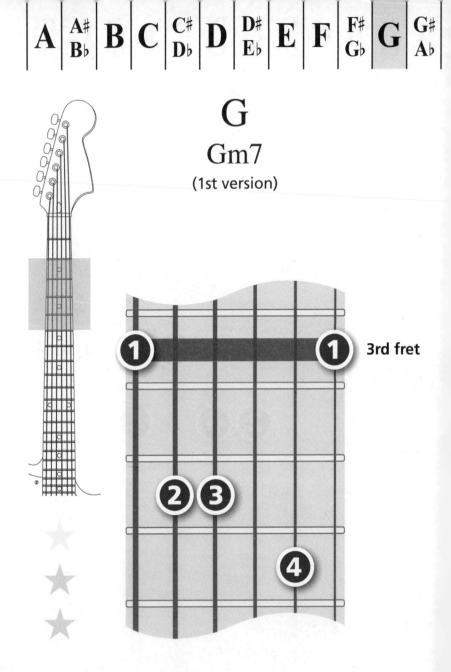

G

Gm7

(1st version)

3rd fret

Notes in the chord:

6: G (root); 5: D (fifth); 4: G; 3: Bb (third); 2: F (dom seventh); 1: G

The 4th finger is hard to position correctly, but the effort is worth it.

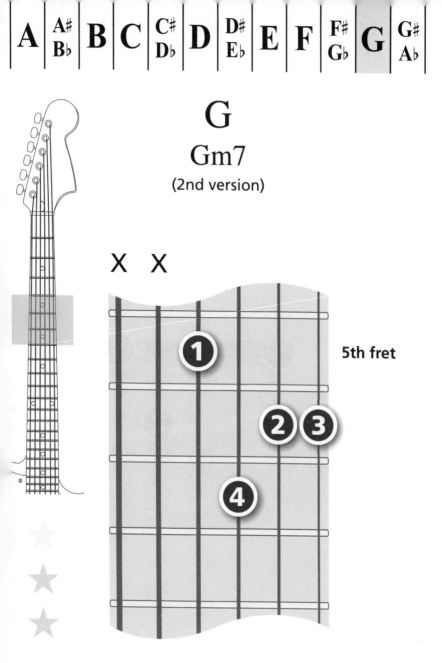

G
Gm7
(2nd version)

5th fret

Notes in the chord:
4: G (root); 3: D (fifth); 2: F (dom seventh); 1: Bb (third)

A tasty Gm7, though it's impossible to supply it with a
lower root note.

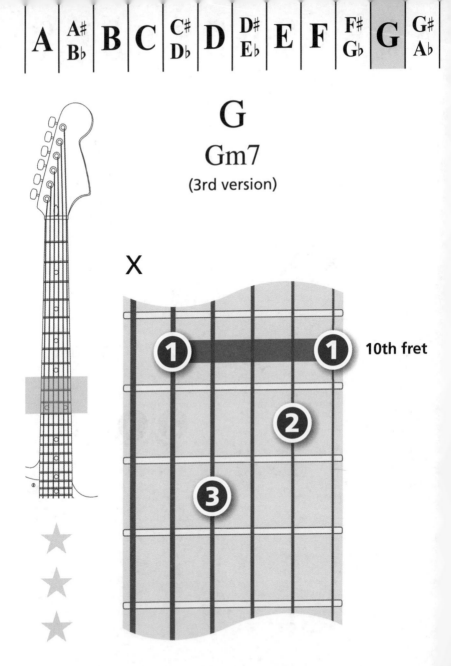

G
Gm7
(3rd version)

X

10th fret

Notes in the chord:
5: G (root); 4: D (fifth); 3: F (dom seventh); 2: Bb (third); 1: D

On guitars without a cutaway, this fingering can be
challenging at such a high neck position.

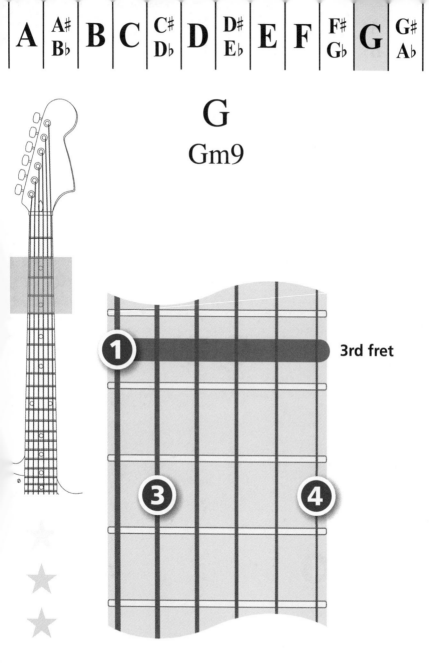

G
Gm9

3rd fret

Notes in the chord:

6: G (root); 5: D (fifth); 4: F (dom seventh); 3: B♭ (third); 2: D; 1: A (ninth)

Quite a wide stretch for the third and fourth fingers…
but the results are worth the effort.

G# or Ab
'Bare' G# or 'bare' Ab
(G#5 or Ab5)

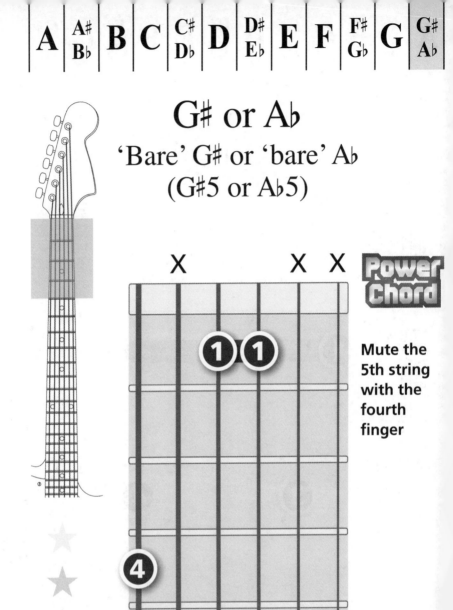

X   X X

Power Chord

Mute the 5th string with the fourth finger

Notes in the chord:

6: Ab (root); 4: Eb (fifth); 3: Ab

If you have large hands, you may prefer to fret the 6th string, and mute the 5th string, with your third finger.

G♯ or A♭
G♯ major or A♭ major
(1st version)

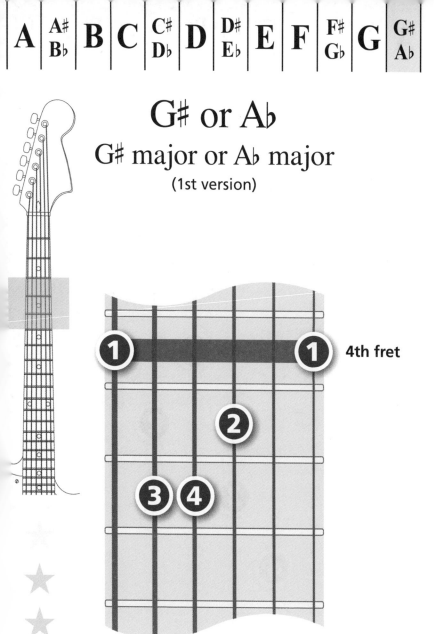

4th fret

Notes in the chord:

6: A♭ (root); 5: E♭ (fifth); 4: A♭; 3: C (third); 2: E♭; 1: A♭

Barrés are regularly required for even simple chords in keys with many sharps or flats, such as G#/A♭.

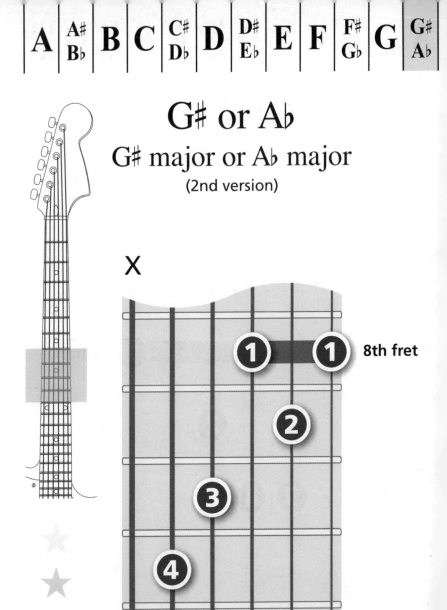

G♯ or A♭

G♯ major or A♭ major

(2nd version)

8th fret

Notes in the chord:

5: A♭ (root); 4: C (third); 3: E♭ (fifth); 2: A♭; 1: C

An effective high-register G♯/A♭ – but it lacks any deep bass notes.

G♯ or A♭
G♯ major or A♭ major
(3rd version)

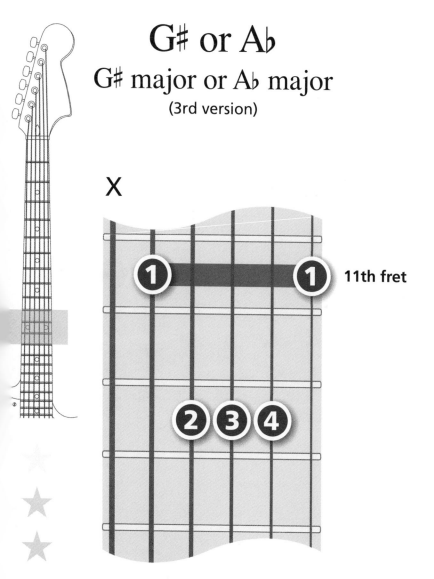

11th fret

Notes in the chord:
5: A♭ (root); 4: E♭ (fifth); 3: A♭; 2: C (third); 1: E♭

This 11th position shape may be a struggle on some guitars; however, it will pose no problems if you have a cutaway.

G♯ or A♭

G♯ sus4 or A♭ sus4

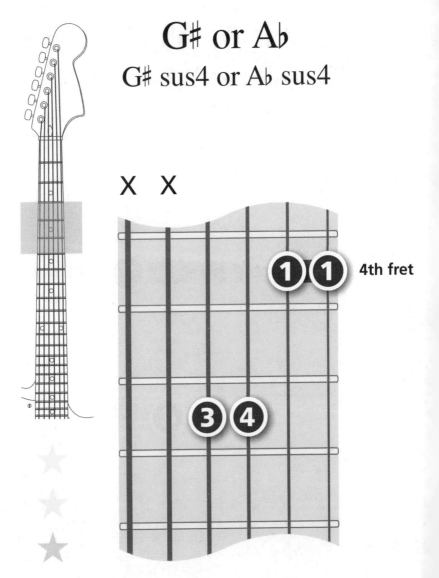

X X

4th fret

Notes in the chord:

4: A♭ (root); 3: D♭ (sus fourth); 2: E♭ (fifth); 1: A♭

Resolve this chord to a four-string A♭ by lifting your fourth
finger, and placing your second finger on the 3rd string
at the 5th fret.

346

G♯ or A♭
G♯6 or A♭6
(1st version)

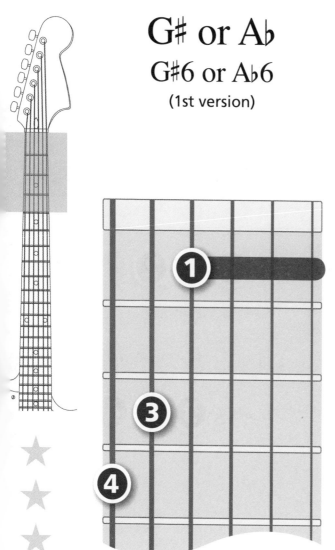

Notes in the chord:

6: A♭ (root); 5: C (third); 4: E♭ (fifth); 3: A♭; 2: C; 1: F (added sixth)

Quite a beefy sixth chord, with the crucial added sixth itself
as the highest note.

G# or Ab
G#6 or Ab6
(2nd version)

X   X

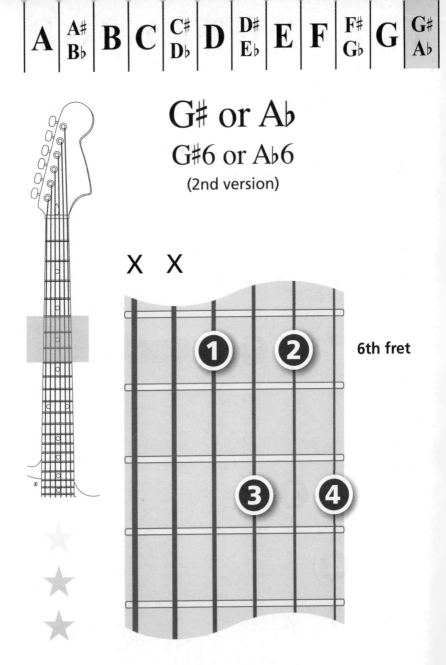

6th fret

Notes in the chord:
4: Ab (root); 3: Eb (fifth); 2: F (added sixth); 1: C (third)

A much lighter voicing. You could barré at the 6th fret
instead of using separate fingers.

G♯ or A♭
G♯6/9 or A♭6/9

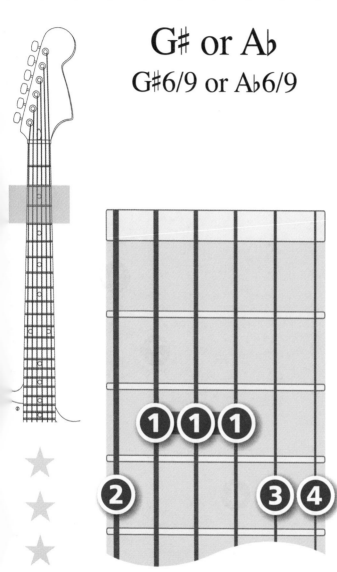

Notes in the chord:
6: A♭ (root); 5: C (third); 4: F (sixth); 3: B♭ (ninth); 2: E♭ (fifth); 1: A♭

One of the standard 6/9 fingerings, placed here in the
3rd position.

G♯ or A♭

G♯ maj7 or A♭ maj7

(1st version)

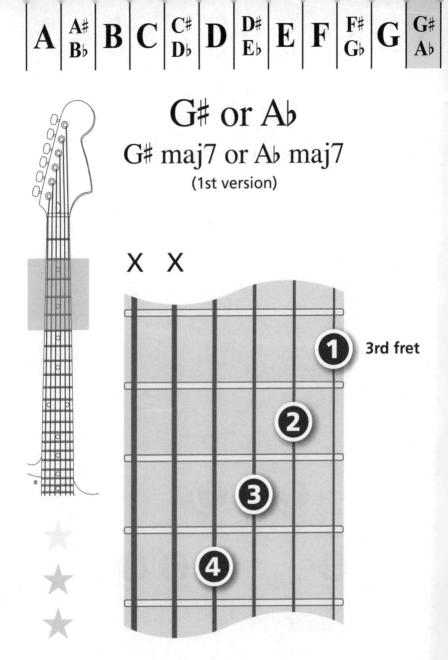

3rd fret

Notes in the chord:

4: A♭ (root); 3: C (third); 2: E♭ (fifth); 1: G (maj seventh)

There's less than an octave between these four notes, and, consequently, no low bass root.

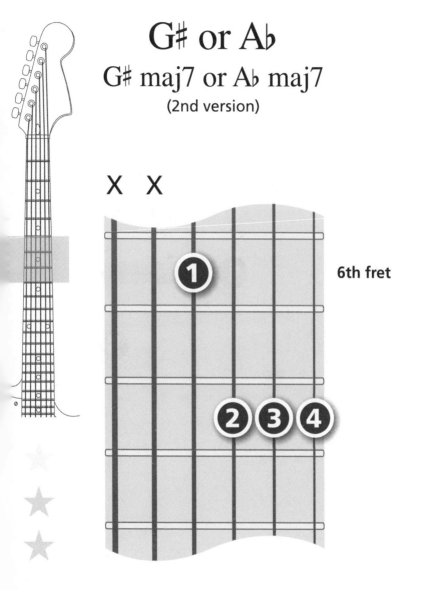

G# or Ab
G# maj7 or Ab maj7
(2nd version)

6th fret

Notes in the chord:

4: Ab (root); 3: Eb (fifth); 2: G (maj seventh); 1: C (third)

A high-pitched chord that can cut through effectively
when struck hard.

G♯ or A♭
G♯7 or A♭7
(1st version)

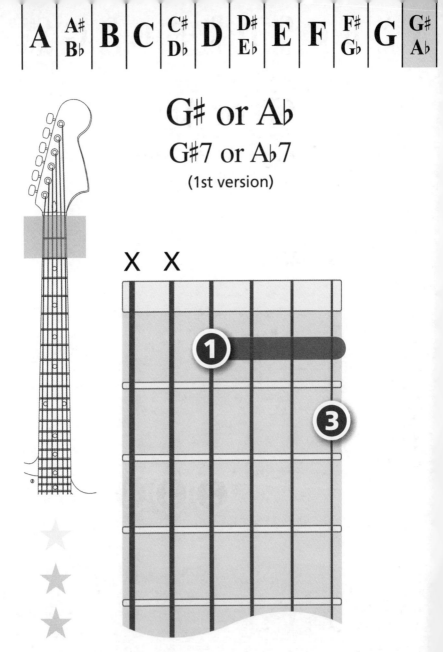

Notes in the chord:
4: E♭ (fifth); 3: A♭; 2: C (third); 1: G♭ (dom seventh)

No deep G#/A♭ is reachable here, but this second-inversion
dominant seventh works well.

G♯ or A♭
G♯7 or A♭7
(2nd version)

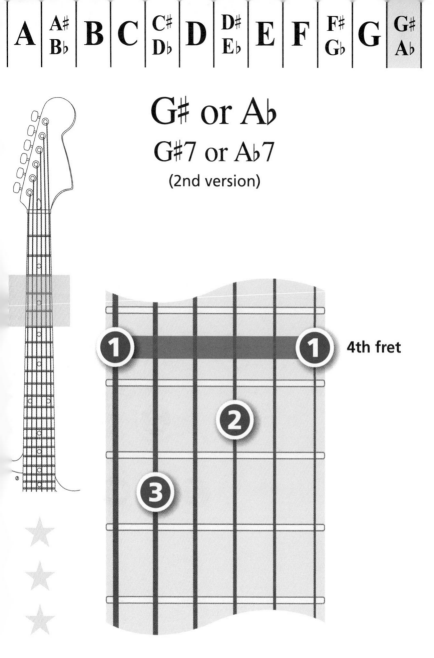

4th fret

Notes in the chord:
6: A♭ (root); 4: E♭ (fifth); 4: G♭ (dom seventh); 3: C (third); 2: E♭; 1: A♭

The best shape to use when you require a six-string, root position G#/A♭7.

G# or Ab

G#7 or Ab7

(3rd version)

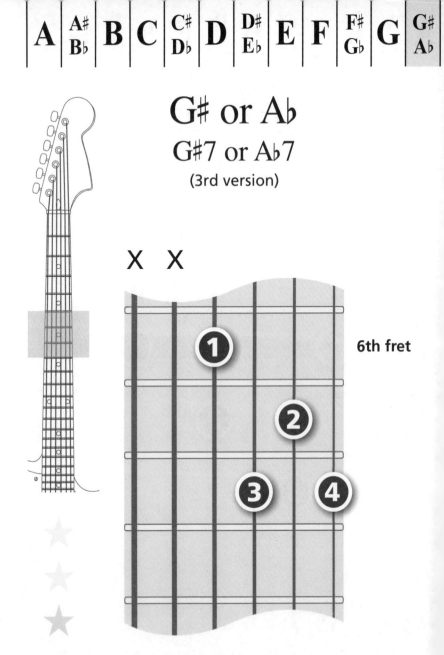

X   X

6th fret

Notes in the chord:

4: Ab (root); 3: Eb (fifth); 2: Gb (dom seventh); 1: C (third)

An Eb is available on the 5th string at the 6th fret, and could be held down by your index finger to create a second-inversion chord.

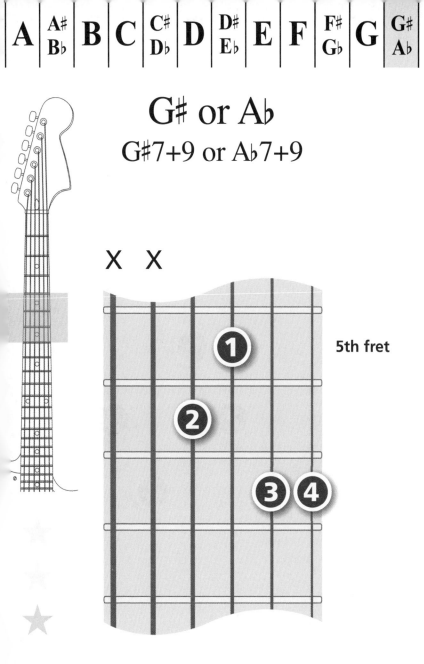

| A | A#
B♭ | B | C | C#
D♭ | D | D#
E♭ | E | F | F#
G♭ | G | G#
A♭ |

G# or A♭
G#7+9 or A♭7+9

X X

5th fret

Notes in the chord:
4: A♭ (root); 3: C (third); 2: G♭ (dom seventh); 1: B (aug ninth)

This fingering can be moved up and down the neck to
wherever a 7+9 is needed.

G♯ or A♭
G♯9 or A♭9

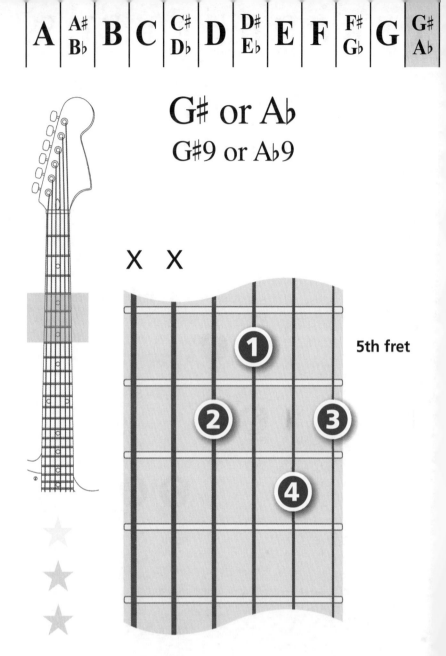

X   X

①

5th fret

②

③

④

Notes in the chord:
4: A♭ (root); 3: C (third); 2: G♭ (dom seventh); 1: B♭ (ninth)

Another readily shiftable shape.

G# or Ab
G#11 or Ab11

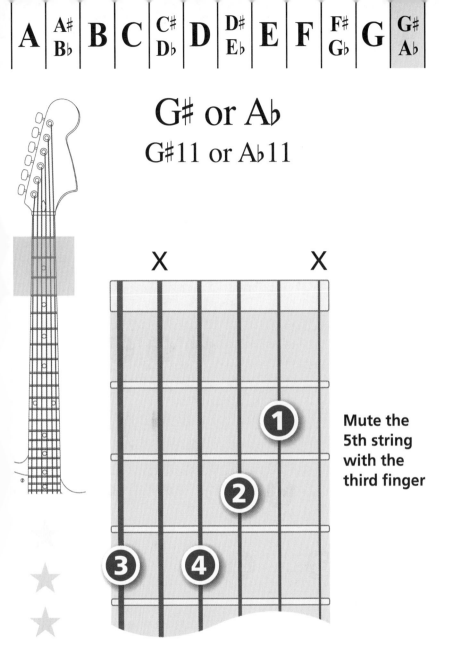

X   X

Mute the 5th string with the third finger

Notes in the chord:

6: Ab (root); 4: Gb (dom seventh); 3: Bb (ninth); 2: Db (eleventh)

Rich and jazzy sounding!

G# or A♭
G#13 or A♭13

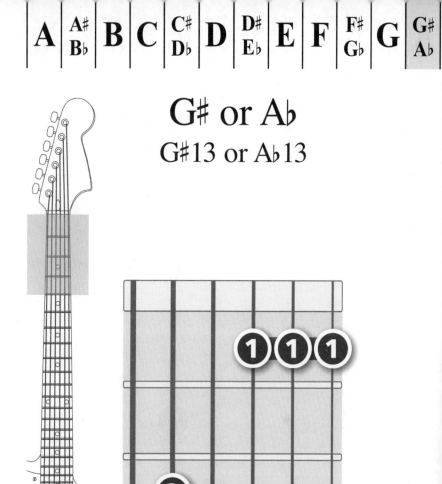

Notes in the chord:
6: A♭ (root); 5: C (third); 4: G♭ (dom seventh); 3: A♭; 2: C; 1: F (thirteenth)

This fingering is – literally – quite a handful, but is ideal if you require a six-string thirteenth chord.

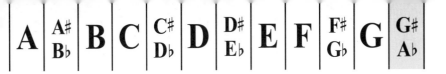

G♯ or A♭
G♯ dim or A♭ dim
(G♯° or A♭°)
(1st version)

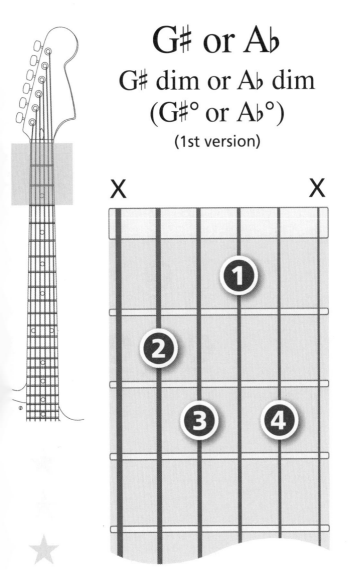

X   X

Notes in the chord:

5: B (minor third); 4: F (dim seventh); 3: A♭ (keynote); 2: D (dim fifth)

An inverted G#/A♭ diminished, with no bass keynote.

G♯ or A♭
G♯ dim or A♭ dim
(G♯° or A♭°)
(2nd version)

X X

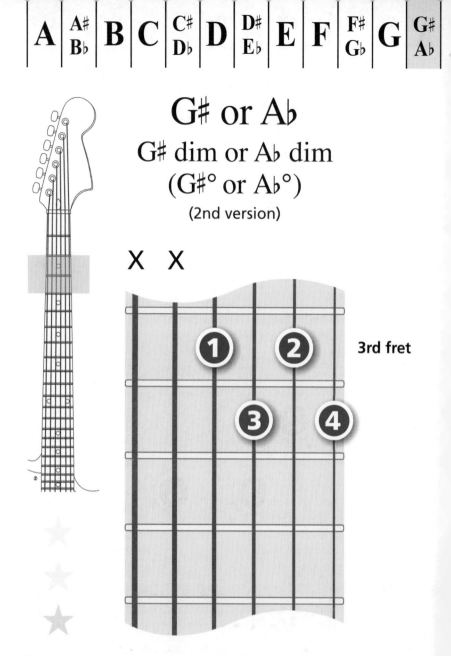

3rd fret

Notes in the chord:
4: F (dim seventh); 3: B (minor third); 2: D (dim fifth); 1: A♭ (keynote)

A higher 'reshuffle' of the diminished chord; A♭ is now its top note.

G♯ or A♭

G♯ aug or A♭ aug
(G♯+ or A♭+)
(1st version)

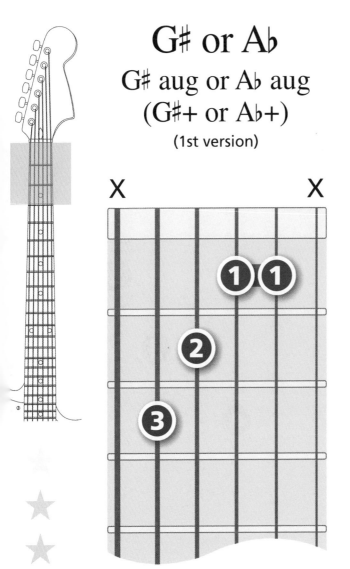

Notes in the chord:

5: C (third); 4: E (aug fifth); 3: A♭ (keynote); 2: C

Here, our augmented chord of G♯/A♭ is supplied by a 'staple' fingering that can be deployed all over the fretboard.

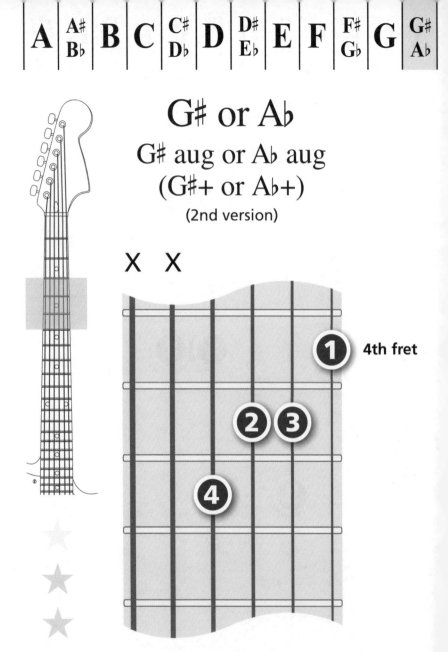

G♯ or A♭

G♯ aug or A♭ aug
(G♯+ or A♭+)
(2nd version)

X   X

① **4th fret**

②③

④

Notes in the chord:

4: A♭ (root); 3: C (third); 2: E (aug fifth); 1: A♭

This shape takes a while to get accustomed to!

362

| A | A♯ B♭ | B | C | C♯ D♭ | D | D♯ E♭ | E | F | F♯ G♭ | G | G♯ A♭ |

G♯ or A♭
G♯ minor or A♭ minor
(G♯m or A♭m)
(1st version)

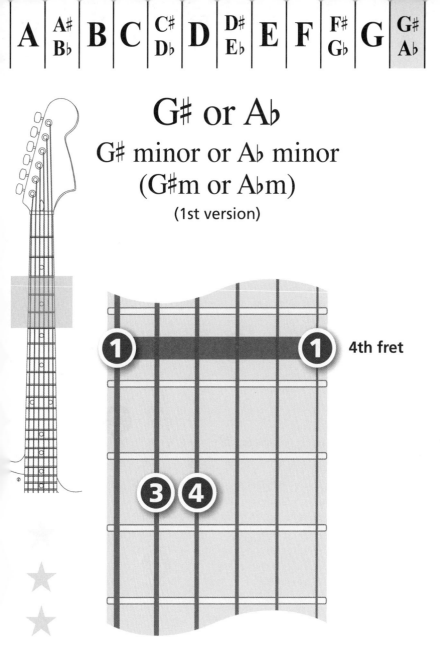

4th fret

Notes in the chord:
6: A♭ (root); 5: E♭ (fifth); 4: A♭; 3: C♭ (third); 2: E♭; 1: A♭

The guitar's lowest six-string G#/A♭ minor chord.

G♯ or A♭
G♯ minor or A♭ minor
(G♯m or A♭m)
(2nd version)

X X

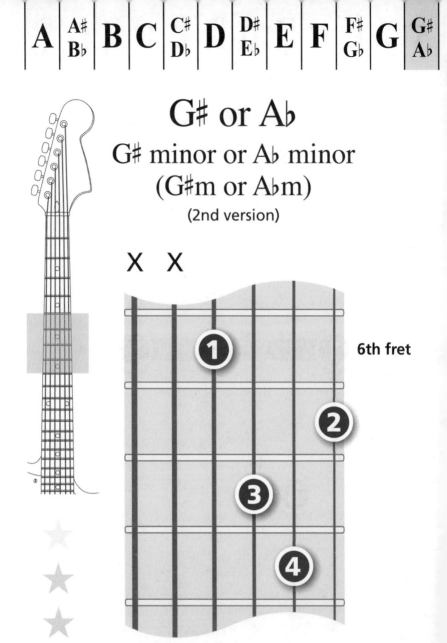

6th fret

Notes in the chord:
4: A♭ (root); 3: E♭ (fifth); 2: A♭; 1: C♭ (third)

A handy middle-register voicing.

A	A♯ B♭	B	C	C♯ D♭	D	D♯ E♭	E	F	F♯ G♭	G	G♯ A♭

G♯ or A♭
G♯ minor or A♭ minor
(G♯m or A♭m)
(3rd version)

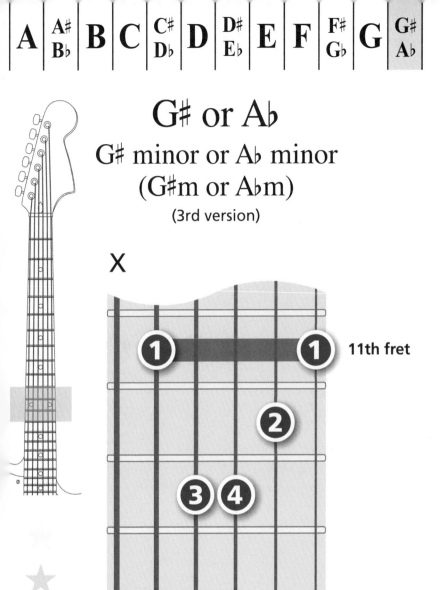

11th fret

Notes in the chord:

5: A♭ (root); 4: E♭ (fifth); 3: A♭; 2: C♭ (third); 1: E♭

Like the shape on page 345, this chord can be tricky on some instruments.

365

A	A♯ B♭	B	C	C♯ D♭	D	D♯ E♭	E	F	F♯ G♭	G	G♯ A♭

G♯ or A♭
G♯m6 or A♭m6
(1st version)

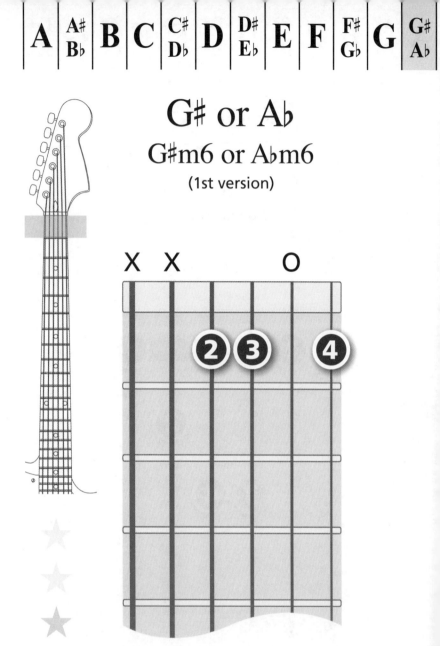

Notes in the chord:
4: E♭ (fifth); 3: A♭; 2: C♭ (third); 1: F (sixth)

A rare chance to play an open string in such a remote key.

G♯ or A♭
G♯m6 or A♭m6
(2nd version)

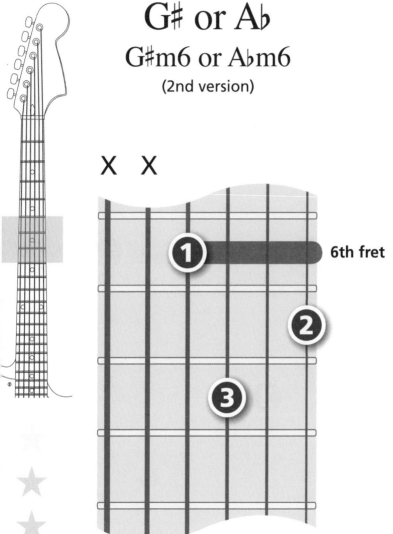

X X

6th fret

Notes in the chord:
4: A♭ (root); 3: E♭ (fifth); 2: F (sixth); 1: C♭ (third)

In G♯ minor, A♭ minor's enharmonic equivalent, this chord's constituent notes are referred to as G♯, D♯, E♯ and B.

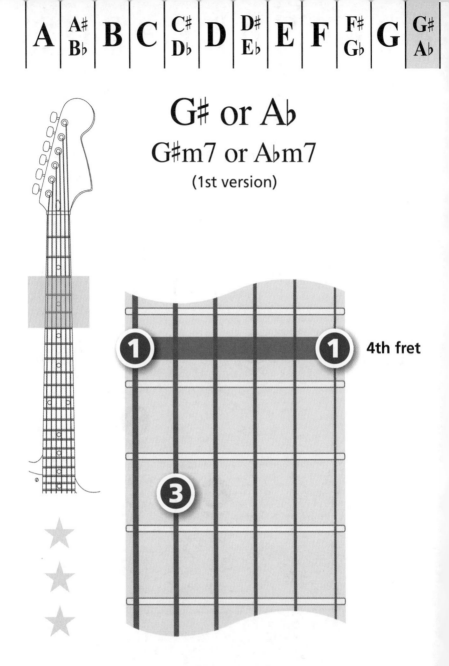

G♯ or A♭

G♯m7 or A♭m7

(1st version)

4th fret

Notes in the chord:

6: A♭ (root); 5: E♭ (fifth); 4: G♭ (dom seventh); 3: C♭ (third); 2: E♭; 1: A♭

A shape with potential for unwanted buzzing!

G♯ or A♭

G♯m7 or A♭m7

(2nd version)

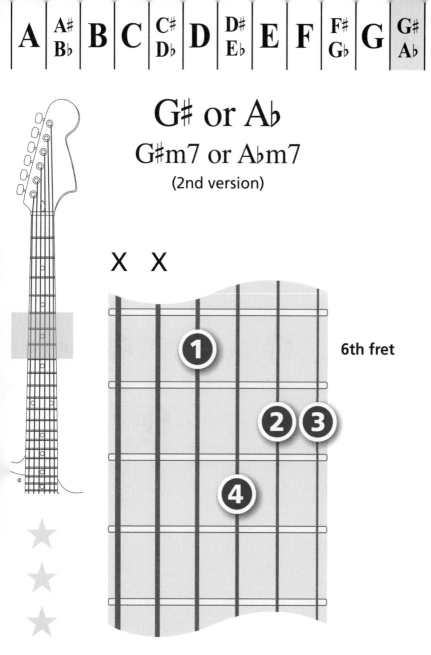

X X

6th fret

Notes in the chord:

4: A♭ (root); 3: E♭ (fifth); 2: G♭ (dom seventh); 1: C♭ (third)

Also fairly hard to finger, despite the absence of a barré.

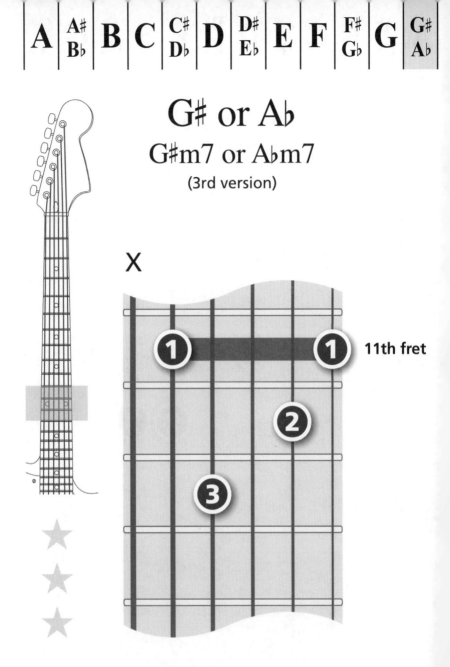

| A | A#
Bb | B | C | C#
Db | D | D#
Eb | E | F | F#
Gb | G | G#
Ab |

G# or Ab
G#m7 or Abm7
(3rd version)

X

11th fret

Notes in the chord:
5: Ab (root); 4: Eb (fifth); 3: Gb (dom seventh); 2: Cb (third); 1: Eb

Yet again, we find ourselves at one of the guitar's very highest accessible neck positions.

G♯ or A♭
G♯m9 or A♭m9

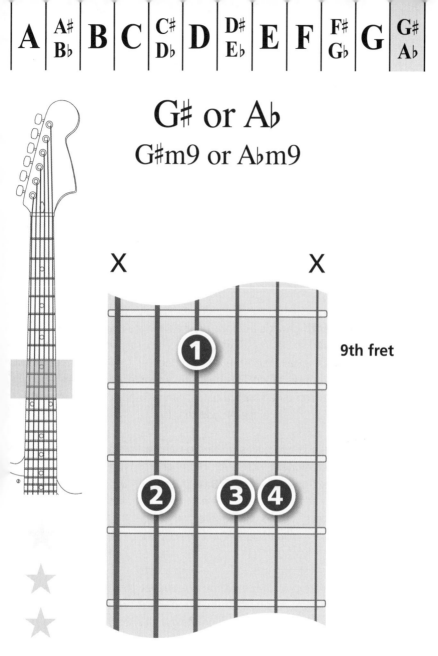

9th fret

Notes in the chord:
5: A♭ (root); 4: C♭ (third); 3: G♭ (dom seventh); 2: B♭ (ninth)

A comparatively easy minor ninth shape.

Other chords

For various reasons, the chord fingerings in the final section of this directory are unusual or exceptional – which is why they've been placed here, rather than in the main body of the book. Despite their special status, however, they're all handy and even intriguing shapes that will give your playing a distinctive flavour. Let's investigate them further…

The **'bare'** or **'open fifth' chords** you've already been shown are also called 'power chords', as they're particularly effective when cranked up and used in hard rock and heavy metal, though they can also be valuable in gentler musical contexts. More examples of them appear on pages 373–6: all are 'three-stringers', which can be shifted up and down the fretboard to produce 'open fifths' in a variety of keys.

The jazzy **eleventh chords** also featured earlier are much subtler than 'power chords', and sometimes involve quite elaborate fingerings, though that certainly isn't the case with the A11 on page 377: a 'five-stringer' that requires no fretted notes at all! This beautifully simple voicing is perennially useful, and, when combined with a barré, can provide you with any other eleventh you want.

For rhythm guitar playing, clear definition and a crisp sound are often essential – but occasionally, rich, even blurry chords with resonating open strings, like the six-note **E/A** and **E/B** on pages 379–80, and the **A/C** on page 383, are what's needed. Try them out for musical size; to play them in different keys, a capo will be necessary to get the open strings sounding at the correct pitch.

Budding guitarists struggling with five- and six-string chords and barrés sometimes forget that shapes with fewer notes can frequently be a more effective choice. A couple of these more **lightweight harmonies** appear on pages 381–2; both can be moved all over the fingerboard, and you'll soon become adept at creating similar chords by adapting and 'abbreviating' other multi-string shapes.

Enjoy your musical explorations!

Other chords

F
F5

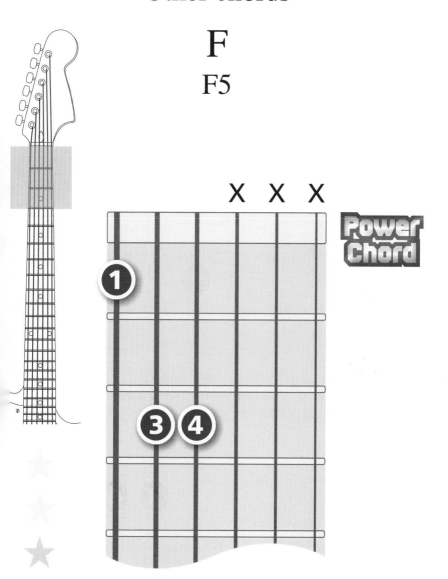

X   X   X

Power Chord

Notes in the chord:
6: F (root); 5: C (fifth); 4: F

Move this three-string shape one fret higher and it becomes F#/Gb5; with the index finger on the 3rd fret it'll be G5, and so on.

Other chords

G♯ or A♭
G♯5 or A♭5

X X X

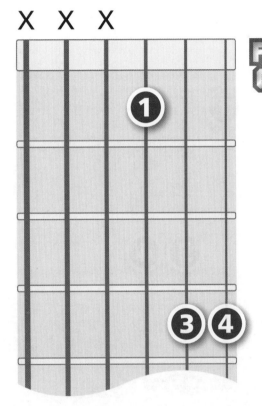

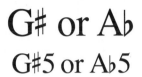

Notes in the chord:
3: A♭ (root); 2: E♭ (fifth); 1: A♭

This fingering can also be shifted up the neck for a succession of 'power chords' (A5 in 2nd position, A♯/B♭5 in 3rd position, etc.).

Other chords

D♯ or E♭
D♯5 or E♭5

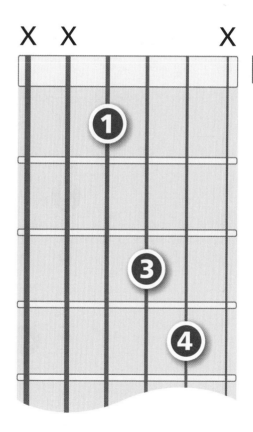

Notes in the chord:
4: E♭ (root); 3: B♭ (fifth); 2: E♭

A movable variant of the D5 fingering on page 162, also seen on page 252 as a 3rd position F5 chord.

Other chords

C♯ or D♭
C♯5 or D♭5

X X X

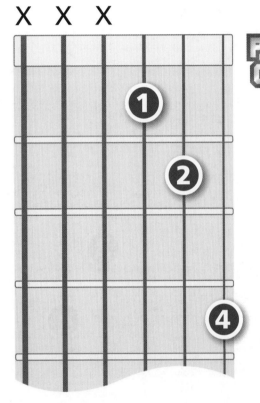

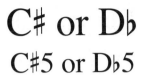

Notes in the chord:
3: G♯ (fifth); 2: C♯ (root); 1: G♯

Yet another shiftable 'power chord': this one is a second
inversion. At the 2nd position, it becomes D5, at the 3rd,
D♯/E♭5, and so on.

Other chords

A
A11

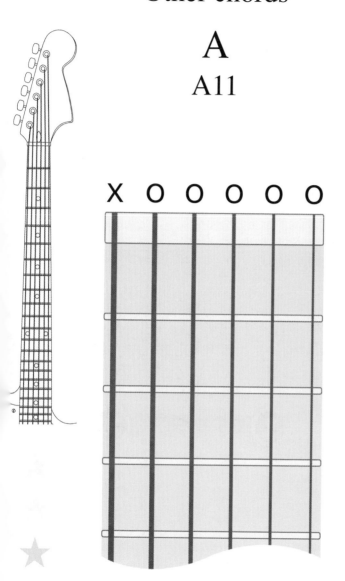

Notes in the chord:

5: A (root); 4: D (eleventh); 3: G (dom seventh); 2: B (ninth); 1: E (fifth)

Can five open strings really generate a proper chord?
Certainly! This is a very useful voicing of A11.

Other chords

C
C11

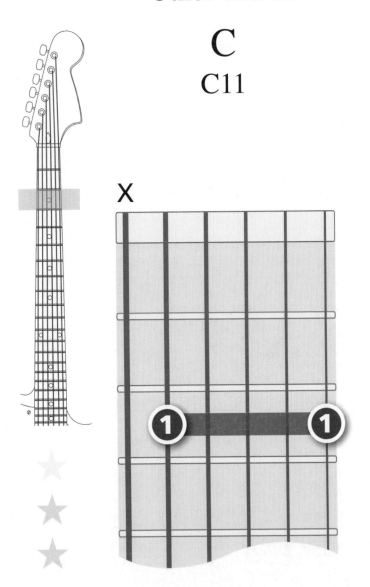

X

Notes in the chord:
5: C (root); 4: F (eleventh); 3: B♭ (dom seventh); 2: D (ninth); 1: G (fifth)

A barré allows us to move our originally all-open-string
eleventh chord freely around the neck. Here, in the 3rd
position, it becomes C11.

Other chords

E
E/A

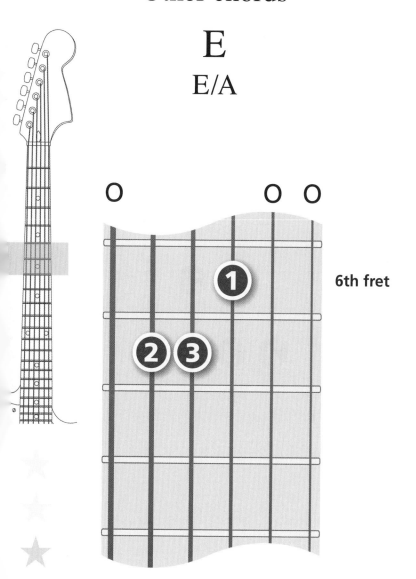

6th fret

Notes in the chord:

6: E; 5: E; 4: A; 3: C#; 2: B; 1: E

Great for vigorous rhythm playing in the key of E. Its mixture of open and fretted strings provides an alternative to a 'straight' A chord.

Other chords

E
E/B

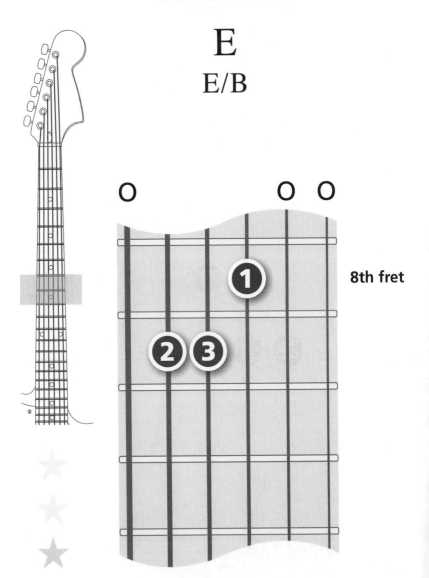

8th fret

Notes in the chord:

6: E; 5: F#; 4: B; 3: D#; 2: B; 1: E

The logical progression from E/A when pounding out rhythm in the key of E: a hybrid chord with elements of both E and B major.

Other chords

B
B7 'slidable' shape

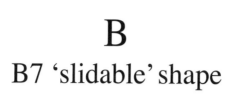

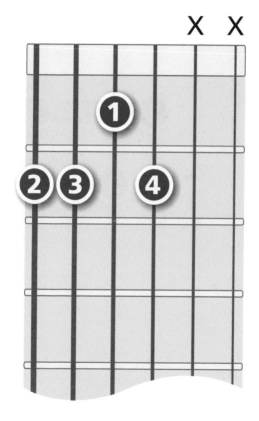

Notes in the chord:
6: F# (fifth); 5: B; 4: D# (third); 3: A (dom seventh)

Not all movable fingerings require barrés; this one
will supply four-string dominant seventh chords all over
the fingerboard.

Other chords

F
F7 'slidable' shape

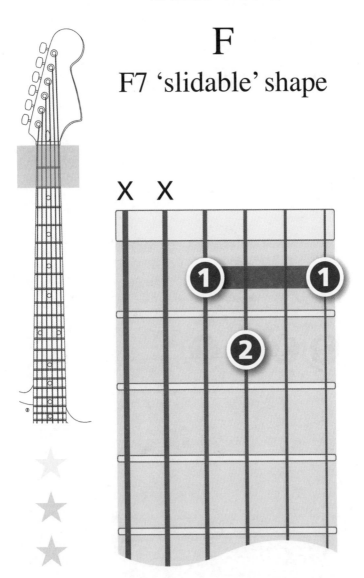

X X

Notes in the chord:
4: E♭ (dom seventh); 3: A (third); 2: C (fifth); 1: F

A higher-pitched counterpart to the previous shape. In the 2nd position, it becomes F#/G♭7; move it up another fret for G7, and so on.

Other chords

A
A/C

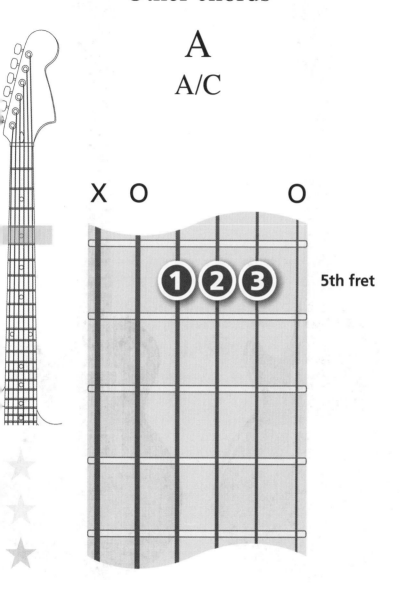

5th fret

Notes in the chord:
5: A (root); 4: G; 3: C; 2: E; 1: E

Similar in its effect to E/A and E/B, and most useful when
playing in A major or minor. The 1st and 2nd strings
supply the same note.